Ten Talents in the American Theatre

TEN TALENTS
IN THE AMERICAN
THEATRE

Edited, with an introduction, by David H. Stevens

Robert E. Gard

Paul Baker

Alan Schneider

Margo Jones

Frederic McConnell

Barclay Leathem

Gilmor Brown

Leslie Cheek, Jr.

George C. Izenour

Paul Green

Norman: University of Oklahoma Press

Library of Congress Catalog Card Number: 57-5960

Copyright 1957 by the University of Oklahoma Press,
Publishing Division of the University.
Composed and printed at Norman, Oklahoma, U.S.A.,
by the University of Oklahoma Press.
First edition.

To the Memory of Barrett H. Clark

lifelong worker in the fields of drama
and friend of all who gave their talents
to increase of the arts in America

ACKNOWLEDGMENTS

ACKNOWLEDGMENTS of help from others in the making of this book could be at great length, for many persons have contributed by advice and encouragement. Among these the most noteworthy are the members of the University of Oklahoma Press. The Press's staff again has demonstrated its deep concern with the advancement of thought and of taste in living society by issuing a book on the margins of trade publication. Alongside it are these writers themselves, persons so engaged in daily duties that stopping to write seemed almost a hindrance to advancement of drama rather than a demonstration of how advancement is to be accomplished.

The more exact acknowledging of help is due two metropolitan newspapers and one individual. To the *New York Herald Tribune* thanks are here given for permission to quote from the tribute of Maxwell Anderson to the memory of Robert Sherwood, printed in the issue of November 17, 1955; also, to the *New York Times* for free use of the admirable sketch of the late Margo Jones that appeared in its columns on July 26, 1955. Maxwell Anderson again has shown his true interest in the drama of this country by permitting a reprinting of a part of his tribute to Sherwood. He also gave the text of his words before the American Academy of Arts and Letters, spoken at a second memorial meeting to the same purpose. These two writings signify what are the ends in our view of American drama here expressed by a few among the many working with plays.

David H. Stevens

January 30, 1957

CONTENTS

ix

Ten Talents in the American Theatre

"From Time's relentless operation, there is only one escape—into the world of Art, a world from which Time is forever banished. . . . Only in a work of art is it possible to recapture and hold the past."
—Fred B. Millett, "In My Opinion," *University of Chicago Magazine*, Vol. XXV, No. 2 (December, 1932), 87.

INTRODUCTION

David H. Stevens

THE TEN PERSONS contributing to this book have spent their lives in the American theatre. A few of them show in their narratives that they had an intense interest in the rudiments of their profession from early childhood, and each has pointed out certain influences and impulses, of later years, that made a devotion to staged drama an inevitable fact of existence. All but one still are at work in the complex process that at last brings a play to public performance. In doing so, each has demonstrated a particular talent in one or several of the forms of dramatic creativeness—as playwrights, technicians, inventors, designers, directors, administrators, or as interpreters by written or spoken word. Several have served their country in time of war as special service officers, an onerous but rewarding line of duty; with no exception the ten individuals have been actively engaged in theatre practice with undivided interest over periods of twenty years and upwards, constantly improving the appreciation of the American public for staged plays. By such creative work they have greatly increased our possessions nationally, in form of discriminating audiences and of experienced workers in all the contributing arts of the theatre.

In the advancing lines of cultural change across this country, these individuals and others of like sort are the frontiersmen who establish new forms of self-expression. They have not followed an east-to-west direction, as was the case in earlier movements of economic and physical kind, but they have been central sources of influence radiating in every direction. They have been able to do this because by some reason each one had become attached to a particular place, to which students and audiences came out of desire for theatre on the levels of interest that these persons were creating.

One distinction common to all ten is a remarkable record for writing or producing new scripts. Paul Green is the one who has done both, over many years, while several have been consistently encouraging new authors by including a definite number of new plays yearly among their classical and modern productions. They could do this because of direct access to their own theatres, operated on a nonprofit basis, in case no commercial houses had opened the way to production for the author of the new work. They were operating theatrical seasons extending over nine months, or more, of the year, and doing so year after year. Some of the theatres directed by these particular individuals have their lights up five nights a week, and in a few—notably in Pasadena and Cleveland —the playhouses have two or more stages in action simultaneously. This readiness to help the new playwright is shown equally to the young actor. In every part of the theatre process, from beginning to finished production, these devoted workers intently watch the development of artistry. Training and teaching, directing or writing, managing and financing—by such forms of personal endeavor

6

they have been creating critically mature audiences over widening areas of this country. While doing this they have also given security in their work and freedom for artistic expression to a very great number of people.

Quite evidently, they are but examples of what is being accomplished by scores of others in all parts of the country. According to individual talents and strength of local support, all who encourage new writers, actors, and directors to produce plays for critical audiences are contributing to the increase of dramatic art. They are helping, unconsciously for the most part, to create a national theatre. It should be recognized that they are contributing to the national wealth, by a systematic plan for cultural growth, quite as definitely as those who produce machines and scientists for service to industry. Society must give toward both of these diverse purposes in order to produce the inventions, discoveries, and imaginative or critical works needed to sustain a growing culture. Herein lies the reason that the noncommercial theatre is now supported by colleges, universities, and many communities. They are producing-centers for individuals as leaders in all parts of this country and in all aspects of the arts. They provide precisely the needed medium for independent work under highly trained and experienced directors.

These workers within institutions have no wish for elaborate playhouses built and maintained by government subsidy, with annual financing from the Treasury. Nor do they look with favor on any plan of management from a metropolitan center: Other than as a means of professional entertainment that takes little account of public taste, chain management offers little for the future of American drama in the sense of originality and diversity. What these individuals and others like them desire is a nationwide interest in artists and in the arts of the drama, which can discover and create under favoring circumstances on a nationwide scale. The need is for such freedom from social and financial pressures as can be given in an independent, nonprofit theatre; for training under specialists in theatre arts comparable to that given in sciences by a university; and for the development of critically mature audiences, by constantly giving them the chance to see good plays, well acted, at costs within reach of each community.

What is needed is greater understanding of the theatre as a national asset, as an expression of the American mind and spirit. These ends are not sought after with the delusions of nationalism, but with the intent to make the arts a part of living. Every person grasps the meaning of a "national" art by his own experiences in the theatre. He keeps some cherished recollections of plays, and of players, that to him represent more than personal distinction. As that sense of values pervades the people of a country, the beginnings of a national theatre are in that country. Always the origin of idea and inspiration is in a spontaneous sharing by many people as they turn toward original values in the work of some artist with full appreciation, and so with the encouragement that gives sharper definition to his talents.

In the year 1955, the American theatre lost three such names from its rolls of living participants in this process of change—those of Margo Jones as a managing director, of Lemuel Ayres as a designer, and of Robert E. Sherwood as a playwright. The first speaks for herself briefly through the pages of this book. The second is remembered for settings on metropolitan stages that were seemingly beyond his years in their taste, originality, and fitness for particular plays. On the third name no comment is needed on why it is in the record of American theatrical history.

At a memorial service in New York City, Maxwell Anderson, in his elegy, placed his comrade in two settings: one was personal, the other universal. In the following passage he recalled their working together. "When we say that we have lost incalculably in intelligence, humor, mordant wit, and human kindness, we can see Bob's face, brooding for a moment before he can find and utter his implacable, unanswerable comment on these trite phrases. It is part of our loss that we shall never know what his comment would have been, and it is part of our human incompetence that we can never convey to one who didn't know him the essence of how he looked to us, how he spoke, how the tacit affection in his eyes could take the sting out of criticism." As a forecast of Sherwood's place in American letters, he added: "When a playwright is trying to write a page, and the characters begin to speak in clichés, let him open a copy of any play by Molière, Shaw, Synge, or Sherwood, and if his dialogue doesn't improve it's not the fault of the models. Only, of these four, Sherwood is the safer guide in modern playwriting."[1]

Then on May 23, 1956, Maxwell Anderson's poetic tribute, "Robert E. Sherwood," was read at the American Academy of Arts and Letters. With permission of the author it is printed here, because the true quality of human friendship and the latent criticism of American drama make these lines wholly within the purposes of this book.

> *Back in the early twenties*
> *Met a young giant.*

[1] From the printing of the full address as given in the *New York Herald Tribune*, November 17, 1955.

As I remember it
He was lounging against a wall
Chatting with cronies
Somewhere in the theatre district.
Tall. Six feet seven I heard later.
Lean. Gangling. Watchful.
A lot of structural steel
In that suave leaning tower.
He put out a hand that had a grip in it.
Spoke slowly. Said few words.
Syllables carefully articulated.
Made rounded sentences when he made any.
Mordant.
Kindly.
A long head. A long face, looking down.
Astute.

Next meeting.
He'd written a play and I went to see it.
I said to myself
Some of these lines are better than Shaw.
Just as witty and more blood in them.
High tension. High voltage. High comedy.
We talked a bit.
He smiled slowly from up there where he lived.
Six foot seven.
He was somewhat dazed.
The play was a hit.
He could quit writing for a boss.
Could write as he pleased.

When Petrified Forest opened I was in
    San Francisco.
Read about it.
Sent him a wire.
That does it. That's the kind of play
    I'd like to write.

Later Idiot's Delight *was on*
With the Lunts—
The whole town infected with its laughter.
It took all the prizes
And deserved them.
Never heard such a glissando of wit.

Bob was president of the Dramatists' Guild
In 1937.
After a tough session
Bob and I sat down with Elmer Rice
To have a drink (not that we drank much).
One of us said
Why don't we produce our own plays?
Well, we were pleased with the idea.
Talked with Sidney Howard and Sam Behrman.
They came in with us.
We made up the Playwrights' Company.
Abe Lincoln in Illinois *was Bob's first contribution.*

From that time on
We met regularly.
It seemed sometimes
That was what our office was for.
We put on plays
But what mattered most
Was talking things over with tough-minded men
Working at the same trade.
Alchemy was our business.
Trying to transmute Broadway into gold.
The result was (and is) mostly frustration.
Or fool's gold.
Sometimes there was a glint of the real metal.
We tried not to fool ourselves.
Bob made a sort of center,
A rallying standard.

If he wasn't there nothing was transacted
Except transactions.

When he was there
The sparks flew.
Mostly in fun.
Sam and Elmer were fast with their rapiers,
But Bob was quick also,
And his reach was—
Well, figure it out,
Six foot seven.
One of the Playwrights said
About a play of his:
"I can't put it off.
I'll be sitting on tenterhooks
Till it's produced."
"What," I asked,
"Are tenterhooks?"
Bob turned to me gravely.
"The upholstery of the anxious seat," he said.

The earth is now altered.
The city is emptier and colder.
Some of its meaning has gone
Out of Broadway,
Out of Fifth Avenue.
Out of the familiar windows along the street.
Somewhere, at a frequented table,
Someone is ordering a Dubonnet cocktail.
No doubt
Someone is speaking slowly,
With laconic wit.
But it's not Bob, and the earth is diminished
  and not the same.
Sherwood is dead.

Those who were younger than he

> *Are still younger.*
> *Those who were older,*
> *I among them,*
> *Are much older now.*

By such writing the reader is led toward an understanding of what creates a national theatre. Two others of similar insight lately have given added views of what lies beyond the temporary in dramatic arts and theatre. One of the two, Agnes de Mille, had been defining the function in society of the teacher. She went on to a conclusion that is equally applicable to her own profession. In part it reads: "It is sad and frightening to think how few people in our culture believe in what they are doing. . . . Work for its own sake brings joy to only a few dedicated groups, and of these it is the priests and the teachers who persevere undauntedly without financial ambition or financial hope. Do not underestimate the value of this point of view. A community that gives its time to working at what brings little joy loses zest and self-respect and can be teased into any kind of foolishness. Our incorruptibles are our hold on sanity."[2] This same spirit appears in a passage by Agnes Moorehead, who wrote: "The theatre is not merely a place of amusement. I believe it can be a great educational medium, teaching an audience many things that would otherwise be lost to them. It widens the sympathies and broadens the intellect and sweetens the heart."[3]

Other signs of the powers latent in drama and other arts appear in the words of three reporters returned home from duty overseas. They had been away in the service of their broadcasting company and had been brought back

[2] *Atlantic Monthly,* Vol. CXCV, No. 6 (June, 1955), 31–33.
[3] Edward R. Murrow, *This I Believe,* edited by Raymond Swing (New York, Simon and Shuster, 1954), Series II, 100–101.

for a review of world affairs, to be given at the end of the year by themselves and their colleagues from other countries. Their comments had national circulation by television. It was at the end of their round-table talk that the chairman, Edward R. Murrow, asked each to tell what, in his country of service, had influenced public opinion most decisively during the past year. Out of that question came answers bearing on this present issue, of what drama and the other arts give in universal measure.

The reporter home from Russia singled out the tour of the American company under Robert Breen. After their European tour they had gone into Russia under nongovernmental auspices to present *Porgy and Bess* before audiences of surpassing size and enthusiasm. He told how surprised were Russian audiences, at these productions, by the friendly spirit of the Americans toward persons of all races. He went further in describing the warmth of feeling and good will shown by all who met the members of the cast socially. Artistically, the work had fascinated its Russian audiences. They exclaimed with pleasure over its jazz movements, its spirituals, and the rhythmic phrasings in the text of Du Bose Heyward and in the score by George Gershwin.

Two other reporters brought comparable evidence from their stations in France and East Asia. The man from the Far East was unreserved in praise of the American symphony orchestra that had appeared at centers scattered along the enormous semicircle that stretches from Japan to western India. The other, returned from France, had a national view rather than one with Parisian limits. He told of the great popular enthusiasm of the French people and of their nationwide gratification over an announcement from their government that the United States had officially invited a company from the Comédie

Française to make a transcontinental tour of this country as an American tribute to France for the exceptional quality of her dramatic art, meriting high international recognition.

Such examples show something more than a desire to give national recognition to artists from other countries. There is no better proof that in the arts lie the universal appeals of mankind. One may labor the point that they are still being used in these instances with a purpose outside the aims of the artists who wrote and presented them abroad; but the essential element in every story of this sort is that great art is universal, with a power to reach the popular level of interest at once and everywhere. Herein is better proof of change toward understanding than can come out of any statistical digest covering the number of plays produced, the size of each audience, or the count of dollars and final profits. These are solid demonstrations of what the arts, and drama in particular, can be as reflections of the living spirit of a nation behind the artist as an individual. They are signs of what belief a people has in that great natural resource, the person, and in the art media that are its truest symbols of inner quality.

Comparison of the recognition of drama as a national symbol in Great Britain and in the United States can be drawn from a few facts of recent origin. These have no relation to the obvious contrasts in length of tradition, number of dramatists, or distinction of the greatest among them. In 1951, an international conference was held at the University of Bristol on the general topic of "The Responsibility of Universities to the Theatre." The three days of discussion brought out views of amateur and professional groups and of representatives of educational institutions from many countries. They came under the sponsorship of the Colston Research Society, clearly concerned with the need to relate formal studies more closely to dramatic writing and stage production. The title itself was sufficient indication of the prime source from which help was expected to come.

Conclusions reached were that theatre history, properly taught, brings all formal studies in the humanities into unity; that a university is the place for uniting theory and practice at the outset of serious studies in the arts of drama; and that the liberal arts are essential for one who would surpass in any phase of dramatic endeavor, be it in the theatre itself or in critical or creative writing. Whatever the field of specialization, the learner was to be told that a wide range of subjects in the arts curriculum must give balance to his studies in dramatic literatures and criticism, to theory and research, and to practice in stage production.

Reporting from the United States was done by Sawyer Falk of Syracuse University. In 1951 he had held for twenty-eight years the post that he still has as head of his department. During that time he had participated in all national programs educationally and had a constant familiarity with the operations of the commercial, metropolitan theatre. His central thesis was that drama belongs in formal education, in varying degree, from earliest schooling to the end of higher studies in the graduate school. He defined its values for adult life in town, country, and city and urged that the commercial theatre do much more to educate the public mind in the arts.

Nothing else at the conference equaled the record of Great Britain, as shown in reports on its National Arts Council and its local and county committees. Other distinction, internationally, lay in its evidence of scholarly concern, exemplified by the ten annual volumes of the *Shakespeare Survey*, edited by Allardyce Nicoll, who likewise has maintained at Stratford, with others, the Shake-speare Institute as a gathering point for students from many countries. A deep and enduring regard for the theatre underlies such continuing projects. Among the oldest of such national symbols is the Shakespeare Festival at Stratford, and the most recent one of high distinction is the Edinburgh Festival. Both of these prove that support of the arts in Great Britain is constant because they are desired by the many, not by merely the few.

A new illustration of that national attachment appears in the plans of the county of Shropshire for dramatic productions during the summer of 1956. There Eric Salmon, county drama adviser, scheduled repeated performances of three plays in the town of Ludlow, where Milton's *Comus* was first produced. The staging of Hofmannsthal's *Jedermann* was in the town church, Marlowe's *Edward II* in the castle, and Milton's *Samson Agonistes* in the town hall. Thereafter, the *Samson Agonistes* was to be given in the Birmingham Repertory Theatre through a full week, and again for another week in September as the concluding work of the Edinburgh Festival for 1956.

Behind these signs is a living tradition. It has existed through generation after generation. No need to wonder why the theatre of Great Britain has steady support from the Treasury, from local and county authorities, and from all the people. The national record gives a complete naturalness to a remark made by Mary Glasgow, back in 1946, regarding the Arts Council, which she admirably served. In conversation, she remarked that the aid of government to the arts was then even more needed than during the years of World War II, just ended, "in order to relieve emotional strains and the losses of social and spiritual strength under the current economic restrictions." Such discernment of the use of staged plays in times of stress is no denial of their significance artistically in a national culture, but an intense recognition of their reality in the lives of human beings. During World War II official circles in this country came to a slow acceptance of understanding in this regard, by admitting that drama could do much for individuals living under the boredom of camp or in the fury of open battle. Yet it is clear that such belief came by persuasion and testing of such individuals as have written the present book, not out of a national tradition of accepting drama as a necessary element in the good society.

Only a few further comments are needed on the reasons behind this contrast. Great Britain has the advantages of easy and economical movement of both players and audiences in a small, compact country having a dense population, by comparison with that of the United States. Across the expanse of a continent, the media of mass communication by air have extraordinary possibilities in supplying substitutes for reality. They possess that added power of using the arts as lures of advertising, thus linking them to profits and the paid time span, which is determined by the buyer. Yet these are secondary to the prime factor in the minds of all who can choose between stage and screen. Live drama remains as compelling and vivid as do living people in comparison with their shadows.

In any society, staged plays succeed in proportion to the levels of intellectual, spiritual, and imaginative power. Their appeal reaches to all who are sensitive to impressions deeper than those of elementary sound and sight. Maturity appears most decidedly as an individual passes beyond the material to the inner quality of humanity. The word "value" then comes to possess abstract and symbolic meanings for him. Applied to his interests in the arts, that advance in perception and sensitiveness brings into his existence a completely new appreciation. He no longer will be satisfied with elemental appeals to his physical senses, which go no farther. As this becomes true of a total society, there can exist within it those higher art forms demanded by the popular, advancing interest in intellectual, spiritual, and imaginative values.

Today, in the United States, the judgments to be passed on the theatre should rest upon the degree to which it serves these three vital qualities in humanity. Or rather, to remove the implication of moralizing, one should ask that these qualities be considered simply as the characteristics of a developed culture to which the drama must make its artistic appeal.

On the constructive account, much evidence of growth toward a national theatre in the United States might be assembled into the forms of history. Biography, seasonal narratives on the urban stage, and assessments of merit by critics all have had a place in cultural histories of the twentieth century. Meanwhile, with annual summary of what has occurred during the calendar year, have come those occasional penetrating judgments that become standard descriptions of passing vogues and exceptional successes on the contemporary stage. As an example, there is that estimate of a British critic twenty years ago passed on a particular American playwright. That successful writer had apparently asserted art to be trivial unless it plead for some social or political cause. His position was taken at a time when such assumptions concerning artists were fashionable within urban opinion held by their followers and themselves. The brusque disposal given that point of view was that the writer was showing "his form of spiritual pride, and so of aesthetic blindness," and would so reduce his world to "an economic ant-heap."[4] This opinion on one individual applied also to a group of writers and critics, but it had its immediate weight because it was attached to the name of a prominent member. It was penetrating in effect because it was a justifiable opinion under the current conditions. Then there are those broad, well-recognized assertions that can stimulate thought and popular judgment because they are based on a very considerable knowledge of the theatre in successive periods of cultural history. One such is the question of another British critic concerning the Victorian period. He wondered whether its lack of new drama might be explained by the necessity for Great Britain to regain coherence after the cyclones of two revolutions[5]—a thought-provoking comment for those who examine the output of nations in the arts between the two world wars of the twentieth century.

These approaches, however, are not useful in searching after the unrecognized sources of a new national theatre in this country. They are to be found beyond the metropolitan boundaries of the commercial theatre. Within those boundaries the valid and the fortuitous elements of historical change have been brought out clearly, if at times with overestimated valuation of what is at the moment popular and profitable. It would appear to be better, as an approach to a national view of growth in theatre, to look for individuals and organizations in American society that are known to have been deeply concerned in an objective manner with the advancement of theatre among the people.

[4] From a review of Elmer Rice's *Other Plays and Not For Children* in the London *Times Literary Supplement*, August 22, 1935, p. 523.
[5] From a review of Allardyce Nicoll's *A History of Early Nineteenth-*

Within such terms, most critics would open their accounts with the name of George Pierce Baker. He was the first and, for many people, the most significant individual of the past twenty-five years to work for a national interest in staged plays. Since the time of his earliest work at Harvard University, he has been a constant influence, increasingly so during his lifetime and still continuing in the lives of his students. They, in turn, have transmitted his beliefs to others. Frederick Koch, one of Baker's first auditors in his "47 Workshop," went back to teaching and sent on Thomas Wolfe from North Carolina for guidance in writing. One can only speculate how much farther that stream of influence went on into American letters through readers and reviewers. Another person, of Baker's last class at Yale University, is today exerting strong influence over all who study his methods of direction or see his staged productions: Elia Kazan had the qualities in his personality for later success before that particular experience, but it altered his conception of drama as it brought him under the influence of that creative mind. The saying of John Mason Brown regarding George Pierce Baker is that he was "the first person to make one realize that a calendar cannot keep those who share interests from being contemporaries."⁶ It was the opinion of Sidney Howard that he "taught students truths more valid than techniques,"⁷ a remark that grows more meaningful when thought on. A third close observer of Baker's mind and meaning, the late Mrs. Edith Isaacs, carried his beliefs into all her writing. With him she helped teachers and workers in drama to organize a na-

Century Drama, 1800 to 1850, in the London *Times Literary Supplement,* January 1, 1931, p. 1.
  ⁶ Wisner Payne Kinne, *George Pierce Baker and the American Theatre* (Cambridge, Harvard University Press, 1954), xii.
  ⁷ *Ibid.,* xiv.

tional association known as the National Theatre Conference, that there might be widespread exchange of values in every phase of theatrical practice.

More general estimate of the uses of drama and all the arts in education has come from two foreign scholars who came to complete their careers in the United States. In his final work, *Vision in Motion*,[8] László Moholy-Nagy set down his recommendations. He asked that theoretical and practical forms of education be joined at every level of the public schools, in colleges, universities, and professional schools. The content of his argument is better understood from intimate examination of what he did in his own field of design, but it can be brought to bear upon any other as well. Much of his exposition can be summed up in the denial of any distinct difference between artist and craftsman. The merit of his method is demonstrated by the way his students were brought to emulation, not to imitation, as they wholeheartedly followed his teaching and practice. Moholy-Nagy was one who came within Gilbert Murray's description of a writer as one who "retains a passionate interest in the present, which he feels cannot be divorced from the past, so that he becomes by his vital power of expression a public force working beyond the strict limits of his own science."[9] Here is an identification of those qualities within a single individual that raised Moholy-Nagy as well as Baker above their specific levels of action into higher places of influence.

The other foreign scholar, now American in every sense except his European origin and inheritance, is Professor Erwin Panofsky. In one of his essays, "Three Decades of

[8] László Moholy-Nagy, *Vision in Motion* (Chicago, Paul Theobald, 1947).
[9] From a review of Ulrich Von Wilamowitz-Moellendorff's *My Recollections, 1848–1914*, in the London *Times Literary Supplement*, May 8, 1930, p. 377.

Art History in the United States," he has brought out the contrasts of European practice in teaching and research. He also has added his reasons why "fine" should not be attached persistently to the word "arts," on either historical or individual grounds of description. Values he placed above facts, saying that in all research and education the aim must be "not for a maximum of knowledge but a maximum of adaptability."[10] Both authorities, in their fields, would call for the union of theory and practice; in the field of theatre arts they would ask for the same approach to reality and abstraction by learners under such masters as was George Pierce Baker during his years of greatest influence.

Baker's full career has recently been under review in a book that brings to light many unfamiliar examples of national consequences from his work.[11] It was his desire to reach the country as a whole that led to the organization of the National Theatre Conference as a means of associating hundreds of teachers and adult playmakers in plans of study and production. That association made effective in action much that the Drama League of America had fostered by group study and recommendation of current plays. Through the pages of *Theatre Arts Monthly* the aims of the Conference were brought effectively into public understanding. Under the inspiration of Baker and a few other leaders, it was made a genuinely national organization serving the interests of adult groups and educational institutions. For the first time a relationship was created among community theatres and colleges. Metropolitan producers and publishers of plays found new markets for their products. As yet, however, during that early

[10] Erwin Panofsky, *Meaning in the Visual Arts* (Garden City, A Doubleday Anchor Book, 1955), 340.
[11] Kinne, *George Pierce Baker.*

period before 1930, little was done to encourage regional writing and stage productions of high quality.

Out of the Depression in 1933 came a new pattern of operation. The subsidy that had given basic support to the Conference came to an end, and local resources lessened. A reorganization was begun, under the guidance of Edward C. Mabie, of the University of Iowa, that led to the creation of a small advisory body giving services of essential kind to the noncommercial theatre. A national office in Cleveland began issuing the *Quarterly Bulletin*, which in time carried to its fifteen hundred subscribers news of fellowship aids and varied opportunities for improving personnel and production in colleges and universities where drama had strong support and in all community theatres combining advanced training with excellent production. Beginning with forty-eight members, by 1950 the Conference had risen to a total of one hundred and had become a recognized medium of action nationally and internationally.

One such demonstration of usefulness came in 1939 as World War II brought demands for aid of its members to the military branches of the government. Twenty members soon entered as special service officers, and these in turn enlisted many others as directors of drama in this country and abroad. The accounts of service rendered by these men were never brought together, but each of them on returning to civilian duties had new, practicable ideas to contribute from his experiences. Much of the maturity to be found in methods of dramatic work today came out of camps and military establishments.

Such gains toward a genuinely national theatre in this country followed the work of the Conference under the leadership of Mabie, Leathem, McConnell, Green, Norvelle, and others. An earlier consolidation of values had in part opened the way for the Conference to become a truly national influence. That had come through the Federal Theatre Project as a branch of the Works Progress Administration between the years 1935 and 1939. Its director, Hallie Flanagan Davis, reported on these years of marvelous success, under obstacles, in her book entitled *Arena*.[12] More graphic, because compressed into a brief address before her fellow members in the Conference, was her statement at the annual meeting on November 25, 1939, when she summed up that record thus: "This is not a time for us to sit down and 'tell sad stories of the death of kings.' The Federal Theatre as an institution is dead; but not even an Act of Congress can kill an idea. What the Federal Theatre stood for and what the National Theatre Conference stands for is very much alive. The dreams of an American theatre national in scope and regional in emphasis, advocated for many years by *Theatre Arts Monthly* and by members of this Conference, took definite form during the four years of Federal Theatre. We know now what many doubted four years ago— that great numbers of people, millions of them, want to go to the theatre if the plays are good and the admission reasonable."[13]

There are other unwritten chapters in this story of American drama. One has to do with the labors in Germany, between 1946 and 1948, of those who carried to audiences and readers the plays and the books needed to depict the cultural life of the United States. Again highly trained personnel were called in from the noncommercial theatre here, as were many professionals from the commercial groups in New York City. It was in Bavaria, dur-

[12] Hallie Flanagan, *Arena* (New York, Duell, Sloane and Pearce, 1940).
[13] *Quarterly Bulletin*, National Theatre Conference, Vol. I, No. 4 (December, 1939), 3.

ing the years noted, that two directors in special services, Jelinek of New York City, and Dawes of Ohio State University, demonstrated what could be done under subsidy to gratify the real interest of a foreign people in American life. In the three years they had 619,630 spectators of their productions in German translations of the following plays, and others: *The Skin of Our Teeth*; *Our Town*; *The Voice of the Turtle*; *Ah, Wilderness!*; and *Mary of Scotland*; also, Job's *Uncle Harry*; Ardrey's *Thunder Rock*; and Lavery's *The First Legion*.

Still another chapter waiting for writing into the record is on the origin and development of the American National Theatre and Academy, today an effective organ for theatre interests at home and abroad. In January, 1934, a group of citizens of Philadelphia appealed to Congress for recognition of the need for a national theatre, with attendant schools developing the necessary personnel in all essential services to such an institution. To a limited degree, this was to be on patterns developed under state control in various European countries. To the surprise of many, a federal charter was granted. No appropriation of funds accompanied it, but under private support A.N.T.A. has become the four-letter name of a vigorous and useful organization, of aid to commercial and non-commercial planning and also to that of the government for foreign productions. The most arresting project of A.N.T.A. thus far was set in motion early in 1956, in the hope of success by the twenty-first anniversary of the granting of its charter on July 5, 1935. The five million dollars sought for was to be used to create a circuit of forty theatres, through which on a weekly schedule musical and dramatic productions would circulate throughout a given season. Here, perhaps on the level of British belief in the social meanings of staged plays, the American believers in A.N.T.A. will prove the existence of a powerful and demanding desire for drama in a new kind of national theatre. If and when that comes about, high credit will be due to all the pioneers and frontiersmen whose lives are exemplified by the narratives in this book.

ORIGINS

1. A SOIL FOR THEATRE

Robert E. Gard

JOHN STEUART CURRY was the first artist-in-residence at an American state university. This one-time Kansas man who had painted pictures that I loved and understood—like the twister striking at the Kansas flatlands, or a brawny farmer standing in waist-high grain with his two children—was brought to the University of Wisconsin in 1937 to paint on the campus and to help Wisconsin artists to interpret the land they lived on and the folks they worked with. It was to some a curious and startling thing to learn that John Steuart Curry had been brought to the university, not by a division of fine arts, but by a dean of the Agricultural College.

This dean was a Dane named Chris Christensen. He was as broad as a door and seemed as tall as a ceiling. When he smiled his face shone with a wondrous light, and when he talked there was often a feeling of earth and stars in his words. One of the paintings John Steuart Curry made when he got to Wisconsin was of this Chris Christensen standing in the middle of a great field of tall corn, with the corn leaves blowing in the wind and curling up around

31

Chris's body. Chris loved the things of earth and had found within himself the will to make the earth things and the men who understood them live in terms of art.

By 1942 I had gotten into gear with the notion that there must be a great theatre of the American people, fostered and nourished through the creativeness of the people themselves. And I visited that summer several American universities in the hope that I might discover promising fields for the development of grassroots theatre. One of the places I visited was Madison, Wisconsin, set down among four blue lakes, with the great dome of the state capitol and the main, pillared hall of the state university facing each other across the city.

I spent most of a day listening while Chris Christensen and John Steuart Curry told me about the Wisconsin people: the downtrodden peoples from Europe who sought freedom; the down-East Yankees and the farmers and tradesmen from New York State who sailed on the packet boats of the old Erie Canal and then came through the lakes to Milwaukee, where they spread out across the woodlands and the prairies like a wave. They told me of the Indians who had left their names and the mystery of the legends across the face of Wisconsin earth, and I heard of the shanty boys and the pinery boys who chewed down the mighty forests to a memory. Dean Chris spoke of the hunger of the people for education, how they had formed the university in 1848, the same year that Wisconsin found statehood, and how, little by little, the university had broadened its services until the whole state was, in effect, the university.

On the walls of Dean Chris's office were paintings of rural Wisconsin, and he told me that an art movement was springing up among the farm folks. Every year there was a large exhibit of rural art in Madison, and Curry

32

described how he would go out into the state to meet these new writers and to talk about their work. Every year, at the exhibit in Madison, the university would purchase a number of these rural paintings to preserve in a permanent collection.

There was a theatre tradition, too. The great days of theatre were gone in Wisconsin, of course, when fine German language companies played the Pabst in Milwaukee, or when great American actresses and actors swept through the towns, barnstorming up from Chicago to the Twin Cities. Wisconsin had the earliest "little theatre" movement, too, when a group called the Wisconsin Dramatic Society dedicated itself to the writing and production of plays of Middle Western life.

Unfortunately, the Wisconsin Dramatic Society was no more, but the university had, for fifteen years, kept workers traveling the state, encouraging play production in the cities and in the country. True, no great plays of the people had sprung to life, but the attitude toward theatre was healthy. Indeed, as they told me about theatre in Wisconsin, it seemed more than healthy. There was a dramatic guild to which many persons belonged. There were hundreds of groups reading plays for pleasure. There were schools and institutes to which persons could go for training in drama. I was overwhelmed by the force of this university that could stimulate theatre so completely and nurture it so well.

And yet I somehow sensed that there was a puzzlement in these men about theatre: that an essential idea of theatre was not clear to them. When painting came into our conversation, the talk sparked up and burned bright, but the descriptions they gave me of theatre were academic. But this was impression only, and I forgot it later that day when I had convinced myself that of all the places

I had visited, Wisconsin had done the most to establish a popular concept of drama. I believed that the pioneer work had been done in Wisconsin, and that there was very little need for my services. And I went away from Madison on a hot July day in 1942, remembering the blue lakes, the gentle roll of the country, and the big barns set hard against the sides of the hills. I remembered the big Dean and the remarkable artist. There was a comfortable feeling within me, too—a feeling that in Wisconsin all was well with the creative expression that was theatre, and that in Wisconsin theatre would flourish.

Three years later, in Edmonton, Alberta, where I was directing a native folklore and literary movement, I received a letter from Madison. To my surprise, it was a discouraged letter. Dean Chris had left Wisconsin to become a director of a large American corporation. Curry was still painting great pictures and encouraging state artists, but the bottom had dropped out of the drama business. The whole structure of people's training in theatre that the university had nurtured for so many years had pretty well collapsed, mostly because of the war. There were few plays of any sort being presented, and though the university still had a person traveling the countryside to aid the people in making plays, it was as though that person were working in a vacuum. "What," the writer asked, "were the reasons for this smash of a vital popular theatre idea? Could anything be done to build it up again? Or should the University of Wisconsin even try? If they did try, what kind of program in theatre should they build?"

I did not know. I thought about it. I walked down through the South Saskatchewan River bottoms at Edmonton one afternoon thinking about Wisconsin. There was a wonderful early spring chill in the air, and the green river was fast and sparkling. But I didn't notice. I was thinking that perhaps no great idea of theatre could ever grow on activity alone. There were millions of plays being produced, gleaned at random from this or that publisher's catalogs, or played because Broadway had enjoyed them; and yet, without meaning, without a philosophy for the plays to sit upon firmly, the activity of drama, of theatre, was a flashing thing that lighted for a moment and was gone, with no more meaning, really, than a flashing impression of life itself. There had been a lot of plays produced in Wisconsin, but perhaps a real meaning for the encouragement of such production was absent. Plays were done for recreation when a group needed a recreative activity, or plays were attempted as entertainment. The plays gave the odd individual play director a chance to create an interesting living picture, and people came to see his work and maybe laugh a little or cry a little, and then the play was over and that was that. It was an activity, sometimes an art, that could be turned on and off. It was in no sense essential to the life of the people. If the plays were good, they were enjoyed. But people could get along without them, and when anything came along with more seeming importance, the people dispensed with the plays.

I knew that this was somehow because living theatre was not now a vital part of the life of the American folk. It became suddenly and completely apparent to me that we could no longer pretend that the living theatre could be fabricated and foisted upon the people as entertainment alone, or as sociology, or as an art form practiced by the few for the satisfaction of individual egos. Theatre must grow spontaneously from the lives and the necessities of the people, so that the great dream of a few men and women who saw true visions might come true: The dream of an America accepting the idea of great popular art expression without question, as a thing inherently American.

America, the artists do not paint on the street corners of your cities as they do in Paris, France, where the humblest passer-by may have an art sense of what he sees on the easel. Nor do good pictures by native artists hang on a multitude of your humbler walls as they do in Norway. You have no great body of national plays and no great national theatre to bring your myth and legend to all the people.

What you have, or have had, America, is the frontier in its many complex and varied manifestations. What you have now is the result of a struggle that has somehow not fixed itself into great plays expressing the vast growing agonies of the frontier, but rather has established the industrialism that lies along your Highway 12 as it roars into Chicago from the east, or along your wide Mississippi as she curves south from Galena to Davenport. Your struggle, America, is the sweeping agricultural machines biting into the yellow foodstuff, or it is the herds of purebred cattle on your range lands and in the comfortable barns. It is your lacings of rails and the hot blasts of furnaces, the telephone wires and high-voltage derricks against the sky, and the minds and hands of your people molded and set by the magnificent achievement and impact of these things.

Your struggle, America, has matured so rapidly that the quaint folkishness of your village has been swept into an almost common molding, and the economic fruit of your struggle has been so plentiful that we, your people, have tended to shun the responsibility of art, sometimes to scorn it, and to look at it askance as a manifestation unworthy of our virile American manhood.

You have put down deep taproots, America, that have given us the stuff of wondrous plenty, but these same roots have starved off the expressiveness of yourself. For those of us who have loved you best have not completely understood your struggle, and the art that is in you has only faintly touched our lives.

I knew that this was particularly so, this faint touching, in the smaller places. And my thought then was that the part I might play in American theatre must be related to the back country, away from the largest centers. My part and work must be with the dramatic impulse, the creative force that is in the people; and it was this force that I must work with, and that, developed slowly in keeping with the way of life of the people, might swell the idea of living theatre to a national crescendo.

When I was called to the University of Wisconsin in 1945, space was the university's worst problem. A few of the old-timers on the faculty had private offices, but most of us who were recent arrivals had to roost where we could. There were twenty thousand students jammed into accommodations built for about ten thousand, and the faculty had grown correspondingly large with the student influx. There were some professors who taught lecture classes with as many as one thousand students, and there were some faculty offices that had so many desks jammed into them that there was absolutely no space to move from desk to desk. It was rough going for some, but it was impossible not to feel the excitement of these waves of young people who sought the university in the days just after the war.

My sense of humor and my intense preoccupation with what I was trying to do saved me from irritations rising from inadequate working space. My office was a corner of the geology museum, and I went to work each morning beneath the skeleton legs of a huge prehistoric monster. Many persons visiting the museum thought that I was the curator and were often incensed at my inability to explain scientifically the geological phenomena of the region. Nor could the geology instructors understand the presence of a theatre person in their domain, and certain of these rock tappers who had less pleasant surroundings than I cast wistful and sometimes baleful glances at me and my corner. But in no place that I had ever worked had there been such a complete sense of freedom. If I asked for advice, whether it was from a dean or a professor, or the president, it was freely and completely given; but no one sought me out with suggestions about how I was to proceed. Indeed, so highly is individual responsibility and initiative thought of at the University of Wisconsin that if I had gone out into the state and had not been heard of for several months, I doubt whether anyone would have questioned whether or not I was doing valuable work. It is wonderful to work in an atmosphere and in a tradition of that kind.

But I did not go anywhere for a time. I sat in my corner and thought and made plans, or I visited around the university with men who had been pioneers in many fields. It was stimulating, and for almost the first time I felt that I had stature and respect among men who had made remarkable achievements in fields outside my own. My status at the university, I found, was rather unusual. I was a member of the faculties of three university divisions, and this, I was told, had been done to give me the support and backing of the entire university.

I had been called to Wisconsin to try to relate all the forces that might have bearing on a consciousness of theatre in the community. I had large ideas about theatre in many phases and on many levels to attract and hold the imaginations of the majority of the people, and a name for my new project was a first concern. I thought of such inept titles as the "Wisconsin Theatre Program," the "Wisconsin People's Theatre," the "Wisconsin State Theatre Project." I discussed possible names with many persons, but nothing materialized. Then one day I was reading a book by a man named Charles McCarthy. This book was called *The Wisconsin Idea,*[1] and it seemed to mean a wonderful sort of expression of good will that arose in the state after 1900—a peaceful means used with intelligence to accomplish reforms and general good for all the people. Later, after the political meaning of the Wisconsin Idea had slipped into disuse, the university became the symbol of its meaning in the undiscourageable quality that had come to mean broad and untiring service and a giving out of the fruits of knowledge by those that have knowledge to those who have a need of it.

I was greatly intrigued with *The Wisconsin Idea,* and it suddenly occurred to me that here was the perfect name for the new Wisconsin experiment in theatre, especially since the name reflected so strongly the university's idea of service.

I therefore had some letterheads printed with the name "The Wisconsin Idea Theatre" along the top of the sheet. It seemed to me that I had found a very unique and original name for our state-wide work. It was a week or so later that I made an interesting discovery. I learned that in 1913, in the very heyday of the original concept of the Wisconsin Idea, there appeared the first issue of a small magazine called *The Play Book,* published by the Dramatic Society of Milwaukee and Madison. Leading figures in this organization, which, as I have already said, was really the first "little theatre" movement in the nation, were Zona Gale of Portage; Thomas Dickinson of

[1] Charles McCarthy, *The Wisconsin Idea* (New York, The Macmillan Co., 1912).

Madison, who later became a leading writer on the American theatre; William Ellery Leonard, who later achieved a national reputation as a poet; and Thomas Wood Stevens, who became a much-loved teacher of drama and play producer. And in this first issue of *The Play Book* there was an article entitled, of all things, "The Wisconsin Idea in Theatre!"

The article was written by Percy MacKaye, who is well known today for his plays and poetry. He wrote:

The Wisconsin Idea which today [1913] is stirring our nation so deeply in government, science, civics, agriculture and the progress of the people's self rule, is big with a promise even greater, perhaps, than that which President Van Hise of the University has suggested so admirably in his work.

The part played by the University of Wisconsin in the development of its idea appears likely to strike even more deeply into untilled fields of man's spiritual nature than the plowshares of the state into nature's loam . . . and the seed being sown in the former is being selected, nurtured with the same scientific spirit as the latter. I refer to the work being done for the art of the theatre by the Wisconsin Dramatic Society.

The policy of the Society is to produce plays of Middle-Western life, written and acted by Americans from the Middle West. Wisely pursued it should achieve a notable success . . . The Society deserves the interest of all Americans solicitous for the growth of the theatre as a social institution. The Society desires . . . to quicken the art of the theatre in the soil of society itself, through technical training of the imaginations, dramatic instincts, and latent art-impulses of the people in all their natural and local variety. I would take occasion only to note the tremendous vitality and importance of this movement as a necessary and inevitable extension of The Wisconsin Idea.[2]

[2] *The Play Book: A Magazine of the Drama*, Vol. I, No. 1 (April, 1913), 8–10. The magazine was published monthly by the Wisconsin Dramatic Society. Its publication ceased with Vol. II, No. 12 (May, 1915).

So in 1913, thirty-three years before my version of a Wisconsin Idea Theatre was conceived, there had been this statement that at least approximated one theory on which Professor Frederick Koch of North Carolina, Professor Alexander Drummond of Cornell, and a lot of other people had been working: that fine playwriting could be nurtured in the regions of America, and that the result would greatly contribute to theatre art.

I was very proud that I had unconsciously chosen a name for a new Wisconsin theatre movement that had such tradition. The gap had been bridged, and it seemed to me that now we were ready to begin on a permanent project, for certainly a great trend in literature was toward sympathetic American portrayals of scene and character. Folklorists were having a field day, and great treasuries of American folklore were actually best sellers in American bookstores—something that had certainly never happened before. The American drama, too, sometimes behind the other arts in the reflection of trend, was trying desperately to catch up, with many musicals and dramatic shows carrying strong native themes.

The drawback, of course, to a mature theatre interpretation of the nation was the lack of good new writers, capable of writing great serious and comic plays. I determined to do what I could about this lack, and to provide as many stages as I could that would be the workshops of the new writers. I envisioned a plan somewhat like Drummond's in New York State, or along the lines of the one I had directed in Alberta, where the materials of the region—the stories and the songs—might be collected and made available to writers. I determined that a playwriting project would be among the first of the many phases of the Wisconsin Idea Theatre that I would tackle.

As Drummond and I had worked at Cornell, it had become increasingly apparent to us that it was necessary to develop a regional consciousness of the state's indigenous materials as a basis for our work. Great drama of the people, we believed, could not be successfully developed without this basic consciousness. We realized that we could not hope to stimulate a reasonable interest in local scene, and thereby in theatre, through pamphlets, books, and plays alone, but that the radio, especially, as well as the other public organs must be wisely used toward the end of informing the people of our purpose. And in New York, because of the geographical factors that break the state into several almost separate regions, we found this communication idea difficult to achieve. There was also no one available who was especially trained to write the sort of regional programs we visioned.

In Alberta the communication job was easier, but Wisconsin—with its state radio system and its several hundred weekly and daily newspapers, with its not too great size, and with no mountain ranges to interfere with radio reception—seemed like the perfect setting for an experiment in communicating the purposes and results of the theatre program to the people. So a radio program based on the living lore of the state was established, and I called the program "Wisconsin Yarns." It attained an immediate and enthusiastic following, and suddenly I was working harder than I had ever worked, writing the half-hour weekly radio show, narrating it, and traveling about the state collecting material for the show.

I was, of course, intensely interested in the Wisconsin land and the lore of the people. From Drummond and from my own natural desires I had learned a delicate sensitivity to the winds and the rains and the sound of places. I had learned to turn my imagination almost at will into a theatre, where the dramatic high lights of the past and present were rolling across the stage of my mind in a sort of panorama that seemed to roll on and on without end. Sometimes, in the middle of a Wisconsin woods, I might stop for a moment to listen to the wind rising in the pines; and the wind would make me remember how it must have sounded in those greater forests before the lumbering days; or how the wind carried the great flocks of passenger pigeons across the sky, darkening the sky, rippling the water, scurrying the clouds, driving the rains, hurling the sleet and snow, casting the storms upon the Wisconsin pioneers. And as the wind would die to a whisper, I could hear voices in the wind. Lonely voices. The pioneer women were lonely sometimes. Perhaps I was hearing their voices. Or perhaps the faint wind was the symbol of a memory of the freedom people sought in Wisconsin, and found. The wind remembers.

I noted the rising land of the Baraboo Range of purple hills and knew an inner theatre that the mystery of their color brought to life. I was seeing the pea vineries in canning time, where Mexican laborers, wearing bright kerchiefs, were working side by side with the Wisconsin farmers; and their movements and song as they pitched the green vines into the shelling machines were the movement and sound of living drama.

One time I stopped to watch a country auction, and I saw the personal belongings of the last member of an old Wisconsin family being auctioned off. The auctioneer lifted from a trunk a yellowed wedding dress, and when he asked for bids there was a titter of nerved-up laughter that brushed across the audience. And then that laughter was still as a very old lady made her way from the back of the crowd and offered her small bid for the dress. It was undisputed, and she took the dress and tottered away with it. At a local bar that night I heard the story, and it was like a play, for the dress had been worn fifty years before by *one* lady, but it *should* have been worn by the old lady who finally bought it.

A feeling for place and at least an instinctive understanding of the lore of the people seem basic to the creative processes of anyone wishing to make sincere and honest interpretations of regional scenes.

At the same time we had better realize that Americans are no longer a quaint or a "folkish" people, and that attempts to make us seem so lack the reality of life itself; for our developing communications have made us socially, really, one people. Rural and urban are, as concepts, inextricably mixed and mingled, and that old controversy, if it exists at all, is almost a paper quarrel. There are sectional differences in speech and behavior, but these are probably minor things, no longer worthy of wide exploitation in creative terms. Thus, we may be much more free of the old arguments of what is or is not folk drama. What we have left is the human being and the basic creative impulse that seems to be present in everyone. While bodies of collected material are useful, they must not be used as levers to force creation. Otherwise, one must face masses of undigested and misunderstood history, attempts to recount events approximately as they transpired without much relationship to the processes of art creativeness. One must face and deal with quaintness, stereotypes of rural courting, phoney dialects, and usually unsuccessful attempts to try to seem regionally unique.

With the old argumentative saws no longer existent to hinder, plague, and classify creative talent, the author or the artist may strive for a sincere and unencumbered grasp of the things he knows and understands, and which he may interpret sincerely. The finest literature in America,

as anyone knows, is in a true sense regional. For our greatest American writers seem to have done their best work
when they were rising from or returning to their native
environment.

The problem of the director of regional theatre programs is to try to clear his mind of old ideas, to let the
one fact of the human being and the creative impulse
that is in him be the only idea. The search must be constantly for ways to unshackle the creative human spirit,
to gain great, rising responses from the people toward
interpretations of themselves through and by themselves.
The whole history of the Wisconsin Idea Theatre, as
well as my own methods of stimulating wide cultural
movements and my troubles arising from such stimulation may be studied in my book, *Grassroots Theater*.[3] I
do not need to relate here that I have encountered black
discouragements in Wisconsin or wherever I have been.
However, I am keenly aware now, looking backward, that
it is the soil of preparation that is most important to keep
in mind. Faith, if one is hardy and tireless, will maintain
itself despite everything. But the full recognition must be
made, as it has been by me, that the struggle is twofold.
It is not merely the playwright and his material and his
attitude and his result. It is the whole community, too.

Before many plays of value can rise from us as a people,
the soil of American communities must be so prepared
that the good works of home-based writers may rise proud-
ly from it. Plays must be developed co-operatively as
community projects between the playwright and the people he lives among and is a part of. The plays must take
their place as part of the essential life of the place of their

[3] Robert E. Gard, *Grassroots Theater: A Search for Regional Arts in
America*, with a foreword by David H. Stevens (Madison, University of
Wisconsin Press, 1955).

making. Then, perhaps, New York will come to the back-country playwrights of America, seeking their products that have come to fruition in a thousand American places. Thus may we have great dramatic voices rising out of the heart of us.

There must be a radical change of public attitude toward all the arts, and the development of such an attitude is a Herculean task that must be faced. Finding ways to accomplish the job is a search that has been the impetus for many of the experiments of the Wisconsin Idea Theatre. We have become increasingly aware that the entire community must be developed, not simply the small segments. Baker Brownell, the American philosopher who has frequently grappled with the problem of the arts in community life, wrote an article several years ago which stated that "the drama should be the formulation, the symbolic formulation if you will, of the integrative unity of man in his community. It should be expressive, as only art can be, of the deep answers in common men to the threat of disaster, human dissolution, and community disintegration. And only in the common man will those answers be found."[4]

These deep answers that Baker Brownell speaks of must somehow be made apparent to the people, or they must see the arts (and particularly the theatre arts) as one means through which such deep answers may be obtained. At the present time the arts do not represent deep spiritual answers and satisfactions to the common man. We have seen the possibilities of such satisfaction in some of the theatre experiments we have tried here in Wisconsin, yet it cannot be said that we have exploded a great and deeply

[4] Baker Brownell, "Community Drama in Montana," *Wisconsin Idea Theatre Quarterly*, Vol. II, No. 4 (December, 1948), 6–10.

expressive movement in the arts—a movement that touches everyone.

Many persons, of course, take the point of view that such a movement is not possible and, perhaps, not even desirable. But in Wisconsin we adopt the attitude that an arts movement touching all classes and levels of human beings is possible and is a desirable goal. We believe that we have made steps toward such a movement in Wisconsin, but we recognize that we have a tremendous distance to go.

It seems to me that a part of the problem is the lack of community symbols of art. I do not mean that we want more museums—places of defunct art—but rather that we need community centers in the small communities, as well as in the large, where art may be witnessed and where persons may participate in an art. Such symbols as we once possessed have almost disappeared, although their relics and the ideas they once symbolized are still to be found. For example, a theatre that at least looks like a theatre, where young persons may get a sense of being in a real playhouse primarily for the production of living theatre, can have great community effect.

I have recently visited in Somerset, England, where the director of education for the county has a strong belief that real theatres must be provided for the rural areas. He has developed a plan through which there will be twelve major playhouses for community use in twelve rural centers in Somerset. One playhouse is already completed, and revival of interest in living theatre is the result.

Unfortunately, in Wisconsin we are not so well off. Menomonie is on the banks of the Red Cedar River, and in Menomonie stands a remarkable building. Not remarkable in beauty, for the Tainter Memorial is not beautiful. The place sprawls; its stone has turned a dirty gray-black color. But if you will go inside and ask a pleasant lady who works at a library desk to open a certain heavy oak door for you, you will suddenly find that you are in a theatre, a wonderful theatre, intimate, beautifully designed so that auditorium and stage seem of a piece, so that the turned up chairs seem occupied, somehow, by the personalities who witnessed comedy and tragedy here throughout bygone years.

Yes, a beautiful theatre. The carpeting of the 1890's is on the floor; the furniture of the lounge is just as it was sixty years ago. Drops hang from ancient lines above the stage, and the paint frame has carried no burden for a generation.

You walk to the edge of the stage, reaching across a corner of the orchestra pit to caress the grand drape tenderly. Idly you look at your fingers. Black. Smoke, grime, dust—accumulation of years and years. And suddenly, awakened by the quietness that is louder, really, than a shot, you realize the meaning of this emptiness, this grime, this futile waiting.

For since this theatre was so lovingly built in 1890, great changes have come to Menomonie, yes, to the lives of the people, to the destiny of this lovely theatre. For the emptiness of theatre means death—the death of the road and the great actors and actresses who played here in Menomonie on their way through, perhaps, from St. Paul to Eau Claire, Madison, and Chicago. There was stock for a time. The Winniger brothers hung on as long as they could. But after a while the Winnigers stopped coming, too.

Here in Menomonie, when this old theatre was in the flowering of its worth and beauty, the people knew about good plays, fine acting. Heard of Shakespeare? Yes! Most of 'em, even the kids, could probably recite from *Hamlet,* *Macbeth,* or *The Merchant of Venice.* Not at all uncommon was the town sot in the tavern reeling off a dozen dramatically rendered or tearful pages of *Richard III.* Ask the town drunk in one of Menomonie's bars today to recite you something from *Richard III,* and he will probably reply with a stale gag from yesterday's radio program.

Brethern and sistern, what do we have? You will venture to say that in or near Menomonie, home of this wonderful theatre, there are young people who have never seen a real play, whose sole knowledge of theatre is the stuff canned up in Hollywood. Further, you may safely venture that there are young persons in or near Menomonie who do not even know of the existence of the Tainter Theatre and all that it meant in the half-forgotten life of this American place. Sad? Sure. And tragic, too, for the theatre doors have been closed to the development of an appreciation of theatre in the children, which means that the children have been shut away from human portrayal of the fascinating characters of the great dramatic literature of the world.

But apparently nobody cares very much. The night that we played *Wisconsin Showtime* in Menomonie some of us were talking with the old caretaker of the Tainter Theatre. He was expounding on the sorrowful demise of the road. He said that he didn't see much theatre these days. It was a shame! Where were the good old days, etc., etc.? I said, "Well, Jack, here are a couple of tickets for our show tonight. We'd sure be honored to have an old-time theatre man like you come and see it."

I handed him the tickets, and he handed them back quick as could be. "Boys," he said, his face brightening up, "I sure couldn't do it tonight! Tonight our Menomonie basketball team plays the All-Stars! Boys, I couldn't

miss that!" Well, I don't know the answers. Maybe basketball is the great cultural expression of the times. As Alex
Drummond would say, "I dunno." But some of us will
keep plugging the theatre idea anyway.

Although there is a vast amount of the old-fashioned and
ordinary process of play production going on in Wisconsin, I have noted here and there many experiments that
seem to show that a new concept of theatre is taking place.
When plays cannot be found that fit the needs of the
people, somebody or a group will make up a play, and in
such playmaking there seems to me to be a wonderful
freshness. I was present one day when a group of thirty or
so persons made up a play that represented life on the
town square at Stevens Point. Stevens Point is a small city
in the heart of a large settlement of Polish people, and
these Poles, as well as others, are in the habit of bringing
farm produce to sell on the town market square. The play
was colorful with dancing and singing—dances and songs
the people danced and sang, and which everybody knew—
and the play used characters and subjects familiar to the
central part of Wisconsin. But so interesting was the
treatment, and so universally good was the story, that
under the influence of this and other similar examples,
I let myself believe that a great free theatre movement is
springing to life.

At least, the seeds of such a movement have been sown.
People in Wisconsin now accept the arts as a part of the
pattern of neighborhood life. A Wisconsin farmer who
does not paint pictures, these days, is apt to be considered
a bit on the strange side, and certainly, in every community of the state, there is more play production sympa-
thetically and eagerly attended. Perhaps one-third of the

population of Wisconsin witnessed a play of some sort last year.

Just what the actual contribution of the Wisconsin Idea Theatre to such development has been is hard to estimate, but we have worked toward the end of popular arts understanding and participation in many ways. Along with a vigorous native writers movement and our public relations work in radio, we have published a magazine, *The Wisconsin Idea Theatre Quarterly*, since 1947. We have conducted research into many phases of the theatre as a community force in Wisconsin. We have helped to develop a young people's rural drama program that last year produced nearly one thousand plays. We have endeavored to develop new theatre techniques, have encouraged new playwrights by arranging productions of their work, and have begun to work toward a state-wide movement in children's theatre. We have worked with the Wisconsin high schools in an effort to raise general standards in play production, and we have worked closely with communities to make theatre a vital force. We have established the Community Arts Workshop for the training of local leaders.

We have helped the organized community theatre groups of the state to develop the Wisconsin Idea Theatre Conference, which is doing important work in stimulating theatre education.

Our aim at the Wisconsin Idea Theatre is to make the arts the great frontier they can be in America.

If I could wish for one thing in this life it would be that I might live long enough to hear the music of the American spirit emerging from thousands of fine civic orchestras in large places and small; see good plays, joyously presented and viewed in every American community almost every night; see fine pictures by native American artists decorating the walls of a multitude of American homes of every economic status. Well, we move rapidly in America. We do get things done. We can become a nation of great interior strength through the arts if we have a mind to do it.

2. THE THEATRE IS A FAITH

Paul Baker

AFTER COMPLETING my undergraduate work at Trinity University, in Texas, and the University of Wisconsin, I went to Yale to study under George Pierce Baker. When I arrived at the Yale Department of Drama in the fall of 1933, the theatre had already reached its maturity, and the remarkable scheme for the training of young Americans in all phases of theatre work was moving ahead in a most admirable fashion. To a young man who had come from a very small school in Texas, the Yale University Theatre and the staff that George Pierce Baker had assembled were absolutely fabulous. It was a living experience in active learning. I believe it was one of the really exciting experiments America has had in the arts of teaching.

I did not finish my course in 1933, but returned again in 1937 to complete my degree. When I returned, much of the life, spirit, and drive seemed to have gone out of the theatre, for George Pierce Baker had gone. I have thought about what George Pierce Baker gave to Yale which made it a living, growing, creative theatre; which made it an irrepressible force in the cultural life of America; which gave an unquenchable confidence to his students; and which imbued them with a physical and spiritual determination to carry his ideas into every phase of dramatic life in America.

I have explained it to myself like this: The Yale Theatre was not one man, but it did have a great guiding force of one dedicated man. That was George Pierce Baker, with his vast experience, his knowledge, his discipline, and his constant devotion to the development of a fine laboratory where creative ability could work, grow, and develop. He had a genius for selecting rich young talents in the fields of design, lighting, stage craft, and costuming who became an extension and enlargement of his ideals and his vision. Hence, the whole course of study and all the activities of play production were a unified extension of the driving, creative ideal for which George Pierce Baker stood. And the striking force of his personality was enlarged, enhanced, and given form through his unified and creative staff. This made of the theatre where I was so fortunate to study in 1933 a living, productive energy.

After that year I left Yale and came to Baylor University, into a vastly different environment. I did not expect an ideal physical plant, or an organized working unit, or a ready-made audience thirsting for drama. It is a good thing, because I was confronted with just the opposite. The theatre was on the third floor of an old firetrap of a building and was called the "Tower Theatre." It consisted of a level floor with 125 classroom chairs and a small platform with a curtain. There were no pulleys, no grid, no hammers or saws or paintbrushes. There were few workers, few actors, and very little desire on the part of anyone to see a play. Our routines there will be familiar to many other college workers. In that small, badly located, and barren hall we did the work on all our productions from 1934 until 1941. For large public performances we had to transfer everything across the campus to Waco Hall, an auditorium with a large stage and impossible acoustics in the great open space of 2,500 seats.

Our typical working day was made up of classes at 8:00 and 9:00 A. M.; compulsory chapel at 10:00; consultations at 11:00; classes and laboratory work from 1:30 to 3:30 P. M.; rehearsals from 3:30 to 5:30, and from 6:45 until 10:45; building of scenery and hanging of lights from 10:45 P. M. until 1:00 or 2:00 A. M. Our scenery was built in the Tower Theatre, with each work session ending in sweeping the floor and replacing the chairs for classroom use. Our one available water faucet was located in the basement, eight flights down from our theatre. So we mixed our paints in the basement and then carted the paint cans to the top of the old building. Lumber, props, scenery elements, and other objects—lights, switchboards, and all else—traveled the same hard route. Sometimes I worked alone. All of us, in every way, were learning the full round of work habits that we were to apply in our teaching under far easier circumstances. We also were strengthening our hold on the idea of what theatre is in the life of our own times.

We went on to rebuild the stage in the Tower Theatre. We installed a gridiron of sorts on the small stage. There was no way to secure a petty cash fund; so students and instructors alike contributed for small purchases. Then when we rehearsed in Waco Hall, no matter how reward-ing our artistic achievement, it all ended with hot water and scrub brushes to restore the fifty- by eighty-five-foot stage and its one hundred faculty chairs for chapel use the following morning. We worked on—through holi-days, football games, and parties. By 1935, the university had given us a small shop and some tools. Even so, work was still more physical than of any other sort or level. Assuming that we were later to prove it important to establish a theatre on this campus, we had taken the shortest and surest road to that end. We had not presented any truly artistic production, and our score in number of trained people was low, but we had opened the way. Our staff consisted of myself and a student assistant. We worked on an over-all budget of $3,300 (including my monthly salary of $150) and had a student enrollment of fifteen.

The second stage in our development came soon. One afternoon during the fall of 1936, I happened by the door of the dean of the university and turned back for a chat. I discovered that he was trying to choose a member of his faculty for a year of advanced study on a fellowship from an outside organization concerned with faculty development in the South. He asked if I were interested; I was. I had seen what George Pierce Baker was doing in the East in theatre education; and after three years of teaching, I had spent a summer in England and another in traveling in Germany, Russia, and Japan. But I knew that I needed more training. The outcome was two years, through 1939, back at Yale.

Another great gain for us in this second stage was the result of a visit of Barclay Leathem to our campus. He was on a long tour of such visits for the National Theatre Conference. Shortly after his visit I was invited to become a member of the Conference and to attend the next annual meeting in New York City. This membership, with chances to meet with important national figures while I was still under thirty years of age, was of utmost importance to our theatre and to me.

Soon good fortune, and some direction, brought me to the acquaintance of a friend of all higher education in our southern states—Jackson Davis. With equal participation of our university administration in the financing secured through Jackson Davis from an outside organization, we received funds for our first real theatre. Other financial aid came to increase the first plan and to improve it, with the result that in 1941 we had a new theatre. It was not just another new theatre building, either. It was of a revolutionary design, allowing a wonderful flexibility in staging. Six connecting stages surround the audience seated in swivel chairs, making possible experimental work on all stages or orthodox proscenium staging; or, by moving the chairs up onto the stage, in-the-round staging. The physical struggle on survival levels was partly over.

Then came the war years, during which time I left the Baylor theatre to work as theatrical specialist in Iceland and later as chief of entertainment for the European Theater of Operations, with headquarters in Paris. After the war, we began to rebuild the work of the theatre on the campus, increasing the selection of courses in the drama department and developing the student and faculty play-production work. The staff of the theatre was increased and now includes a designer and technical director; a teacher of playwriting, film and television, and religious drama; an instructor in acting; a children's theatre director; a business manager; and special guest lecturers on theatre subjects, such as movement for the stage and film. Our enrollment has increased to include in 1955 some fifteen graduate students, about ninety undergraduate drama majors and minors, plus approximately three hundred nondrama majors. The budget for 1955–56 was $50,500. The play production for the 1954–55 season included two faculty-produced original plays, eight advanced student productions of full-length plays, and twenty-five student productions of original one-act plays.

After twenty-one years, I now believe that a theatre can grow anywhere if the right method of applying energy is used. First, and foremost, one must never take "no" for an answer. I have always tried to propose an idea for suggestions to perhaps five to twenty people; when one shows any interest, develop that interest into a "yes," and then into action. I have never asked for much at first. Our present theatre, built in 1941, grew out of an agreement that we could move an old tin warehouse from a spot of prominence on the campus to another spot not quite so prominent, and attach it to an antiquated frame house. Somehow a stagehouse was added, then an auditorium, and presto, we had a fine concrete and steel building attached to the house. Two years ago we asked for a five-thousand-dollar entrance to the theatre, and it gradually grew into another flexible theatre with a ninety-foot lobby, large eighty-five- by twenty-five-foot workshop, offices, rest rooms and dressing rooms, and air conditioning for both theatres and work areas. If you cannot get action, work in a tent, work in a garage, but wherever you work, make it solely yours. Then start asking.

I have worked in the Baylor theatre to prove three things: theatre can be good for a university, a town, or a region; theatre need not follow the Victorian patterns of culture heavily laid on the region but can create its own superior artistic life wherever it finds a place to work; and theatre can be the leaven that changes the philosophy and life of a region. The Baylor theatre is built on a strong faith in the unquestioned creative talent of the youth of every region. We accept quite easily the fact that an all-American athlete may turn up in the most remote corner of the most remote farm or ranch in America; yet few people accept the same criterion for our theatre artists. Perhaps we are looking too near the surface. Perhaps we are giving only a copied, traditional, lifeless training to our young talent. When the theatre entered the university as a subject and began to try to become more academic than the deadliest academic standard in order to be accepted, something died—usually both the professor and the student. Taste developed—copied style-taste, cultured tones, deadly scholastic readings; productions became an exercise in techniques and forced styles. The theatre was not a place of co-operative creative discovery, but a place where a professor brought the discipline and formal attitude of the classroom into a deadly, cut and dried dictatorship in the theatre. Even with all these hindrances, the theatre somehow managed to peep through, to appear, in contrast with most of the other departments in the college or university, to be partially alive.

In order to avoid these pedantic pitfalls, we have tried to keep our courses very simple and direct. We do not teach "a course"; we teach each student—trying to find out where he is in his personal discovery, and helping him then to say what he has to say in his own way. The courses are integrated, and extensive files of student work are kept so that each professor can study the progress of the individual student in all phases of his activities. We believe that each student has a unique individuality and that he must first locate himself in time and space. He must believe in the moving power of his own energy. He must learn to use his energy on many levels and in many forms. But, always, he must have an abiding faith that his energy is needed.

The student is not taught that his ideas must be worked

out on a confining, tradition-deadened, and crowded stage. For me, a theatre stage is an empty space surrounded by, or enclosed in, four walls. Lying dormant in that space are the basic elements of time-rhythm, silence and sound, movement, and darkness and light. While these primary elements have areas of difference, the ingredients that make up these elements are similar and parallel. For example, movement has direction, rhythm, silhouette, intensity, texture, timbre, and color. Sound simulates color and has movement, intensity, direction, rhythm, pitch, timbre, texture.

The raw material of the theatre is each play. This raw material must be brought to life to make its own statement through the use of space, direction, silhouette, sound, silence, light, and dark—each receiving the emphasis and the importance that the director and actors have discovered through experimentation and work. The designer acts as a creative energy in the heart of the play. He does not put up backgrounds or represent places. He puts the plan into its physical shape; he catches the energy of the play in living forms. He projects the space of the stage into the silence of the auditorium.

The director challenges the designer and the actors with his ideas, but he does not confine them to his imagination. He does not if he has belief in their creative abilities. And he does not if he has belief in his own ability to channel their energies into a positive and growing form.

For me, at least, the theatre is a faith. It is based on the firm belief that man needs to see his actions presented, in sharply delineated form, in terms of life that he can understand. It is the faith that each one of us must find his individual creative force and make it grow and take form. It is the faith that this individual creative force may be used to change and improve our lives and our perspective toward contemporary living. It is a faith developed out of experimentation and expenditure of every form of energy. It is a faith that must be expressed in action. In this faith is the positive belief that herein lies the living theatre of our time.

3. A TALE OF TWO CITIES

Alan Schneider

THE TWO CITIES where I have often been obstinate and occasionally objective in some rather up-and-down conditions represent, in terms of the present pattern of the American theatre, two separate worlds: New York City and Washington, Broadway and off off-Broadway. They represent the amateur and the professional, the communal and the commercial, the university and the college of hard knocks.

For fifteen restless years I have journeyed back and forth between these often-alienated and yet not always alien worlds. I have lived and worked in both, served an extended apprenticeship in both—replete with enthusiasms, seriousness, and all the other youthful diseases—physically and artistically fed, and been fed by, both: a kind of shuttling common denominator making the best of two possible worlds.

Alternately, for reasons of faith or despair, I would leave New York or Washington "for good," only to return as the tides of my theatrical fortune washed me back. Whenever Manhattan pavements grew too hard underfoot and outer-office secretaries too forbidding, I would board the ever available Pennsylvania Railroad for the green landscapes and easier ways of the nation's capital. Whenever a production of mine in Washington happened to be worth seeing, someone would usually skip luncheon at Sardi's to come down (or is it up?), see it, and beckon me up (or is it down?) again. For a few years I tried commuting weekly—studying and working (without pay) with various off-Broadway groups in New York, and teaching and directing (with pay) in Washington. This procedure I do not recommend. The physical part was all right, and one may even grow to love the Pennsylvania. But the psychological strain of functioning simultaneously as an unemployed pariah and a working messiah was almost too much to bear.

A young would-be director, who recently came to me for advice on how to crash Broadway (and I often wonder why I should be expected to encourage competition), informed me that he considered my career crowned with success because he had read much about me in the newspapers. I gently suggested that success in the theatre is not measured in column inches but in personal satisfaction, a rare bird of a commodity and not easily caught. I explained that success, at least in my case, came neither from fame, which is always somewhat ersatz, nor from monetary reward, which is certainly pleasant, but from the opportunities I had had for more or less continuous work. My specific advice, by the way, was that he stop reading newspapers and start directing plays. Anyhow, whatever success I have had did not come to me the night of my first Broadway production; it came from a succession of opportunities through fifteen years of work on a variety of more or less congenial directorial assignments that let me practice and grow in my craft.

Good, bad, and who knew at the time, a total of nearly one hundred productions have come my way—from Saroyan's *Jim Dandy* in the early years of the Catholic University theatre (for which some eight lonely graduate students showed up at tryouts) to the "Salute to France" production of Thornton Wilder's *The Skin of Our Teeth*, so happily blessed with the combined talents of Helen Hayes, Mary Martin, George Abbott, and Florence Reed. (George, since everyone wants to know, not only took direction nobly; he asked for more.) I have rehearsed in attics, lofts, storerooms, washrooms, gymnasiums, and even theatres. I have worked in tiny auditoriums where the actors tripped over the first rows of spectators and in amphitheatres that would have been too vast for Reinhardt. I have worked indoors and out, on classics and first drafts—good and bad in each category—in front of and behind the proscenium arch, and sometimes with no arch at all.

The main thing was that I kept working, instead of tramping the streets or trying to sell my talents in a theatrical office (at both of which processes I am constitutionally bad). Instead of suffering in silence, I worked in silence. Instead of bemoaning the lack of proper opportunity, I looked up some improper opportunity some place else. On some occasions I wound up having to create my own opportunity. And this process invariably and inevitably paid off—in terms of more opportunity. Besides, and fortunately, there was always Washington.

The essential ingredients for theatrical survival are talent possibly, persistence probably, and luck certainly. My luck started with my first real directing job at Washington's Catholic University theatre, then (1941) beginning to acquire its reputation and status. Washington just happened to be my home town; I knew most of the theatre people there personally. The director of the Washington Civic Theatre, Day Tuttle, for whom I had worked both off stage and on, had been encouraging me to work for a graduate degree in theatre so that I might be qualified to teach and direct. Walter Kerr, now drama critic for the *New York Herald Tribune* and then a recent addition to the Catholic University faculty, was similarly helpful and had suggested Northwestern University in Illinois or Cornell University in New York State. I had become aware of Catholic University's theatrical prowess largely through Walter's productions of *Murder in the Cathedral* and *The Comedy of Errors,* and we had spent many a tavernous night discussing matters of theatre aesthetics and history.

No sooner had I completed my work for the degree at Cornell, and was awaiting the conventional call from some state teachers college in the wilds of the Middle West, when the lucky lightning struck. Father Gilbert V. Hartke, head of Catholic University's department of speech and drama, was going away for a year to work on his doctorate; at the last minute, the person he wanted could not come. Was I interested? Was I! I came down on the Pennsylvania and got the job. Up again to pack, I heard someone on the train saying that the job had been given to a Yale man. That was one of the longest train rides I ever took, but the Yale man turned out to be from Cornell. And instead of one year, I stayed off and on for eleven.

From that accidental association came not only the rewards of the actual work and the people with whom I was fortunate enough to work, but one thing eventually led to another. A graduate of the department started Arena Stage, which turned out to be one of the country's most interesting theatres-in-the-round, and I became production director for cofounder Zelda Fichandler. A friendly visitor from England's Dartington Hall Arts Centre some years later invited me over for a return visit; I went and became so enamored that I have since returned three times, at steadily decreasing intervals. The university put on several productions that went to New York, and many others that brought New York down to see us—and to get acquainted.

When Theatre, Inc., in the person of board member Norris Houghton, now coproducer of the Phoenix Theatre, asked me to come to New York as casting director, I was a trifle hesitant. I was not exactly sure just what a casting director did, and I was terrified about the world of the commercial theatre. But Theatre, Inc., seemed an especially enterprising organization. It had just brought over the Old Vic, which, paced by Olivier and Richardson, had scored an artistic triumph no other company had ever equaled. It had plans for new playwrights, young actors, a children's theatre, and a few other somewhat unorthodox ventures. I decided to take a chance on New York—and casting directors.

In between casting a wide variety of productions, none of which got farther than Philadelphia, we held weekly auditions of talent, most of which, in the usual manner, continued to languish in our copious casting files. Largely through Norrie's moral support and that of another board member, actress Beatrice Straight, I organized an acting workshop for some of the more talented people who had auditioned and were still languishing on cards. We called ourselves "Studio 63," because our address was 63 West Forty-fourth Street, and the word "Studio" had just come into prominence with the formation of Elia Kazan's

Actors' Studio. Among our members—some did not stay very long but graduated to *the* Studio and/or Broadway —were Julie Harris, Maureen Stapleton, Darren Mc-Gavin, Lee Grant, Charles Nolte, and Vivian Nathan.

One of our early projects consisted of four different simultaneous productions, with four separate casts, of Tennessee Williams' one-act *The Long Goodbye*. Two of these productions were to be staged conventionally, with flats set up at one end of our rehearsal room; the other two, partly as expedient and partly as experiment, were to be done "in-the-round." I had heard vague rumors of Margo Jones's early work in Dallas, but I had not previously been attracted by central staging techniques.

We rehearsed in shifts, with actors shuttling back and forth among the various casts because of commercial engagements that cropped up. Then Norrie went off to England to direct *Macbeth*. Neglected and almost forgotten by the rest of our board of directors, we had no help, no budget, no hope. Only a kind of actors' persistence kept us going, plus the guiding light of an occasional small moment of good work. Many times, in those long weeks of endless midnight stands in that cold, bare upstairs room, we were tempted to quit. But somehow we did not. Somehow we managed to arrange a "demonstration" of our work for an invited audience of agents, producers, and the board.

The day before the "demonstration," our remaining juvenile lead got a paying job, and we had to replace him with a hastily rehearsed walk-on. He turned out to be wonderful in the part. And the "demonstration" demonstrated that once seen, many of the members of Studio 63 could get jobs—even though not all the agents came, nor, particularly disappointing, did Tennessee. The board was most impressed. New faces battered at our gates. We went to work on another project with renewed enthusiasm and drive.

Out of this came something totally unexpected. Randy Goodman, a young playwright whose adaptation of *The Lower Depths* was scheduled for production in A.N.T.A.'s Experimental Theatre Series, had watched some of our rehearsals. He offered me his play. I liked the script very much, begged Theatre, Inc., and Studio 63 for a leave of absence, and went into rehearsal. I had been in New York four months, and I had expected to wait four years for this kind of opportunity.

The ensuing production of *A Long Way from Home*, as the adaptation was called, while it neither revolutionized Broadway nor brought me hordes of offers, proved a valuable and special kind of experience. In addition, I received four good notices, including one from Brooks Atkinson, which I especially cherish, a nice note from Margaret Webster, and a telephone call from a rising young producer named Robert Whitehead. The rest was silence. I went back to Theatre, Inc., to find a cast for Norrie Houghton's *Macbeth*. Studio 63 continued to work and grow and give other "demonstrations" and lose more people—until Theatre, Inc., itself, buffeted on all sides, quietly faded away. Years later, some of the ideas it had had, but never carried out, became part of the Phoenix Theatre on Second Avenue. The theatre is predictably unpredictable.

For days that grew into weeks that grew into months, I walked the streets of Broadway, part of the lonely crowd looking for a nonexistent job. I lived on unemployment insurance and died several times daily. Then one dark day a cable from England wondered whether I could come to Dartington Hall for a year as a guest director and lecturer. I swallowed once and answered that I could come for only six months: I had "commitments." The next day, almost, I was offered a beginning director's job in television at what seemed an absolutely astronomical salary. I struggled with my conscience for about five seconds and then chose England and the theatre. I have never regretted that choice. (And since that time I have tried more and more never to let the question of money affect such a decision.)

Those six months in England had many consequences, including a strong desire to work more continuously than I had been working in New York. I went back to the security and continuity of Catholic University. Only when I was offered an even greater continuity of production, though somewhat less security, at Arena Stage, did I leave. I liked the idea of working for a permanent resident professional theatre in Washington. I liked the idea of its being an arena theatre as well, with an excellent staff and a high level of imagination in its productions. Here, as before at Catholic University, I was able to work happily and fully, learning from each production and gaining from each a satisfying theatrical experience.

How long this process might have gone on, I do not know, but some years and many ups and downs later, I received another telephone call from a now-established producer named Robert Whitehead. Bob had a good memory, the courage of his convictions, and a heart of gold. He offered me a new comedy, *The Remarkable Mr. Pennypacker,* which I reluctantly turned down because I did not think that I could direct comedy. The job went to another director, and I forgot about it, eating my heart out when my wife and I read the script again and realized what a good, warm, wonderful play it was. Two weeks later, the telephone rang again. It was Bob, again asking me to direct *Pennypacker*. The other director had gotten a film offer. Fate does not often telephone twice. I took the next train to New York and my first Broadway job. As Eddie Cantor is supposed to have said, "It takes twenty years to make an overnight success." Or fifteen.

Some people are born to the theatre, some achieve it, and some have the theatre thrust upon them. I came into the theatre by osmosis. Until after I was graduated from college, the thought of working in the theatre never occurred to me, although I had "played" in it since childhood. At different times in my increasingly distant youth, I was going to be a doctor, a writer, a physicist, a foreign correspondent, and, I suppose, a fireman. Somehow or other I became a theatre director. Even then, when finally led to try my hand at directing plays, I chose the supposed stability and permanence of a teaching career in a university theatre. The constant uncertainty and insecurity of the professional stage always frightened me. Yet here I am now right in the middle of it.

How this transformation took place, I do not really know. As the fortuneteller in *The Skin of Our Teeth* says, "It's easy to tell one's future, but who can truly explain the past?" I was born in Kharkov, Russia, in the middle of what is probably as theatrical an event as the overly theatrical twentieth century has produced: the Russian Revolution. On the evening of July 4, 1923, my mother and father and I arrived in New York Harbor—with some fairly theatrical fireworks making us think that we had left one conflagration for another. When I was four or five, I spent many happy Saturday afternoons at the Moscow Children's Theatre, watching casts of talented adults play Kipling's *Jungle Tales*, Hans Christian Andersen's *The Emperor and the Nightingale*, and the *Nutcracker*.

Needless to say, I loved them all, over and over again, and to this day I feel that what the theatre needs more than anything else is a generation or two of youthful spectators. At the same time, my parents went regularly to the Moscow Art Theatre, often braving gunfire in the streets. I was evidently too young for Chekhov, a loss that saddens me to this day.

Once safely in the United States, however, I seem to have neglected the theatre. Whether it was because of the change, the language, or perhaps the absence of a theatre to be seen, at any rate, I can recall no youthful excursions to the local stock company, no glimpses of the great scurrying into carriages, nor even a visit to *The Student Prince*. My parents both being physicians, specialists in tuberculosis, we lived mostly in a succession of "Magic Mountain" sanatoriums, remote from even the smallest small town and the smallest touring company. My chief recreation consisted of reading every book in whatever library happened to be near by—especially Tom Swift and G. A. Henty's succession of historical romances—and populating the superabundant fields around us with the heroes of Agincourt and the "old abandoned mine shaft."

There must have been the usual number of back-yard theatricals for pennies and pins, but I do not remember any special occasions. Actually, the "theatre" of my childhood was the silent movie. Three or four nights each week the patients and staff saw the latest films absolutely free of charge. Three or four nights each week for years I went to the silent movies, except when an oversexy title or parental punishment kept me at home with Henty. I knew them all intimately and inside out: Thomas Meighan and Milton Sills, Chaplin and Keaton, Vilma Banky, and Rod La Rocque. My first "crushes" were on Betty Bronson and Billie Dove. But I had never heard of the family Barrymore—neither John nor Ethel. Once a Sunday supplement advertised a projector and several reels of film to anyone who could sell some fantastic number of packets of needles (plus $3.50 in cash). I sold them all. My mother still comes across an occasional packet at home.

When I was ready for high school, we moved to Baltimore and to the sudden, shattering experience of having to pay for each movie. My evening excursions lessened in number; besides, libraries were more convenient and still free. After a succession of little red schoolhouses, the size of my new school made me more than normally shy. Not until I had been persuaded by my English teacher, a Miss Angela Broening, to participate in a city-wide oratorical contest on the aims and merits of the National Recovery Administration—a contest that I eventually and rather surprisingly won—did I emerge from the cocoon. I was a cheerleader. I ran on the track team and got my letter. I even got interested in student politics. I participated in every activity possible, except the dramatics club. For some inscrutable reason, I was sent to art school twice a week, and twice a week I hated art with an ardor that has only recently abated. And I remember the usual trials and errors in studying *Julius Caesar*. But although Baltimore at that time had two or three theatres for touring shows and a flock of amateur organizations, including the Vagabonds, neither theatregoing nor theatredoing interested me. Then one day during my junior year, a close friend, finding himself with an extra ticket, invited me along to see Ina Claire in S. N. Behrman's *Biography*. I had never heard of either Miss Claire or the play in question, but I went along. Getting free tickets was, after all, a habit.

That accidental journey to a matinee has left me never the same. The play was charming, its language poised and gleaming in a manner no longer fashionable, and Miss Claire was absolutely irresistible. Twenty years later I happened to sit next to her at a Broadway *première*. By the end of the second act I had screwed up my courage enough to lean over and introduce myself, adding, with something of a schoolboy's tongue-tiedness, that she had, without knowing it, started me in the theatre. She smiled politely and went on talking to her partner, obviously assuming that I was a little drunk or eccentric or both. But I had told her the simple truth. That afternoon I had been overwhelmed by the magic and radiance of her performance, by the flavor of the total event. I had discovered that the theatre, at its best, was an experience more satisfying than books or movies or running the hundred-yard dash in ten seconds.

From then on, I went as often as I could afford it and sometimes when I could not, going without meals or ushering for my ticket of admission. I saw Walter Huston in *Dodsworth*, Ethel Barrymore in *The Constant Wife*, and the Group Theatre productions of *Men in White* and *Awake and Sing*. I had finally discovered America, or at least the theatre in America. (It took me years to discover that the theatre in America had anything besides a second balcony; I still feel not quite at home sitting downstairs.) For the first time I began to be interested in reading plays and hearing about plays—although I had not yet read any books on the theatre, or the Sunday *New York Times* drama section. I joined the dramatics club at school, played the title role in *Hernani* in French (!), organized a group of friends to do one-act plays around Baltimore, and snared the coveted leading role in our Senior Class production of *Seven Keys to Baldpate*. Most sacrilegiously, I once chose to go to a rehearsal instead of track practice. Under Miss Claire's spell, I was beginning to be lost.

Extracurricularly lost, that is. No thought of the theatre as a livelihood entered my mind. My favorite subjects remained mathematics and physics, and I was set on being a research physicist. The book I chose for graduation was Sir James Jeans's *The Mysterious Universe*. (I have still never read it all the way through.) I entered the Johns Hopkins University to study projective geometry and advanced physics. On the side I wrote for the newspaper, including occasional drama reviews, and played a small part in the "Barnstormer" show. To my great amazement and despair, I soon discovered that advanced physics proved much too advanced. I had to struggle to get anything better than a passing grade. But the required freshman course in English literature, which seemed to bother the collection of Einsteins with whom I was closeted daily in the physics laboratory, proved a delight. I reveled in *Beowulf*, in Marlowe's *Tamburlaine the Great*, and in most of Mr. Shakespeare, while I struggled with assorted laws of mass and gravity. Thoreau seemed to be clearer than thermodynamics. Obviously something was wrong.

That summer I retired to Glenn Dale sanatorium near Washington, where my parents were then working, to think and read—and to find out what was wrong. Near by was the University of Maryland. I filled in the summer with a couple of English courses: writing and play production for teachers. The handwriting, though somewhat indistinct, was on the ceiling. In the autumn I transferred to the University of Wisconsin, far enough away for me to lick my wounds in privacy, and equipped with, I was told, an excellent journalism department. I had decided to become a newspaperman, preferably a foreign correspondent. For which romantic aberration, please blame 1936, Vincent Sheean, and John Gunther.

Eventually, as I became impressed with the value of substance over form, I abandoned journalism and moved downstairs in the same building to international relations, supplemented by comparative literature under Philo M. Buck, who made a page of prose seem the most beautiful work of man. I worked on the *Daily Cardinal* as reporter, feature writer, and assistant drama critic. I was on the debating team, benefiting from the coaching of Andrew Weaver and Henry Ewbank. I sampled courses and instructors in other departments, evidently in a fairly judicious manner, for three of those instructors are now college presidents.

Most important, there was the drama society, the Wisconsin Players. Each year the Players occupied a larger proportion of my time and interest, a drift that the political science department had some difficulty in understanding. I tried out for almost every production and wound up carrying every kind of spear in mankind's and the costumer's arsenal. Occasionally I spoke a line or two. At one point I was playing Macduff. I still recall the reverberation I could get on "O hell-kite!" I also collected props, including a caldron eight feet in diameter. (Since then, I have always told prop crews that they could find *anything*.) Sometimes I was playing in two or three shows at the same time; once I managed to study for a final exam on-stage while playing a blind beggar in *The Desert Song*.

Had I been a few inches taller, my role in the theatre might have turned out quite differently. But since all the university theatre directors seemed to feel that I was too short to be very romantic with those lovely tall Wisconsin females, they cast me in such a procession of young boys and bearded ancients that I sought refuge in writing, directing, and radio. (I played Mio once in a laboratory production, but it was too late to show them.) I won a Wisconsin Drama Guild contest with a play that I wrote, directed, played the lead in, and gave away tickets for. I wrote and acted in radio shows for University Station WHA. I took a course in contemporary drama, learned about a "production book" from Joseph Smith and Lowell Lees, and ventured to direct *Hedda Gabler*, which was a step above my first effort, a comedy called *Squaring the Circle*, in both content and method of work. Naturally, this unorthodox activity did not result in a Rhodes Scholarship, although I tried.

But the activity still remained extracurricular, and my knowledge of the theatre largely pragmatic. It was all basically fun, social and creative, but not a serious attachment. I knew nothing of the history or theory of the theatre, nor did I particularly want to know. Totally lacking was the sense of the theatre as an art form, or as a legitimate life occupation. On vacations, of course, I was able to stop off in New York on my way home to see a few plays. I liked the musicals: *Babes in Arms, On Your Toes, Pal Joey*. I went to *Boy Meets Girl* and *Three Men on a Horse* rather than to the social dramas of the period about which everyone was talking—although I did see and was impressed with the acting in the Group's *Johnny Johnson* and *Golden Boy*. The high points of those years seemed to be Gielgud's *Hamlet*, Cornell's *Saint Joan*, and Orson Welles's modern dress *Julius Caesar*. But I missed *Our Town, Victoria Regina*, and *The Shoemaker's Holiday*. Selection was largely a matter of accident, availability, and whim. Taste was yet to come.

Getting a job of any kind on a newspaper in the summer

of 1939 was not too simple. Papers were folding up, and staffs were being reduced. Experienced journalists were walking the streets, or trying to get to Europe for the war that was coming. I tried every angle and followed up every contact. I wrote feature articles, documentary radio scripts, short short stories, and essays for the *Atlantic Monthly*; one or two were sold. I pursued a dozen schemes: experiments in color television for CBS; a column for the Baltimore *Sun* papers; a program of adult education in drama for Baltimore. Nothing seemed to work. I labored like a mountain, while directing a one-act play for a small country school in the wilds of the Bowie Race Track, and brought forth a little mouse of a job: a lowliest-of-the-low announcer on WBAL in Baltimore, mostly commercials and station breaks, and twenty dollars a week. I took it.

To take my mind off some of the day's commercials, I tried out for the Washington Civic Theatre's production of *Merrily We Roll Along* and wound up with one of the leads. Since I was living at home in Glenn Dale—my salary was not large enough to justify moving to Baltimore —I took an early morning train to work, ran after work to catch an evening bus to Washington, and ran after rehearsal to catch the midnight bus back to Glenn Dale. That was a lot of running. Finally the director, Day Tuttle, Yale man and real gentleman of the theatre, suggested that I room with him in Washington until the show went on.

We got to know each other. He encouraged me to read and to think seriously about the theatre for the first time. Through his efforts, I left WBAL to become public relations director for the Civic Theatre. Soon afterward, I got a job writing radio scripts for the Office of Education and ghostwriting speeches for Postmaster General James

A. Farley. I learned about the productions at Catholic University and became a frequent visitor and friend. Piscator's version of *Saint Joan*, which he directed for the Civic with Luise Rainer playing Joan, also impressed me —even though through Luise's insistence I was demoted from Brother Martin to one of the monks. (I was not powerful enough for Miss Rainer; perhaps she was right.)

More and more I was becoming aware of the possible satisfactions of actually working in the theatre as a director. I realized that I knew very little about the theatre, but for the first time I wanted to know more. After years of resistance and indecision, of avoiding the theatre as a primary interest, while getting increasingly involved in it, I made up my mind: The die I had held so long in my hand but had been afraid to throw would be finally cast. I would go back to college, get a degree, and try to get a job teaching and directing in a university or in a community theatre.

I chose Cornell, partly because of the presence of A. M. Drummond, and partly because I should need no undergraduate credits in speech and drama. It was a fortunate choice. What Drummond gave me during the next year and summer was a revelation. Led by "the Boss," as we affectionately though secretly called him, I explored the terrain of the theatre on my hands and knees, with his vision as a magnifying glass. I discovered the fascinating dichotomy of "representational" and "presentational" theatre—a separation that I have been breaking down ever since. I found out about Craig and Appia, those Siamese twins of the modern theatre, about the theatricality of Nicholas Evreinov, about Bakshy's *The Theatre Unbound*, about Copeau and Stanislavsky. I read Cheney, Mantzius, Aristotle, Stark Young, Simonson, Gorelik, Macgowan, and Jones. I exchanged *Stage Magazine* for

Theatre Arts. Henry Myers of the English department gave an insight into the nature of tragedy that went far beyond the boundaries of the theatre. I lived in the library and wore out a dozen typewriter ribbons. I wrote my thesis on Evreinov's concept of "the theatre-in-life," and was given the opportunity of helping to direct a production of *The Chief Thing*.

Drummond, although he occasionally seemed gruff and distant, made us aware of a thousand facets of theatre art and history. He demonstrated the importance of imagination and curiosity. He showed us not how to hammer nails but how to follow ideas. We did not always agree with everything he said or did. We all missed more specific attention, perhaps, to the everyday problems of acting and directing. But he encouraged us, drove us, goaded us, and loved us—and made us love him and the theatre. More than anyone else up to that time, he prepared me to make the most of the chance if and when it came.

The bookcase in my study, where most of my theatre books are kept, has four shelves. The first is what might loosely be called the theatrical or "new stagecraft" shelf: Craig; Reinhardt; Moderwell's *The Theatre of Today* and Macgowan's *The Theatre of Tomorrow* (tomorrow, it seems, as in *Waiting for Godot*, never comes); Cheney's *The New Movement in the Theatre*; Hallie Flanagan's *Shifting Scenes of the Modern European Theatre*; Norris Houghton's *Moscow Rehearsals*; Gorelik; Gassner; and so on. Below this is the "acting" shelf, mostly by or about or derived from Stanislavsky: *Acting: The First Six Lessons*, by Boleslavsky; the Rosenstein-Haydon-Sparrow manual; Cole and Chinoy; Chekhov, Redgrave, and Arthur Hopkins; as well as Archer, Calvert, Dolman, and Selden, ad infinitum. A few books on production have intruded. The third shelf is my English shelf: various studies of the Old Vic and Stratford; biographies of Gielgud, the Oliviers, Peggy Ashcroft, and Sybil Thorndike; the daily and Sunday columns of Agate, Harold Hobson, and some others; histories of various repertory theatres. The shelf is getting crowded. Already I have had to move the magazines and the beginnings of a "European" shelf in French, Italian, and German. The fourth is my "modern art" shelf. It contains only one or two books on the theatre—Margo Jones's slim volume on theatre-in-the-round and Edith Isaacs' *Architecture for the New Theatre*. Here are mostly Frank Lloyd Wright, Moholy-Nagy, Gropius, Kepes, Dorner, the Bauhaus, and a horde of its disciples—books and authors that theatre people read all too rarely for their own good.

In a curious way, without conscious plan or realization, that bookcase suggests the pattern of my life in the theatre. From theatricality to reality, from America to Europe, from the classics to the moderns—this is more or less the path I have taken.

Cornell first made me aware of the potentialities of theatricality; Catholic University let me practice theatricality and gave me a chance to find myself as a director. The policy of the department was to present experimental plays, new scripts, and classics (a policy more unique in 1941 than today) on as high a level of production as possible. I worked on all three kinds, from Saroyan's surrealist-lyrical *Jim Dandy* to several original musicals, and such eternals as Sophocles, Shakespeare, Racine, and Chekhov. The breadth and intensity of this experience was responsible, I am sure, for much of my subsequent work and thinking. The faculty (notably Father Hartke, director Walter Kerr, and interpretation "coach" Josephine Callan) was at that time primarily concerned with the nonrealistic theatre, as well as with certain decorative and stylistic aspects of speech and movement. Consciously and unconsciously, but quite willingly, I followed their lead. The design of my early productions tended to consist of the scenic elements, music and dance, patterns of movement, arrangements of levels and platforms. I planned each movement and position carefully in advance and marked it exactly in my production script, coming to each rehearsal with elaborate notations, arrows, and zig-zags—"blocking" the actors within an inch of their stage lives. (Block, by the way, also means to obstruct.)

My early productions were strong in stage pictures, the fluid use of vertical space, a wide range of movement— logical or not—carefully designed rhythmical relation-ships, and actors who were little better than puppets, and not always too happy about it, although they did not always complain. I remember that I was especially happy with the patterns of slapstick in *The Doctor in Spite of Himself*, the choreography in *Jim Dandy* and *The Importance of Being Earnest*, and the significantly formal patterns I evolved for the choruses in *Athaliah* and the prop men in *Lute Song*. I would take notes during dress rehearsals about an actor's being a foot too far right, in-stead of concerning myself about the meaning of what the actor was doing in the scene. In other words, at the time Meyerhold seemed more important than Stanislavsky.

Like almost everyone else, of course, I had tried not too successfully to read *An Actor Prepares*. The exercises in *A Manual of Acting* seemed to make sense, but I had difficulty in using them outside of class. The Clurman history of the Group Theatre made a tremendous impression on me, as had the Group's productions, but still I had little idea of how to apply what I had read about or seen.

When I came to New York for a short time in 1943–44 to play a small part in Maxwell Anderson's *Storm Operation*, "the method" was considered a kind of big joke by everyone except a dedicated few. I was interested but ignorant, and the show did not run long enough for me to find out very much. When I came to Theatre, Inc., in 1947, the joke was wearing off a bit. New York was dotted with acting groups, most of them guided or at least sparked by former members of the Group: Clurman, Stella Adler, Lee Strasberg, and Marty Ritt. Sandy Meisner had been teaching at the Neighborhood Playhouse since the mid-thirties.

Dissatisfied even in the years of their commercial success with the lack of a common vocabulary and a common way of working, Elia Kazan and Bobby Lewis had joined forces with producer Cheryl Crawford to found the Actors' Studio, a "theatre place" for professionals to work together and continue their development between jobs or during long runs. Included among the first "students" were Marlon Brando, Montgomery Clift, Julie Harris, David Wayne, Kim Hunter, Karl Malden, Maureen Stapleton, Eli Wallach, and others of similar caliber. No one laughed at that; they were too busy trying to get in. Today, after nine years, the Studio is probably the single most important influence in American acting, directing, and, perhaps, playwriting. The talent it encompasses is unequaled by any other group. Its possibilities in terms of the American theatre are enormous and, now that it has just acquired its own permanent home, closer than ever to some kind of realization.

Somewhat skeptical at first but always curious, I drifted

toward the edges of this fermenting activity. I watched the "demonstrations" at the Neighborhood Playhouse and at a host of lesser breeds without the law. I collared everybody I knew who was teaching or studying, and picked their brains till all hours of the night. Studio 63 gave me a place to try things along the lines of what I had heard. But I was not satisfied until I had literally begged my way into the Actors' Studio itself (thanks to the basic generosity of "Gadge" Kazan). There I proceeded to do everything from an improvisation with Marlon Brando and David Wayne, which almost killed me, to sweeping the floors, directing scenes from time to time, and watching at close range the best young acting talent in America. As I had, a few years previously, been introduced to the idea of theatricality and the use of the stage, so now I was enabled to discover the concept of reality and the use of the actor. I found, for the first time in my experience, a coherent and practical point of view about the craft of acting—with which the craft of directing is, after all, closely connected.

Primarily responsible for my conversion was Lee Strasberg, although personal contacts with Sandy Meisner, Danny Mann, and Kazan must also have contributed. One of the original three founders of the Group, Strasberg had long made his living as a teacher in those periods when he was not directing. Lee had studied with Richard Boleslavsky and Maria Ouspenskaya at the American Laboratory Theatre and had absorbed directly from them the basic principles espoused not only by Stanislavsky but by his great interpreter Vakhtangov. He joined the Studio soon after it was organized and quickly took over its day-by-day artistic leadership. I have listened to Lee talk for over eight years, have taken his advanced directing course in the American Theatre Wing's professional training program, and know of no one else who can speak about acting so cogently and so creatively. One may agree or disagree with him on specific details. One may like or dislike his personality. One must respect his continued presence and his enduring contribution to the American theatre. His diction may not always be Oxonian, but his mind takes top honors, and his knowledge of the technique and history of acting would earn him a dozen doctorates. There is no question that he is a theoretician par excellence, the St. Paul of the Stanislavsky "system."

Lee might on occasion be exasperating, but never dull. He taught me more about acting and, therefore, about directing than anyone else has, before or after. In a sense, he was even more of a teacher to me than Drummond was. Drummond made me generally aware of certain aspects of the theatre; Lee made me aware of certain specific problems of the actor and the director. Exactly what he taught me may not always be definable; all I know is that he made me think altogether differently. He made me think, for the first time, about actors and about how actors accomplished what they have to do. "Conscious preparation for an unconscious result," he quoted his own teacher, Boleslavsky. Truth in acting does not mean just naturalness or casualness or underplaying or saying lines sloppily out of the corner of one's mouth. Truth means actual physical and psychological aliveness—in the sense of actual sensory awareness, actual responsiveness to the stimuli, real and imaginary, that surround the actor on the stage. It is actually using the senses, the muscles, the sensitivity, the imagination of the actor. Truth means actually talking and listening to the other actors. I had read something of this in Lee's article on the training of the actor in the Gassner anthology, *Producing the Play*, but somehow it had not meant nearly so much as it did when it came directly from him.

Lee also made me think differently about what a director does, as well as about how and why he does it. He made me consider not just the lines of a play but the life of a play, out of which the lines spring. A play is like an iceberg, he would say, eight-ninths of which never rises above the surface of the water; but the exact size and shape of the one-ninth that does rise above the surface is always determined by the eight-ninths that remains below. He convinced me that the director's primary job and responsibility is to stimulate the sensitivity of the actor, not simply to steer him up and down the stage. He caused me never to be satisfied with the conventional, the cliché, the surface of truth—even when it "worked," even when it was supposedly "successful." I owe much, more than I can ever repay, to Lee Strasberg. And there are hundreds, perhaps thousands, of actors and directors who can say the same.

From the time I went back to Catholic University in 1949, I no longer mapped out each movement so rigidly in advance. I began to veer away from specific ordered "blocking," except in general outline, or in a Greek chorus, or a complex group scene such as the sequence at the end of Act I in *Pennypacker*. (But even then, in the case of the Greek chorus, I found that the less mechanical I was in my demands, the more effective the chorus movement turned out to be.) I concentrated instead on relationships, motivations, meanings, and a carefully thought-out floor plan. The battles of stage movement may well be won or lost on the drawing board.

Today, I tend to consider what each character wants

and what he is doing, thinking, sensing at the moment, not what he happens to be saying or where he has to move; that is, I consider what is *really happening* in terms of the circumstances surrounding the scene rather than the lines. Naturally, I still plan basic essentials of position and movement, but I allow the actors to fill in and change things as we go along. This does not mean that preparation is less intensive or that I will necessarily accept the first thing that happens in rehearsal. On the contrary, I must now be much more fully acquainted with the script's needs and requirements. And, in various stages of rehearsal, we may try many different ways of getting the desired results. Frankly, I may not know what I want until I see or hear a number of alternate possibilities. I may suggest what is wrong with a specific move, gesture, or manner of interpretation. I may ask the actor to try another kind of response in order to justify a circumstance or a meaning of which he may not even be aware. But I rarely tell him, for example, to get up or sit down on a certain word. I simply suggest that by the end of a given speech he should be near the window so that he can be seen by someone outside, or that somewhere during the scene he ought to find two or three places to examine the letter. I have found that this sort of approach frees the actor to exercise his own individual personality and talent.

While some actors thrive, some are just confused by this method of work. If they are young and relatively inexperienced, I generally urge them on to try—often with results that prove to be astonishing (as, for instance, in the Catholic University productions of *The Cherry Orchard*, *Othello*, and *The Skin of Our Teeth*). If they are established performers or stars, I try to adjust my way of work to their needs.

In *Anastasia* I had a company that was willing to work,

in fact, led me to work, in this way. Many of the best scenes and moments in that production came directly from the actors' finding things for themselves. On the other hand, Burgess Meredith in *The Remarkable Mr. Pennypacker* wanted me to give him an exact pattern of movement, which he adapted to himself, as well as the reasons for each move. George Abbott, himself accustomed to ordering each line and movement, liked me to tell him when and even how to stand or move, but he rarely wanted to know why; he preferred working that out for himself. Mary Martin constantly sought out specific suggestions for gestures, moves, bits of humorous business. She took those she liked and made them absolutely and brilliantly her own. What did not seem right to her, what she could not do, she would not do. Florence Reed always asked me to rehearse the exact moves over and over again until they became comfortable and part of herself. But Helen Hayes, once she knew the general plan of a scene, liked to feel her own way toward the "how." She was a tiny bit different in each performance, yet fundamentally always the same. Her second-act Atlantic City speech was one of the most exhilarating moments I have come close to in the theatre—specific, yet universal, precise yet completely spontaneous, the distillation of truth plus her comment on the truth she had discovered. The basic thing is that all actors work differently, and it is the director's job to reach them the best way he can.

When I first began directing, I would normally start to stage a script on the first or second day of rehearsal. This was partly because in the university theatre there was never enough time, and partly because I thought that was the best way to work. Since coming into contact with Lee and some of his colleagues, I like to spend the first few days reading the play, talking about it with the actors, exploring and finding out about the values of the script, as well as about the individualities of the performers. In the case of *The Cherry Orchard*, I took more than a week on this stage of rehearsal, including a day or two in trying various improvisations with different floor plans. This was in order not to get the actors accustomed to any particular movements and was designed to make a heavily Irish and youthfully optimistic cast understand and successfully interpret a Russian dramatist and behave like Russians—whatever that means. When we finally got on the stage, we had progressed to the point where it was possible to work out the movements in each act in one evening, a rate that I had never been able to reach before. And the degree of reality—looking, listening, behaving, reacting—was greater than I had previously been able to achieve with equally talented casts.

The use of improvisations during rehearsals may or may not bring about the desired results. It is worth trying. So are many other directorial procedures and devices. I have, for instance, tried playing music to see whether it might influence or stimulate the actors involved further than they had been able to go without music. I have experimented in all sorts of exercises to arouse the actor's imagination or physical responses. Sometimes I have had actors playing a scene at a distance from each other or with their backs turned, to produce a greater urgency in communicating. Once I had a cast running up and down the aisles of the auditorium, playing a given scene at full volume, in order to lend the proper vitality to the scene. Interestingly enough, both these devices had a pronounced and immediate effect.

I have also become a great believer in rehearsing privately with groups of two or three actors. This removes any shyness or inhibition that may exist, even subconsciously, and helps the actor to work freely and spontaneously. In the case of the "recognition scene" in *Anastasia*, I believe that a definite factor in making it come off so well was the fact that we rehearsed it in my apartment, over numerous cups of Russian tea and to generous doses of Russian music, long before the rest of the cast saw it played.

Every play and every performer poses specific problems, which must be approached organically, and with as clear a perception of those problems as possible. I suppose that this is the core of what I learned from Lee.

At any rate, after I returned to Catholic University, it was obvious to all, including myself, that something had happened to my work. It was not just that I was a better director. I was a different director. It was not just that scene designer Jim Waring and costume designer Joe Lewis were both extremely talented, and that we worked well together; it was that the very texture of the shows we did together was different. The productions were just as full of effective stage pictures, but the movement and the grouping seemed more organic and more satisfying. The rhythmical relationships were as explicit, but the sense of life was deeper, not necessarily more realistic, but definitely more real. The actors were no longer semi-puppets. They were creative and were contributing the fullest measure of themselves, and, therefore, they were more able to grow in their craft as actors. There was no question that something had happened to make me grow in mine.

After World War I, the Mecca for most theatre voyagers was, in the twenties, Germany, with its Reinhardt, its Jessner, its Piscator; and, in the thirties, Russia, with its Meyerhold, its Vakhtangov, its Stanislavsky. The effect of those now distant voyages has been deeply evident in the work and writing of many American theatre people.

After World War II, the Mecca shifted westward to Great Britain, with its London, its Stratford, its Edinburgh; and the effects of this new pilgrimage are only just beginning to be felt. If the Actors' Studio, for example, forms one wing of a new American art of acting and production, the graduates of the Old Vic School and the Royal Academy of Dramatic Art and the scores of returning Fulbright and G.I. scholars must be reckoned with as the other wing. While London's West End continues to send us her melodramas and small-scale comedies of bourgeois manners, it mainly impresses us with the scope and seriousness of its nationwide theatre.

I first went to England in 1949 at the invitation of Dartington Hall, a rather unique blend of rural economics and the seven arts, nestled in the lovely rolling moors of Devonshire. If there is a Shangri-La west of the Himalayas, this is it. Besides lecturing and directing a few plays under Dartington's rather overpeaceful conditions, I was able—through the great generosity of Mrs. Dorothy Elmhirst (mother of Beatrice Straight of Theatre, Inc., and Broadway)—to spend part of my six months in journeying the length and breadth of the United Kingdom, reveling in the traditions and craftsmanship of the English theatre. It was a feast of Herculean proportions, more than making up for the food rationing and the food that was not rationed. I have been going back for dessert ever since. In fact, I fell madly in love with the English in general and with one English girl in particular. (Subsequently, I married her, this being a perfect example of the influence the English theatre has had on my life.) Like Ina Claire, the English stage won me with its brilliance.

The brilliance is not one of performance alone, although the record there is tremendously impressive. The amount and variety of English theatre activity, even in what they call a bad season, has always seemed positively staggering to me—and wonderful. Its top echelon of talent—Olivier, Gielgud, Richardson, Redgrave, Scofield, Guinness, Thorndike, Evans, Ashcroft, Hiller, Johnson, Leigh—is a golden dozen that would be hard to find in any other theatrical environment. Some of its best productions—notably those of Peter Brook, Anthony Quayle, and Tyrone Guthrie—seem to me to rank with the finest in the modern theatre. Guthrie's rendering of *The Three Estates* on the apron stage at the Edinburgh Festival remains especially in my memory as a classic blending of medieval pageantry and brilliant comic invention. The three or four productions of his that I have seen would lead me to rank him as today's most imaginative theatrical director.

While contemporary British dramatists seem generally too tame or too frisky, British theatrical thinking and organization remains consistently energetic and sane. The record of the Arts Council remains unequaled by anything we have been able to develop here. Our off-Broadway theatre has not yet managed to evolve a group like the Arts Theatre or the Lyric Theatre, Hammersmith—although, I admit, the Phoenix is trying. Broadway is a long way from an Old Vic Company, and our regional theatre has need of many more Bristol Old Vics, Birmingham Reps, and Glasgow Citizens' theatres. Any similarity between Stratford-on-Avon and Stratford, Connecticut, is geographical rather than artistic.

But the theatre in England as a whole has a strength greater than the sum of its individual parts. What impresses me most and has most affected my thinking is its primary virtue of functioning as a nationwide habit and not as a local luxury. With whatever weakness or fault, it is an institution and not a free-for-all, a landscape and not a jungle, a meal and not a cocktail party. It is important rather than incidental to the nation's daily life and outlook. Always sensed by theatregoer and theatre worker alike is (I quote Guthrie) "the implication that the imaginative stimulus which good theatre can supply is a necessity, not merely an amenity, in a healthy community." Or as George Jessel once put it to me when I bumped into him at a matinee at Wyndham's: "Every show has a chance here because they like the theatre. We have to wait for the reviews."

I have always wanted to be part of a theatre, whether in New York or Washington, where we did not "have to wait for the reviews" before we knew whether we had a job. Not that I am against reviews or reviewers; some of my best friends are drama critics. But I am for continuity of work rather than stop-and-go, hit-and-flop; permanence instead of production-in-transit; a theatre that could be a home and not a motel. I prefer a theatre operation with a reasonable amount of stability to one with an unreasonable amount of chaos—even if I could not make a fortune in the former kind. As I once told a *New York Times* reporter, "I don't expect to make a million dollars; I just want to work in the theatre." In England, a permanent theatre operation with an organic point of view and a reasonable amount of balance seems to be more or less normal; in the United States, or at least in New York City, it is the ideal and the exception.

While our amateur stages multiply in alarming quantity, if not necessarily in quality, the professional theatre outside the marketplace of New York still awaits the millennium and sometimes labors mightily for that millennium to come. A few notable playhouses across the land have somehow managed to survive and suit the changing times; what they contribute besides survival and a chance for a few people to work is not clear to me. A few others have come and gone; without doubt, more will come and go. Margo Jones has shown us what can be done. And such theatres as Washington's Arena Stage, Nina Vance's Alley in Houston, and the theatre-in-the-round in Rochester obviously owe their existence to her example. There are now, after all, three Stratfords instead of one. There are also Antioch, Manteo, Ellenville, and points west. Next summer, next year, there will be other names on the theatrical maps.

The success of each new venture helps the next and the next. And ten people with Margo's drive and organizational gifts could perhaps remake the theatrical pattern of the continent. But then what? What happens when those ten tire, or retire? Must there always be ten more? I do not mean to be critical when I say that the basic question remains: Do the American people want that much more theatre? Do they care as much about it as they do about movies, television, or ice-cream sodas? Do they really need the living theatre as nourishment, as constant accompaniment to their lives? Or are they satisfied with theatre as an occasional incident—or accident—in life? Is the theatre, as one film critic has written, "in its older form" dead and continuing to exist only by inertia? That is the theatre's sixty-four-million-dollar question.

There was a time when the rise and development of the university theatre, a uniquely American contribution, seemed to presage a golden age of some kind or other. A generation later—and tireder—the hopes remain not entirely fulfilled, wrapped up in some old lecture notes. The basic contradiction between the university as a place for knowing and the theatre as a place for doing has not yet been satisfactorily resolved; classroom and stage remain somehow incommensurate. University theatre plants are unrivaled by anything on Broadway, and more and more are being built each year. Productions are tending to be more interesting and even more "professional," but the level of acting inevitably leaves much to be desired. How do these potentially valuable resources best fit into the future of the American theatre? Where do we go from here? I used to think that it was fine for a school to have a theatre; now I have come round to thinking that perhaps it might be more logical for a theatre to have a school, as the Old Vic does in Bristol, and as Michel St. Denis is working out in his Centre d'Est in Strasbourg. After all, we hang early Picassos in the library and invite Horowitz to come and play Beethoven for us; why should Hamlet always be played by a sophomore premed rather than, for example, an early Laurence Olivier?

In New York City, the theatre's showcase, the glass has of late been considerably shattered. The steadily increasing pressures and inner contradictions of commercial Broadway have produced an off-Broadway movement stronger and more extensive than at any time since the early twenties. Opportunities abound for the supposedly experimental and offbeat venture, and especially for the showcasing of newer talent. The Village and the East Side are full of them: Circle-in-the-Square; the Phoenix Theatre; *Three-Penny Opera* at the Theatre de Lys; *Othello* or *Macbeth* at the Shakespearewrights. Again, they come —and go. I have, in the past, thought that a permanent theatre in New York, repertory or long-run, was an impossibility. If "permanent" does not mean forever, a number of them may yet prove me wrong. But failure, even off Broadway, usually means a quick death and new tenants. Success, off Broadway, means an inevitable dispersal of the talents and energies that made the success possible. The very organs of publicity and exploitation, which automatically make a theatrical event in New York seem more significant than something done in Washington or Seattle, in the long run prevent the theatrical event from really becoming as significant as it might otherwise become. Off-Broadway is good for the soul and for the career. Whether it does anything constructive for the American theatre in the way of a new playwright or a new style of production remains to be seen.

In Washington, during the war, I remember a cultural attaché at one of the embassies telling me that when he wrote to his friends back home saying that the capital of the United States had no permanent professional theatre (in the European sense of what a theatre is), they not only did not believe him but thought that he was trying to make anti-American propaganda. While we were presenting *The Skin of Our Teeth* at the International Theatre Festival in Paris, our most difficult job was not to explain the play but to explain that the players were not members of any permanent company: that they had been selected for this production only and had never played together before. The Peking Opera that was so acclaimed in Paris had been rehearsing, we used to say, for five hundred years; the Berliner Ensemble of East Germany, which brought over such splendid productions of *Mother Courage* and *The Caucasian Circle of Chalk*, for five years; we rehearsed five weeks, one more than customary. The German Communist government spent hundreds of thousands of dollars on the costumes alone. The richest capitalist nation in the world had to depend on the generosity of a few private contributors to send us over, and we did a television show to pay them back. As

William Saroyan says at the end of *My Heart's in the Highlands,* "There's something wrong somewhere." Until and unless enough people care, there will continue to be "something wrong somewhere," no matter how many new theatre buildings we put up, or how many new productions we mount. In England they care. That is why the English theatre, in terms of its character and degree of organization, its contribution to the lives of its citizens, seems to me to be the most important theatre I know.

I remember that I have gone to the theatre in England more than 150 times, and that only once have I left before the curtain fell. I remember that I heard and understood every syllable, no matter where I happened to be sitting. I remember—and I treasure—not only the individual productions and performances, not only what went on on-stage, but the comfort and convenience of playgoing, the courtesy and cleanliness I found everywhere, in the box office, in the auditorium, and backstage. Most of all, I remember that the opera glasses I once rented for sixpence (seven cents) had no umbilical cord riveting them to the back of the seat in front of me. The management assumed that I liked the theatre. They were willing to trust me.

If awareness of theatre came relatively late in my life, awareness of art, modern or otherwise, came even later. Until about ten years ago, I rarely entered a museum and knew little or nothing about the history of art—par for the course among most theatre directors. During the war, however, New York's Museum of Modern Art lured me inside with its silent film series and kept me inside looking at works of Picasso and Brancusi and Calder's mobiles. Accidentally I discovered Kepes's *Language of Vision* and Moholy-Nagy's *Vision in Motion* and have found them continuous sources of wonder and delight. Gradually I found out more and more about the Bauhaus and its varied successors. I had already known *Architecture for the New Theatre* and was acquainted generally with some of Norman Bel Geddes' work. *The Fountainhead* introduced me to Frank Lloyd Wright and made me sorry that I had not become an architect. The postwar building boom introduced me to varieties of modern architecture and graphic art. (Hallie Flanagan Davis once told me that she thought Alexander Dorner's *The Way Beyond 'Art'* was the most valuable book she knew of. It remains a bit beyond me, but I am trying.) The entire visual landscape around me seemed to be changing, and I wanted to know more about the causes and effects. I remember, a few years ago, riding in a car past a new, ultramodern ranch type house in the suburbs. I parked, rang the bell, and asked the lady who answered if she would mind showing me around. She was surprised but flattered—and obliged. Since that particular experience, I have taught a course at Catholic University, somewhat cosmically entitled "Theatre, Art and Civilisation," dealing with some of these newer relationships and changes that I have observed. We explored many books, none of them on the theatre; yet we discovered many things about the theatre. It was one of the most stimulating teaching experiences I have ever had, and I believe that the students felt similarly invigorated.

My interest in modern art is responsible to a great extent for my interest in arena theatre, and, of course, vice versa. The so-called "open stage"—four-sided or arena, three-sided or in a corner of a room—is no passing fancy, although it has had a relatively brief history and, as yet, no fixed aesthetic. It represents in the theatre the same search and some of the same tendencies that have taken place in the past half-century in the arts of sculpture, painting, and architecture. Like the other arts—but, as always, a generation or so later—the theatre is turning, or rather returning, to simplicity, to essentials, to the primitive. Like the other arts, it is trying to extend itself beyond the rigid framework established by the conventions of the recent past. It is looking for fluidity and freedom. It is groping for organic form just as much as the Lever House or the latest Swedish sofa is. Between Frank Lloyd Wright and Stanislavsky, after all, there is a great similarity. Both seek to relate things to their environment. Both urge truths of expression in their own specific forms of creative work. The key to both lies in their faith that inner life should determine outer form.

Even more, the theatre's growing interest in and experimentation with the open stage represents, alongside the other arts, a concern with revealing and utilizing instead of concealing the basic nature of its own materials. The texture of woven cloth, the roughness of stone and the smoothness of metal, the natural grain of wood—these are elements that the artist of today tries to reveal rather than conceal. So, in the case of the theatre, we are abandoning peephole illusion for the frank make-believe that is the theatre's essence. Unfortunately, a theatre building happens to last longer than an ashtray or an armchair. That is why we are so far behind.

I became involved with arena by accident and stayed involved by design. From Theatre, Inc.'s upstairs room, I searched everywhere for the new-found world of theatre-in-the-round. For a while I thought of trying to interest the Museum of Modern Art in letting me have an arena group functioning there. The Museum seemed the most logical place. Fordham's scrim-surrounded ellipse bothered me more than a little, but a production of Saroyan's

Sam Ego's House (with four actors "playing" the corners of the house) showed the potentialities of the medium. The supposed "arena" at the Hotel Edison was more opportunistic than organic and successfully killed the chances for professional central staging in New York for years to come. The various "Music Circuses" I found wonderfully theatrical and, strangely, almost Elizabethan in the total experience they provided. I directed at the Playhouse in Houston (don't *ever* have a *round* stage!) and spent my time in Houston admiring the Alley Theatre's imagination and resourcefulness. In Dartington's "Round House" greenroom, I gave the British Drama League samples of arena technique with productions of Wilder's *Happy Journey* and *Pullman Car Hiawatha* (which I have also directed at the Actors' Studio, Catholic University, the Neighborhood Playhouse, on color television, and almost every place else).

But my real involvement came through Arena Stage in Washington. My first show there was *The Glass Menagerie,* and it turned into the most satisfying production I have ever done. Somehow all the ingredients were there, including the lighting and the music, and the play perfectly fitted the form we chose for it. And the freedom to work made me use my theatrical imagination more fully than ever before. For example, instead of the father's framed picture on the table, I had an actor carrying a picture frame come into view down an aisle and light up with a smile on cue. The audiences loved the idea, and again I became acutely conscious of how many fresh values and relationships were possible in this medium.

Eventually I left Catholic University to devote my full time to directing for Arena. It was not so much a job as an exploration. I directed the widest possible variety of plays there—from *The Hasty Heart* to the world *première* of Robert Anderson's *All Summer Long*—and watched many more in all stages of work. Each production taught me a bit more about the nature of arena and the nature of theatre. Everyone says that only certain types of plays work satisfactorily in the arena form, but no two people agree on which types. I am inclined to think that any play will work if properly done, to a greater or lesser extent. But that is true of any type of stage; no stage is ideal for every kind of play. The only feeling I do have is that plays of strong theatricality—Shakespeare, Molière, Wilde—and plays of strong illusion—Ibsen, Chekhov, Williams— work best.

That good old proscenium arch seems in general to be taking quite a beating, both in Europe and America. Everywhere one hears about open stages, platform stages, flexible stages of all sizes and shapes. During the summer, especially on the Continent, the theatre more and more tends to leave the darkness of the picture-frame auditorium and move outside into the sunlight—in front of palaces, into church courtyards, in tents, on hillsides, and in town squares—searching by instinct, if not always by design, for the kind of stage it had in periods of its greatest achievement: a platform in space.

To me, this movement represents the ultimate in theatricality and the most significant development in the theatre since the invention of the electric light. Robert Edmond Jones once said something to the effect that if only our writers, our directors, and our actors were given a bare stage on which to work, in no time at all we would have the most exciting theatre in the world. Thornton Wilder, of whom I am personally and professionally a great admirer, recently wrote that the most important trend in playwriting is "breaking down that box set, abolishing that curtain, getting rid of that museum-visit that is suggested by the proscenium." Certainly the most exciting productions that I have seen in recent years have, in one way or another, resented the separation that the proscenium arch forces between actors and audiences: *The Three Estates* on a huge tongue of a stage, which nakedly and yet beautifully found its way into the very heart of the audience; Stratford's *Richard III* on an adaptation of that same stage; in Avignon, Jean Vilar's Théâtre National Populaire presenting *Lorenzaccio* on a broad platform in the medieval courtyard of the Palace of the Popes; and in Paris, on the apron of the Sarah Bernhardt, Brecht's tumultuous *Mother Courage* played on a half-bare turntable—in a breath-taking production which blended the finest Actors' Studio realism with the most eloquent of Japanese theatre "style."

And what of the proscenium? It remains, of course, but perhaps a little less certain of its powers. So recently a liberal, it has, in the usual course of history, become a conservative. Once so obviously the norm of the relationship between the playing space and the watching-and-hearing space, it has now become one of many norms, many relationships. Hardy the architect today who would design a theatre without adequate provision for varying, enlarging, breaking through—if not entirely eliminating —that artificial, transparent barrier through which the modern theatre increasingly threatens to hurl itself. No one, of course, tears down theatres for aesthetic reasons, only for more parking lots. So that good old proscenium remains, a respectable though illegitimate grandchild of Renaissance painting and Baroque elegance. It is not completely crumbling, but—watch out for falling plaster.

In a bookshop in Rome, I bought a new study of the twentieth-century theatre. On the cover is the profile of Eleanora Duse, probably the finest realistic actress of our century, and the floor plan of Gropius' project for a "universal theatre," a flexible arena designed some thirty years ago but yet unbuilt. What more suitable symbols of reality and theatricality—and of the two sides of my theatre adventure.

And now the adventure brings me to Broadway. My long apprenticeship is over. A couple of shows ago, I stopped being self-conscious about doing a Broadway play, forgot about that seventy-five or one hundred thousand dollars riding on my head, and just concentrated on directing. I cast the play as well as I could, trusted the actors, and tried not to think about the stakes involved. That was the best job I have done, and it has paid off. The scripts that I am being offered these days are getting better and are coming oftener. More people are willing to give me better chances, and I cannot ask for more than that. If I continue to be lucky, the next ten years of my life should be the most interesting and productive. I am looking forward to those ten years. But I have learned not to predict anything, nor to expect anything. Ten years ago, I would never in my wildest dreams have imagined that what actually did happen to me would happen. The next ten years will, no doubt, weave a pattern equally unexpected and unforeseen. All I know is that I hope to go on working. I have had failures and have learned from and because of them, and I expect to continue having failures. In the theatre, anyone who can be right more than fifty-one per cent of the time is a genius, which I am not, by a long shot. I have had some successes, too, and I hope, fingers crossed, to have a few more. The important thing is that I am no longer afraid of either; that in Jean, the wife I was lucky enough to find in London, I have a life partner who has made me unafraid of failure or success—or of anything that the future may bring us.

For most of my existence in the theatre, I have worked and earned my living at what I liked doing the most: directing plays. Whether this happened to be in New York or Washington did not really matter; there are certain satisfactions in both worlds and certain frustrations in both worlds. All in all, I consider myself to have been more fortunate than most people in this respect, and I would not trade my troubles for anybody else's. We are each, as someone has said, the sum of all the signatures that our life and times have written on us. I, for one, cannot complain about my autograph collection. In each of my two cities I have worked with some of the worst and some of the most wonderful people in the theatre, and perhaps in the world. The inflated egos and the nasty dispositions you forget very quickly; the real artists and the real people are there to be remembered for the rest of your life.

In these past fifteen years, I have learned a great many other things, not easily classified, summarized, or itemized. I have learned, most of all, that the theatre, in a way never dreamed of by Heraclitus in his philosophy, is always in a state of flux, always in transition, always changing. You can never stop learning, finding out, investigating, doing something new, trying something different. There are very few absolute rules or absolute standards of judgment and action. You have to take your chances on your own tastes and your own instincts. I have learned that the theatre anywhere and everywhere may best be described as a series of overlapping crises, and that any two individuals in it are rarely, if ever, in agreement on possible courses of action to be taken to solve these crises. You have to be objective, patient and strong—not easily swayed, for whatever reasons. You have to fight when you feel that you have to and not fight when you know that you shouldn't. I have learned that everything one does in the theatre has consequences far beyond what one wants and expects, and that everything is the result of indirection or even chance, more so than of careful direction and planning. As I have said before, the only sure thing about the theatre is that it has no sure things. So you learn to live with uncertainty and unpredictableness knocking daily at your front door.

People are always asking me if I expect to go back to Washington to direct. I don't see why not. I have both roots and hopes there, and I do not feel any different about them than I did two years ago. I went back right after *Pennypacker* opened to direct a production of *Summer and Smoke* at the Arena, and I hope to go back after many more New York openings to direct many more plays in Washington. That does not mean that I intend or want to give up my hard-won beachhead on Broadway. It only means that I hope and expect to direct plays wherever there is a proper opportunity for me to do it—or where I can help to create such an opportunity. I believe that those two worlds in which I have lived and worked for so long can be part of the same world, and that those two cities in my life can be part of the same theatre, the American theatre. Perhaps, after all, that is the only way we shall ever really have one—an American theatre, I mean.

4. THEATRE '50: A DREAM COME TRUE

Margo Jones

IN TELLING THE STORY of how Theatre '50 came into existence in Dallas, Texas, how it was dreamed of, planned, and brought to operation, I want to point out that this theatre should not be a unique venture. We should have at least one hundred such theatres in these United States, so that a cross-country traveler could stop off every night to see a different play—not just a play, but a good play, well produced and beautifully acted.

With imagination and a tremendous willingness for hard work, it is possible to create a great theatre, a vigorous and vital theatre, in the second half of the twentieth century. We must have more plays, and we must have better plays; and, too, we must have outlets for these that will match the quality of the scripts. I like to think that within the next twenty-five or thirty years we shall have a resident professional theatre in every large city of the world. Am I asking for a miracle? I do not think so. I believe it will take courage and determination and a genuine eagerness to see the theatre take root everywhere, but it can be done, and it must be done.

Audiences the world over are starved for good theatre, and only in the larger centers are they more or less satisfied. They crave more theatre and better theatre. In many localities there is no theatre whatsoever. Who is to bring it to them? Is it not our responsibility? Is it not the obligation of every person who is working in the theatre today? Are we going to wait, and if so, for what? We must realize and fulfill this great duty that we have, to create fine theatre and to create it at once.

I remember how impressed I was—and still am—by Robert Edmond Jones's very inspiring book, *The Dramatic Imagination,* in which he said, "I know that there are young people in this country who will really create for the theatre of their time, who will bring something into existence there that never has existed before."[1] Yes, we must bring this something into existence, and we must stimulate the next generation of theatre people to follow in our footsteps and to do even better.

We should adopt a basic philosophy in the theatre— that theatre must be good at all levels. There is no reason to say, for instance, that a certain play is not good enough for Broadway but might "go" in a college theatre. If it is good, it is good enough for Broadway; if not, it is not good enough even for the college stage. There are two kinds of theatre, good and bad. Much as I should like to see theatre in America, I would rather have no theatre than bad theatre. What we must strive for is perfection and come as close to it as is humanly possible.

When we speak of decentralization in the theatre, we mean that there must be theatres everywhere, not only in the large centers. But decentralization should never be

[1] Robert Edmond Jones, *The Dramatic Imagination: Reflections and Speculations on the Art of the Theatre* (New York, Duell, Sloane and Pearce, 1941).

interpreted as opposed to professionalism. I think it is high time that all of us in the theatre adopt the philosophy of "One theatre—a good one," without arbitrary distinctions concerning the level at which the theatre is organized. It would be easy to adopt this philosophy if every person would ask himself what he wishes to accomplish in life. That goal, then, would be closely related to what he hopes to attain in the theatre.

In my lifetime I should like to be a member of the world. I should like to know and to partake of the joys and sufferings of my fellow men. I should like to have the great experiences, human and artistic, that life offers. I should like to see material progress accompanied by a cultural development that would give true distinction to our civilization and make it a great one. I should like to hear great music, see great painting and sculpture, read great books. And I should like to find great plays and put them on magnificently.

I do not think it is possible to be too idealistic. The higher we aim, the better we can do. If we lower our ideals, we shall land in the inferior regions of art. Idealism has often been condemned because it has been associated with impracticality. But it should not be so. I believe that to create great theatre you must be an idealist and you must be able to convert your ideals into realities—practical realities—and you must never be content until your ideals have all come true. You will not be content then either, because by that time you will have new and still higher ideals, and you will have an incentive to go on and on.

We have seen too much defeatism, too much pessimism, too much of a negative approach. The answer is simple: if you want something very badly, you can achieve it. It may take patience, very hard work, a real struggle, and a long time; but it can be done. That much faith is a prerequisite of any undertaking, artistic or otherwise.

The American theatre, too, has been accused of a lack of idealism. I do not believe that this is true. It is enough to read the wonderful books of Kenneth Macgowan, of Hallie Flanagan, of Robert Edmond Jones, of Harold Clurman, of Stark Young; to go through the files of *Theatre Arts* and find the great ideals expressed in fine terms, and most of the time by people who have been active in the theatre—people who made their dreams work. We have to thank these people and others whose idealism helped to create that vigorous movement in the American theatre around 1920, when the Provincetown Playhouse and the Theatre Guild were beginning and Eugene O'Neill's plays were first appearing on our theatrical horizon. We have to thank them for the efforts that appeared afterwards, too, notably those of the Group Theatre and of the Federal Theatre Project, of the community theatres, the college theatres, and the regional theatres, and for that constant infiltration of new blood into the professional theatre of Broadway.

For myself, I know that it would have been far more difficult to formulate my ideals, my standards, and my practical plans without the inspiration that I received from the work of these men and women, as well as from my reading of plays of the past and present.

I believe in a playwright's theatre. I am a director, and I have wanted to be a director since I was eleven years old, but I think that theatre begins with the playwright. It might be argued that the dramatist needs a place in which to have works performed, and that if there is no theatre, there will be no playwrights. But while I see some point to this argument, I maintain that no theatre would last without plays, the example of the *commedia dell'arte* performances notwithstanding. The theatre is a co-operative venture in which the author, the actor, the director, the designer, and the technician collaborate. But they cannot begin to collaborate until the playwright has set down his basic idea, his story, his characters, his mood, and his words. This is the starting point.

Much has been done to encourage playwrights, but not enough. We must find a way to develop more and better playwrights. I believe that the best way to do this is to give them opportunities to see their plays presented in a first-class theatre. Shakespeare developed alongside his theatre. Perhaps it is an academic question to ask whether he would have been a great playwright had he not been associated with a performing company. The fact remains that he was. Molière, too, was an actor. Goethe had a theatre to work in. So did Ibsen, Strindberg, and O'Neill. Chekhov regained confidence with the Moscow Art Theatre; the Group Theatre produced Clifford Odets.

I say all this because I believe that a theatre should present new plays and classics, with emphasis on the new plays. It is an important element in my philosophy of the theatre, and I have tried to put it into practice in every theatre where I have worked. In Dallas, at Theatre '50, I made it an absolute policy, and I think it would be a good policy for every theatre to adopt. I think that audiences deserve to participate in the discovery of new talent. I think that the only way a theatre can be progressive is to do new plays. At the same time, I do think that it should present the classics, because these have been proved through the ages to be literary and dramatic masterpieces. They must be kept alive for our audiences of today.

These beliefs have been the foundation of my theatre experiences, and they are my guides in every undertaking. Perhaps I cannot pinpoint a particular moment in my life when I decided on them, but in tracing my work, I can say when they gradually became more and more important to me. I knew in the spring of 1944, when I first set about my plan to start a resident professional theatre in Dallas. Then these beliefs were already formulated in my mind, and I was eager to have an opportunity to put them into practice.

I put down my beliefs in writing. "This is a plan," I wrote at the head of the first page, "for the creation of a permanent, repertory, native theatre in Dallas, Texas; a permanent repertory theatre with a permanent staff of the best young artists in America; a theatre that will be a true playwright's theatre; a theatre that will give the young playwrights of America (or of any country, for that matter) a chance to be seen; a theatre that will provide the classics and the best new scripts their chances for good production; a theatre that will enable Dallasites to say twenty years from now, 'My children have lived in a town where they could see the best plays of the world presented in a beautiful and fine way'—where they can say, 'We have had a part in creating theatre and working in it.' This theatre will go beyond the dreams of the past—and they have been wonderful. It will be a theatre to mean even more to America than the Moscow Art Theatre meant to Moscow, the Abbey to Ireland, or the Old Vic to England. It will be a theatre that will carry on, but adapted to our country and our time, the ideals of the Stanislavskys, the Copeaus, the Craigs, and be a theatre of our time."

I had faith that our country had in it people with an intense interest in seeing the theatre develop in different parts of this country and of the whole world. I had met such persons at annual meetings of the National Theatre Conference. I knew that there were idealists who respected practical accomplishment. My hope was that my plan would not sound to them too fantastic to be helped, for I needed their assistance in order to get started on my project.

What impelled me to want a resident professional theatre? I felt that I could, and therefore should, do something about finding a new way to produce the best plays in the best possible manner. I had worked in a community theatre and in the drama department of a university. Both experiences had taught me much. But I was eager to have a theatre in which actors and staff would devote their entire time and energy to the creation of theatre, and where audiences could be provided with continuous professional theatre with the best new plays and classics expertly produced. I wanted to obtain a fellowship in order to do some specific observing and studying before launching the theatre in Dallas. I reviewed my experience in the theatre and my reasons for this great desire to embark on a new venture.

I knew very early in my life that I wanted to be a stage director, as I already have mentioned, and I went to college with this definite purpose in mind. I was fortunate to have the opportunity to direct many plays during my undergraduate years. Since the Texas State College for Women did not at that time offer a master's degree in drama, I majored in psychology. I wrote my thesis on the abnormal ways out of emotional conflict found in three Ibsen heroines—Hedda Gabler in her play, Ellida in *The Lady from the Sea*, and Irene in *When We Dead Awaken*. Experience and study were joined.

One of my college instructors guided me to reading the great plays of the past, and I then started a practice, continued without break, of reading at least one play a day. To read the Greek playwrights, the Romans, the mystery plays of the Middle Ages, those of the Elizabethans—and so on—gave me a wonderful feeling of personal discovery. It was as though these plays were something new, that I was finding them for the first time. Most of the plays read in later years have been new scripts, and with even more reason I have this same attitude of discovery toward them. Opening a new script is a challenge; you may be able to discover a great play or a great playwright in the making. To read a play is a pleasure, but it also involves a responsibility if you are in a position to give that play life in a theatre. I can think of no greater excitement than finding a good play and knowing that I can put it on, that the words on paper will become words and action on a stage.

The day I was graduated from college I applied for a job at the newly formed Southwestern School of the Theatre in Dallas. I felt that there I could learn by watching the work of classes; also, I knew that while living in Dallas for a year I could see the road companies that came there as well as the productions in the Dallas Little Theatre, then at its peak under the direction of Oliver Hinsdell. My job at the school was mainly secretarial, but I attended some of the classes and watched a fine director, Louis Veda Quince, at work.

The following summer I enrolled in the Pasadena Summer School of the Theatre, and there I directed several plays under excellent professional supervision. I had other stimulus toward my reading of plays from Gilmor Brown, who once came to class with a long list of plays that I never had heard of. He made me realize that you never can be complacent about the number of plays you have read, for even in a lifetime of reading you cannot cover all the fine plays that have been written before your time and that are being written today by good authors all over the world. You must read, and read, and read, in the hope of finding those best plays.

After this summer in Pasadena, I was given my first directorial job, with the Ojai Community Players. There I directed a full season of plays, and I was especially happy because I had the chance to do *Hedda Gabler*, already one of my favorites. A trip around the world followed the year at Ojai, California, and that experience lifted many new horizons. I had then an opportunity to see theatre throughout the Orient and Europe. I do not think that I exaggerate when I say that I saw a play every night when not on a boat or a train.

While I was away, the Federal Theatre Project was started. I heard of it on the boat coming home, in 1935. It seemed logical to me to become a part of this great undertaking, and also logical to do that in my home territory of Texas. I promptly went to Houston and became the assistant director of the local project. That was among the most short-lived of these enterprises; yet it was one that made me see another aspect of the entertainment world and acquainted me with the bitter plight of the theatre in our country during the Depression. When our project collapsed, I made a trip to Europe, mainly in order to see the Moscow Art Theatre Festival and then to write a series of articles on it for the *Houston Chronicle*.

Upon my return I went to work for the Houston Recreation Department, my job consisting of teaching the playground directors how to stage plays. Although I felt that this work was necessary, I wanted to direct plays myself and to start a theatre. Then I discovered that the Recreation Department had a theatre and that it was being used only for square dances twice a week. I persuaded the officers to let me use it for the production of plays; next I made the announcement in the daily papers that the Houston Community Players had been formed, and that their first production would be *The Importance of Being Earnest*. Nine persons attended the tryouts, and they were cast in the nine roles of the Wilde play. This was in 1936.

During the six years to follow, the Houston Community Players grew to a membership of about six hundred people. We produced six plays every year, in addition to laboratory studies, special readings, and radio scripts. I did two original musicals by Cy Howard and Richard Shannon, as well as a play about newspaper life called *Special Edition*, the work of Harold Young, a Houston newspaper man. Then I heard of a play by Edwin Justus Mayer, called *Sunrise in My Pocket*, that dealt with episodes in Texas history. I read this play during a visit to Los Angeles and decided that I must get the rights to do it.

I did not know how to get in touch with Mr. Mayer, although he was only a few miles away from where I was staying. But I had met Brooks Atkinson, and I decided to telephone to him for help. (Mr. Atkinson wrote a Sunday article about this, which I appreciated. It was a source of great encouragement to me.) Mr. Atkinson at once telephoned to introduce me to Mr. Mayer. I met the author and obtained his permission to present the world *première* of *Sunrise in My Pocket* at the Houston Community Playhouse. That was my first experience with a new script by an established author. I had discovered that the only way to find good plays is to go after them. I am not saying that any play you wish to do will be available, but simply that you never will have a chance to try something new if you do not attempt to get it.

It was during my years with the Houston Community Players that I first was introduced to theatre-in-the-round techniques. I had gone to a theatre conference in Washington and had seen a production staged in that manner by the Blue Room Players of the Portland Civic Theatre. This group had been formed by a former student of Glenn Hughes. On my journey home, it occurred to me that here was the solution to my hot weather problem. It was impossible to put on plays in our regular playhouse during the summer months, having no air conditioning there. But in the round! Why not do it in a hotel room? We did, and the summer season was a tremendous success.

With the beginning of World War II it became difficult to maintain the Houston Community Playhouse. Our young men were leaving for the service. I felt that my place was with the younger people who were not yet going off to war and who were being trained for a postwar theatre. James H. Parke, head of the department of drama at the University of Texas, invited me to join his faculty, and I did. I found the work in a university just as exciting as in a community. People all around me were eager to learn by working on the production of plays. It was important to develop in them a sound attitude, to teach them that good plays must be done in the best possible way. My first assignment at the university was to produce Maxwell Anderson's *Eve of St. Mark*, which the author had released to the National Theatre Conference prior to its Broadway production. I also directed the staging of two new scripts by a graduate student of playwriting and several lesser plays. Two of these I staged in arena style.

While at the university I began to think very seriously of the future. I wanted a theatre of my own, where I could do new plays and the classics. I wanted to offer security and permanent, or continuous, livelihood to actors and other theatre workers—in short, to have a professional resident theatre. During a visit to Dallas, I had discussed all these matters with John Rosenfield, head of the amusement section of the *Dallas Morning News*. He remarked then that Dallas might be the ideal city for my theatre. I was happy to hear him say that, because I had already thought that Dallas would be my choice. His judgment and his encouragement led me to try for a fellowship from a national foundation, and I was successful.

As set forth in my application for the fellowship, my purpose was to travel throughout the country making a study of existing theatres and meeting as many people with theatrical interests as was possible. I began with a summer at the Pasadena Playhouse. As director in its summer school, I staged three plays, one of them being Tennessee Williams' one-act play in verse, *The Purification*. Earlier I had directed, in collaboration with Donald Windham, another Williams play that was based on a story by D. H. Lawrence. We had staged his *You Touched Me* at the Pasadena and Cleveland playhouses while I had been on leave from the University of Texas. After the summer in Gilmor Brown's Playhouse, I set off on my fellowship travels—looking for new scripts, meeting with actors and other theatre people, and formulating a plan for a professional resident theatre in Dallas.

It was during my travels in 1944 that *The Glass Menagerie* was bought for Broadway production and I was invited to direct it with Eddie Dowling. I had had no experience on Broadway up to that time. I felt that I should have it and that this was my great opportunity. I was to work on a play that I loved, written by an author in whom I had always believed, and in company with some of the finest artists in the profession. That eventually led to the Chicago production of the play. It also brought me the direction of two other plays on Broadway before Theatre '50 opened: Maxine Wood's *On Whitman Ave-*

nue and Maxwell Anderson's *Joan of Lorraine.* While I was away for these assignments, the office in Dallas was in full operation. Scripts were being read, and studies were under way of possible buildings for our use.

It was on my return from New York City, after the opening of *The Glass Menagerie,* that a committee of Dallas citizens organized a board that would conduct a financing campaign. Mr. and Mrs. Eugene McDermott gave this group ten thousand dollars, a wonderful start toward the seventy-five thousand dollars believed necessary for the program. But the real-estate market was unfavorable to new construction, because of the shortage of materials and high costs, and no downtown section had an existing structure that was available. We found, however, that the Old Globe Theatre, built for Shakespearean productions at the Texas Centennial, might be remodeled with a flexible stage suited to productions in many different styles, Jo Mielziner was invited to draft blueprints for the reconstruction, and the financial campaign began. Suddenly, the Old Globe was condemned by city inspectors, and all planning stopped. Hoping against hope, I started looking again for a theatre. I would not let the project collapse. I knew that if I failed, other people would be held back from embarking on similar ventures. I must go through with my plans.

I do not remember when or how I thought of it, but at a certain point in the search I knew that it was not essential to have a proscenium arch in order to do fine plays. I had done it in the center of a room in both Houston and Austin. Why not in Dallas? I knew that this type of theatre would not restrict my imagination; on the contrary, it would put greater demands on it. I knew that if I could create exciting drama on a proscenium stage, I could do it in an arena with the audience surrounding the action. I knew that I could produce any play in that medium, provided that it was a good play.

There was an attractive stucco and glass-brick building on the Fair Park grounds belonging to the Gulf Oil Corporation. This, I decided after much consideration, could be adapted into an adequate theatre-in-the-round. The look and feel of a theatre were created by installing standard theatre seats and lighting that could create the mood and special effects of each play. There we invested the forty thousand dollars from our fund-raising campaign. Then I was off to New York City, to take options on the new plays for our first season and to engage an acting company.

That first season was a short one. We produced five plays, four of them new ones. By the time of our third opening, we knew that the city had accepted us. For the second season we sold twelve hundred subscriptions, double the number of our first one. We therefore planned a twenty-week season, with eight productions running two weeks each and the final four weeks given over to repertory. I soon found rehearsal time inadequate. Also, our subscription list grew, calling for more performances. The consequence was that our third and fourth seasons had thirty weeks, with eight plays on for three weeks each and six weeks of repertory. Of the six, the final two weeks were devoted to a festival of the best plays of the season.

With imaginative direction and staging, and with no fear of taking advantage of the imagination of the audience, there are no limitations to productions in a theatre-in-the-round. We have done Shakespeare, Molière, Ibsen, Chekhov, Wilde, and Shaw, to make a total of eleven classics and eighteen later plays. We have done plays with complete naturalism or with great stylization, depending on what the play required. We have done scripts with many changes of scene, others with simultaneous sets. Costumes, lights, music, and, above all, imagination have worked wonders.

Our staff consists of a managing director, who, in present time, is also the stage director; a business manager; a technical director, who is also the lighting designer; a costume designer; a production manager as assistant director; a treasurer; four production assistants; and an acting company of eight, at times augmented to nine. Our actors and production assistants are members of Actors' Equity, all of the requirements of that organization being met; the same is true of the stock contract recommended by the Dramatists' Guild, under which we pay royalties on all the new scripts that we produce.

Theatre '50 is now an accomplished fact.[2] There is no smugness in this statement. I am ever aware of the need for improvement. We must find better plays every season. We must perform them better. We must seek for constant improvement in artistic and technical presentation. But because of the soundness of our policies and the invaluable initial assistance given by a national foundation and all those who made it possible for us to establish Theatre '50, we are an operating theatre that provides Dallas audiences with thirty weeks of productions every year.

My dream is to see such resident theatres starting all over the world, for I believe that in them is the hope for a young, vital, and creative theatre in the future. But I use the word "future" with limitations of meaning. I mean a future that should start not next year, not with the next generation, not in the year 2000; I mean a future that starts *today*.

[2] [The numeral is advanced with the change of year. This gives immediacy to the spirit of the enterprise and also gives a unity to productions of each season.—Editor.]

DEVELOPMENT

5. THE INNER QUALITY OF A WORK

Frederic McConnell

THE WORDS are Stanislavsky and Sean O'Casey—the actor is the monarch of the theatre and the box office its tabernacle. This paraphrase epitomizes the duality between the work of the stage and the receptivity of the audience as the prime consideration in the operation of a theatre. The artistic and technical processes of the theatre can survive only in the fluid atmosphere of public appreciation. The whole creation is an indivisible amalgam. With this concept, a trio consisting of K. Elmo Lowe, the late Max Eisenstat, and this writer faced the problem of the Cleveland Play House when they arrived on the scene in 1921, and during more than three decades, with the aid and stimulation of hundreds of others, it has been adhered to as the basic principle in the making and preservation of a theatre.

Cleveland then, as now, enjoyed a favorable social and cultural climate. Tom L. Johnson, through victory and defeat on behalf of the people, had planted the seeds of social welfare and civic progress at the turn of the century, later to be fostered by the inspired leadership of Newton

D. Baker and others. Community wealth and energy derived from American industry and enterprise came to the fore in the founding of a fine symphony orchestra and a museum of art, as well as schools, universities, and institutions for music and art. It was the beginning of the Cleveland Foundation and the Community Chest, both of them pioneer activities in America. The spirit of liberal reform was, of course, manifest throughout the nation during the first decade, but much of it here came from within the city's own soul.

The tyro theatre emerged in 1915 from a drawing room where players and audience were one. A small group of writers, artists, teachers, lawyers, social workers, and businessmen met to read and discuss plays and to raise a misty curtain of curiosity on certain new scenic techniques that were then beginning to flower in Europe. A revolution was in being. The theatre of the Shuberts and the Erlangers did not satisfy. The group was sparked by an inchoate desire to participate in a new venture, to light a new fire, and to carry a new torch. The objective was not clear or fixed, and soon conflict arose, the basic difference being between the concept of democracy in art and of art in democracy. Meetings passed from house to house until within a few years an old church was acquired and a stage house built. Leadership was hesitant and confused, and soon came schism and disorganization, bringing with it lag and failure in production. In the welter of group participation an audience was lost. Here, as elsewhere, a lesson was learned; a theatre cannot work for its people. They must work for it, and they must know their way. The real meaning of the Moscow Art Theatre, of Appia, Craig, Copeau, Reinhardt, and the new theatre renascence was on the threshold of discovery. The time was ripe for the practice of a theory.

Despite difficulties, it was determined that the struggling theatre should not fail. An intelligent, loyal, and enlightened board of trustees was reconstituted from recalcitrant factions that stood ready to support—skeptically at first, but enthusiastically later—the plans of a new administration. The call for leadership and organization had been sounded.

These plans and objectives were not made on the spot but had been maturing for years. Education, training, experience, and instinct had formed a goal that was fixed. Precedents were ample, intention manifest, idealism aglow. From forces at hand and others yet to be acquired, the task of cementing an ensemble theatre on concentric lines did not seem difficult. It was a day-by-day challenge wherein the hidden resources of the mind and heart went to work, to group, and regroup, co-ordinate, and assemble the elements, big and little, that eventually would complete the puzzle.

More than his lofty screens, Gordon Craig's concept of the universal director opened the door to a rearrangement of forces in the conduct of the stage and in the management of a theatre. A director need not be either a martinet or a paragon to unify the various techniques that comprise a theatre in the composite. What was needed was disciplined vision coupled with complete authority to translate into action. The actor, the director, the scene designer, and the technical assistants are indeed all one in the fusion of the magic crucible from which the finished stage production flows. The director may have accurate knowledge of all the processes and be able to compose them into a single pattern, into a unified and harmonious whole, but such prowess is useless unless at the same time he has control of the economic and social forces, as well as the artistic, that bring these techniques into being and fruition. Therein Craig's thesis holds firm.

Training and guidance under inspired teachers, such as Thomas Wood Stevens, Donald Robertson, Padraic Colum, B. Iden Payne, and William Poel, in a school of the theatre organized to teach all the elements of theatre production, in which the student would become a personal participant, provided solid ground for the future. The young student at the Carnegie Institute of Technology in Pittsburgh was exposed to the theatre in its wholeness. He became conscious of every facet that made it live before an audience, not only of those elements that must project from the stage but of those that constitute and formulate the audience in the first instance. It was a sound experience to learn that the verdict of an audience is real and fateful.

Early in the evolution of the Moscow Art Theatre, when the days and hours of romantic discussion exploded into action, an integrated theatre ensemble slowly grew to luster and glory. That is now history. And there were others at the turn of the century: William Poel's Elizabethan Stage Society; the repertory theatres in Birmingham and Liverpool; the state theatres of Europe; the Meiningen ensemble in Germany; Copeau's Vieux Colombier in Paris; the timorous and soon abortive attempts at the Art Institute of Chicago; Maurice Browne's Chicago Little Theatre; and finally the distinguished and flourishing stock companies of Augustin Daly, Charles Frohman, and A. M. Palmer in New York during the nineties. The significance and meaning of these enterprises could not escape the attention of an inquiring student. His subsequent determination to realize the fundamental idea of it all in a new community might be an ambition to be pardoned.

Practical application came through an all-too-brief association with Samuel J. Hume of the Arts and Crafts Theatre of Detroit, of which he was founder and director, and then later with him at the Greek Theatre of the University of California. Sam Hume was ingrained with the "new spirit," derived in part from work with George Pierce Baker and Gordon Craig. His imagination was dynamic and fertile, and his theatrical taste impeccable. He felt the theatre in composite; his skills covered management, direction, design, and an occasional diversionary attack on Thespis. The Detroit theatre was not a group effort but a consecrated dedication of a few well-informed and skilled individuals working in an atmosphere of charm and artistic achievement. Associated with the theatre was the late Sheldon Cheney, who in an adjacent cubicle of an office was turning out the first issues of *Theatre Arts Monthly* and carrying the torch for the theatre to come.

The spell and span of the above association were broken abruptly by a call to help quell a riot in Europe engendered by a late German kaiser—a fateful experience indeed, which contributed as much as anything else before or since to self-control and a knowledge of life, as well as of those human qualities that both endanger and endear it.

George Bernard Shaw once defined the professional as "one who does his job superlatively well." The first step toward that goal in the theatre under review was to work for a condition whereby the actor and other workers could learn their craft, could practice their art by a constant and continuous association with the work in hand, and, in the final analysis, earn their living by it. The leaders who brought the young theatre into being were expert and proficient in their own fields but were amateur in the development of their new discovery. The actor is a play's prime exponent; when his performance fails, the whole edifice collapses. Effort was made at once to establish in the minds of the local group that their "amateur status" was not sacred and incorruptible, and to win acceptance of the principle that a theatre should exist for its own sake and not merely as a forum for social participation and self-expression. By constant emphasis on theatrical creation, the creeping ideal of a creative ensemble of players took hold and soon gripped the imagination of the entire organization. Rehearsals became more in number and longer, and fewer teacups had to be washed. In consequence, performance improved and audiences increased. By slow transition, the people within became conscious of their part in the unfolding of an ancient tradition, and they became the means to that end.

The late Charles S. Brooks, who helped found the organization and presided over the eventual metamorphosis, echoed the thought of many when he wrote in the August, 1926, issue of *Theatre Arts Monthly*:

At the start there were four productions to the year, each of three or four performances, and these at times drew but a meager audience. On a rainy night, perhaps, the heroic speeches rattled back from empty chairs. This was the period of Maeterlinck and purple lights through which most private theatres ran, filmy plays of moving shadows and things unrealized. . . . Perhaps at first the theatre was too conscious of its mission to reform the public taste. It was too quarrelsome with the past. The pulpit of its tiny church was but shifted from religious to artistic text. The town was to be forced to swallow culture, Maeterlinck and purple lights. All plays must be tagged with artistic moral, and if the audience found them stupid it was deemed to be their sluggishness toward the stirring of a future drama. Art was a slate rubbed clean for our chalk alone.[1]

[1] *Theatre Arts Monthly*, Vol. X, No. 8 (August, 1926), 517–18.

In six years, beginning in 1921, the audience at the little theatre on East Seventy-third Street expanded from four thousand to fifty thousand. Some sixty plays were produced—of these, thirty-three for the first time in Cleveland and ten for the first time in America. The aim was catholic, varied, and balanced; and the gamut covered such playwrights as Wilde, Synge, Schnitzler, O'Casey, Shakespeare, Shaw, Pirandello, Galsworthy, Sudermann, Hauptmann, Barry, Chekhov, Ibsen, Marlowe, Milne, Vildrac, Chesterton, Ervine, Dunsany, Dostoievsky, Capek, D'Annunzio, Fitzgerald, and many others.

The term "misplaced persons" was not then current, but clearly there were people here whose usefulness to themselves and to society would have been increased if they had found employment in the theatre and, therefore, had been enabled to devote their lives to that which they could do best. A nucleus of full-time players and other workers was thus slowly formed, at the calculated risk of arousing apprehension among some, for fear that democratic process and the amateur spirit were being violated, which in fact they were. The pre-eminent fact, however, was that the theatre, by virtue of such policy, was gaining in public esteem and was able to hold its own against fretting dissidence. As Mr. Brooks once said, "Nor has the mingling of amateurs with professionals under pay worked to a disadvantage. Regardless of money status the soul of the undertaking is amateur, but with trained skill and guidance. Experience here dictates that the heart of the theatre is a director and staff, and that only by their superior quality can a general company grow to excellence."[2]

The infiltration of former volunteers has continued through the years, and the theatre has benefited from their

[2] *Ibid.*, 519.

continued devotion and maturing experience. Together with them has come fine talent from university and community theatres, young people with good training who need and deserve the outlet that only an active producing theatre can provide. To build further from within, a substantial part of the active company has been recruited from the ranks of student apprentices who have come to the theatre from everywhere to learn, and who subsequently have formed the bulwark of its strength. At the outset there was avoidance of quick and arbitrary importation of personnel from the so-called "commercial" theatre, not because of disregard but because such a policy would impair the essential dictate of indigenous growth from within.

In retrospect, the principle of repertory and an ensemble organization has had its reward for those who have come and gone, as well as for those who remain. Writing in the August, 1926, issue of *Theatre Arts Monthly*, this reporter said:

Repertory is a hard-working experience, an experience, incidentally, which the trained European actor takes as a matter of course. It makes for agility of mind and body, for resourcefulness and responsiveness to the wiles and whims of characterization; it demands and enforces concentration in study and in performance, and, above all, it keeps the actor freshly alert and alive to spontaneous and creative effort and guards him from the limbo of type and routine work. Repertory also permits of a type and degree of composite expression such as is difficult of attainment elsewhere. The building up of an ensemble takes time and permanence; also variety, shift, and change. In an ensemble, the general scheme dominates and triumphs, and too often in our American theatre this virtue is lost in the struggle for special predominance. An early lesson in the theatre, though sometimes it is never learned, is the sense of sympathetic coordination of individual work with the larger scheme that is going on about. The practical dictates of repertory playing enforce this valuable lesson upon the young player from the start. So that while he is growing into an understanding of his individual technic, he is also learning the relationship of that technic to the greater rhythm of the complete theatre.[3]

The new spirit in scene design found favor on a new stage. The arts of production, together with a style of direction that fostered the elaboration of stage movement into fluid and pictorial form, joined with the flexibility and cohesion of a maturing acting ensemble. The viability of a stage alive with form and movement gave scope to unfettered imagination and theatrical illusion. There could be no escape from the truth of Appia's interpretation of the plastic stage, nor anything richer than the impact of architecture through the persuasive force of light and shade and the noble puissance of significant form. Light became an instrument of action, an interpreter of mood, a means of accent and selection. In the fluid and cosmic architectonic of the stage cube, the actor found his rightful place in the arena of the third dimension. In the whole round form of the theatre there is nothing more compelling and penetrating than the implicit power of suggestion, the march of a hidden rhythm, which, as Plato said, "finds its way into the secret places of the soul."

In a city of one million people it was no miracle that a theatre of two hundred seats should outgrow itself and its facilities. Aside from novelty and uniqueness, there was a solid premise emanating from an established ensemble performance, artistic and often novel staging, and a liberal policy in selection of repertory. These values produced a

[3] *Ibid.*, 613.

common bond with the public and made possible an appeal to it for aid in the realization in 1927 of a new and modern theatre plant, a plant that would meet the functional needs of an institutional theatre wherein production is conceived and built within the premises and by an ensemble of workers who find it their home. There soon were two theatres parallel to each other, and in between (servicing both) were shops, dressing rooms, foyer, and administrative quarters—a circulation plan that has met the test of time. The larger of the auditoriums, seating 530 persons, represented a departure from the then current plan and taste. The lines were simple, formal, and devoid of decoration, but softened by pleasing plastic contour. The proscenium was practically eliminated by means of its width and height and a blending into the auditorium by way of complementary side portals and descending steps from the stage to the auditorium floor. And the footlight trough was eliminated. In a real sense the conventional barrier between actor and audience had been removed. That sense of intimate singleness and exciting phenomenon of two-way participation was realized in its place. Twenty years later this principle was to be extended and refined in a type of theatre based upon ancient theatre—which was not then moot, but now is.

The next two decades were crowded and compact years of prime activity. Artistic and economic problems were accentuated by the incursion of external affairs, such as panic, bank closings, depression, the draft, and finally by a world at war. To survive, a theatre institution needed the efficacy of a firm foundation and the devoted loyalty of its friends. It needed to cement and extend its contact with the community, form adjuncts of its main work that would benefit the community and, in the end, greatly enhance its own prestige.

A children's theatre was organized, enlisting five hundred children from all ranks. Weekly classes were held
under the guidance of the theatre staff, and this was supplemented by a series of plays for children in which they
were the sole participants, before an annual audience of
ten thousand. It was not the intention to develop actors
and artisans but rather to instill poise, confidence, and
some degree of social responsibility. Natural and native
talent, however, was frequently discovered, and some of
this talent has subsequently found place in the adult theatre in Cleveland and elsewhere.

"I have never seen a Shakespeare play before, but now
I wish I could see more." Thus wrote a high-school student after attending the Shakespeare Festival, an annual
affair of one month of weekday matinees, which the theatre produces for some twelve thousand high-school students in co-operation with the boards of education of
public and private schools in the area of the city and
county. For most of them it is the first contact with the
living stage, as well as an introduction to Shakespeare in
action, and on a stage where, as Brooks Atkinson expressed it, "he can be rescued from the cultural crimes
of the 19th century."[4]

Learning by doing seems the logical way by which a
student might find his way in the composite art of the
theatre, and for twenty-five years an apprentice school has
been in operation for this purpose. The student soon
learns what he can or cannot do, and his development is
controlled by this discovery. There is a legion of testimony
from those who have come and gone on the value of their
association, during a formative period, with the complex of theatre production. It is a reciprocal arrangement
wherein the student pays nothing for the opportunity to

[4] *New York Times,* May 23, 1950.

serve the theatre, by working with his elders and learning his craft in the flesh. Five hundred or more have passed through the portals. Many are professionally employed in the American theatre, some are leaders in university and community theatres, and a segment today is strategically placed in the producing organization of the parent theatre.

The theatre has long since won a place in the liberal arts curriculum of the university, and it is recognized now that it must have its rostrum and workshop where the student may have personal association with the expressive arts involved in stage production. Working first within the established boundaries of a speech department, Barclay Leathem, through patience, tact, and dedicated purpose, has created at Western Reserve University a graduate department in theatre and drama that attracts students from all over the country. With the precepts of practical theatre in his mind, he has accomplished a task in theatre education the story of which he best can tell. One result has been the development of an *entente cordiale* between the university and the Cleveland Play House, a collaboration of mutual interest that has attracted national attention.

This joint leadership has brought focus on Cleveland as a center of theatre activity, one manifestation of which has been the location there for over a decade of the central headquarters of the National Theatre Conference, an association founded by the late George Pierce Baker that is made up of prominent university and community theatre directors and now representative of important work performed by their institutions. Active, far-flung, and guided by a professional concept of what the theatre can mean and do in terms of a hundred local communities,

134

this organization and its members are contributing to the rise of a national theatre in the truest sense. The ministrations of the National Theatre Conference and kindred organizations give emphasis to the fact that while there may be only fifty thousand seats available each night in the thirty-three theatres of New York City, there are approximately one million more waiting to be used in cities and towns throughout the land.

Economic and artistic considerations gave rise to a project for a second Play House theatre—a project that was twelve years in the making. It was found that a second theatre of the same seating capacity as the existing main theatre would make possible a more efficient and profitable administration of the already accepted and tried operation of the dual-theatre program. Further, a new type of theatre was wanted, one that would depart from the narrow conventions of the current proscenium structure. That theatre, completed in 1952, follows the general plan of an Elizabethan stage and of the theatre in the late Greek period. New freedom is gained by means of a large open stage with an extending apron, with no proscenium or curtain, and with the audience seated in a high-tiered semicircle. The actors and audience, as Frank Lloyd Wright has expressed it, are brought together in one room.

The new stage does not enforce the doctrinaire policy of performing only a certain type of play, nor does the theatre require expensive and clumsy elements of adaptation to make it workable for a variety of play forms. The simple fact is that a great free and open space exists in which the director and designer may compose as they will or must. Realism in the theatre pertains more to the nature of the drama than to the structure of the theatre itself, and realism can be suggested in many ways. It does not necessarily need a curtain or a proscenium, both of which antedated it by several centuries. The essential ingredient and potentiality here is that the apex of the stage action is turned toward the audience instead of upstage and back, away from it. The apron is not merely an appendage added to an existing stage; it *is* the core and soul of the whole zone of playing. The stage—any stage —is merely a place occupied by the word and action of a play, and nothing can or should hide that fact. The only consideration is that which gives such word and action the utmost of freedom and eloquence. For this, space is the prime requirement. Max Reinhardt perceived it when he said, "There is no one form of theatre which is the only true artistic form. . . . Therefore, do not write out prescriptions, but give to the actor and his work the atmosphere in which they breathe more freely and more deeply."[5]

Once the way is found, the new stage becomes a pliable instrument, as has been experienced in the production of the following plays during recent years at the Euclid and Seventy-seventh Street theatre of the Cleveland Play House: *Crime and Punishment, The Voice of the Turtle, Marseilles, Detective Story, Anne of the Thousand Days, Born Yesterday, The Cocktail Party, Darkness at Noon, The Lady's Not for Burning, Come Back, Little Sheba, The School for Scandal, A Tree Grows in Brooklyn, The Consul, The Crucible, Othello,* and *Hamlet.*

The characteristics of this second structure may be summed up in these words of Brooks Atkinson:

Although the new theatre is deliberately unostentatious, it may turn out to be one of the most creative in America. It restores the relationship of audience to stage that existed be-

---

[5] Toby Cole and Helen K. Chinoy, *Directing the Play: A Source Book of Stagecraft* (Indianapolis, Bobbs-Merrill, 1953), 242–43.

fore the conventional box stage dominated the drama. It can liberate production and play-writing from some of the arbitrary restrictions that have become basic in most work for the stage. In fact, the relationship of audience to stage is so normal that a playgoer hardly has time to realize that it is novel and revolutionary. Theatre artists have dreamed of a theatre like this for more than a quarter of a century. Now the Cleveland Play House has built it.[6]

Meanwhile, artistic achievement is dependent upon administration and management that, although vital to the end result, do not shine with romance and color. A director or his complement in that work must do many things, and space here permits only a summary. Royalties must be negotiated and paid, budgets carefully prepared and balanced, personnel engaged, controlled, mollified— and also paid. Plays must be selected that meet the standards and over-all patterns of the theatre, one of which is that management itself must have heart in what is done and therefrom must derive satisfaction and comfort. The gratuitous strictures and insults of minority groups and of self-appointed guardians of public morals must be faced with tact and discretion, as well as with determination to preserve the ancient right of the theatre to speak for itself.

It is found that when for the first time an audience is being indoctrinated with the values of the living stage, particularly an audience that is a cross section of a big city, clear avoidance must be kept of the snobbish doctrine emanating from ivory towers elsewhere that popular plays, especially comedies, because they already have been done in New York theatres, should be denied to this audience. Otherwise, audiences of cosmopolitan type would not see them at all and thus would be deprived of the pleasure and profit that the American theatre, in

[6] *New York Times*, October 17, 1949.

its large estate, has to offer to the people. It is a part of management to understand and to appreciate the responsibility of the art form in a democratic society. An administrator, for that reason as well as others, cannot confine himself to the premises but must give due regard and attention to correspondence and to the speaker's platform. Finally, he must carry his colleagues and trustees along with his dreams and his projects by means of confidence and good faith, as well as by the tortuous tasks of reports and estimates painstakingly written and documented. Imagination may be said to consist, for the administrator as for the artist, in the instinct to conceive and in the intuitive sense to resolve every detail.

As was said by one of the founders of the Play House, "A theatre is not in its essence a building, but a group of men and women who work with intelligence toward an idea."[7] In this case, Fortune, indeed, has given her gracious nod to the select company of people whom it has been a privilege to serve and whose service has made possible whatever has been done. They have been activated by the belief that a national theatre must be implanted locally, and that the artistic process must be preserved by whatever means are at hand or that can be devised. They have accepted and have subscribed to the principle defined by Élie Faure: "The inner quality of a work is measured by the quality of the relations which unite its elements and assure continuity of ensemble."[8] The existence of that sort

[7] *Theatre Arts Monthly*, Vol. X, No. 8 (August, 1926), 520.

[8] In translations by Walter Pach, the writings of Faure have been issued in several editions. A reading of various volumes brought up no English translation in this form, but the following quotation has in it the same ideas. "None of the methods created to symbolize form have reality save through their spiritual relations with the expression of an idea, the ensemble of which lies in the intention of the creator. . . . The ensemble does not radiate unless it forms a whole from which nothing can be taken away." Élie Faure, *History of Art: The Spirit of Forms*,

of unity has made unnecessary here, and impossible of existence, that ambagious system prevailing elsewhere, under which everything depends upon laborious reference to separate and sovereign agencies, each of which through collective action stipulates how things are to be done and on what terms. The elimination of this confirmed and authorized confusion saves energy, turmoil, time, and money.

The instinct for theatre is universal. Talent, brains, and skill abound everywhere to bring it to all the people. It is not a private domain, or dependent on any given coterie. Ways and means may vary, plays may vary, but the genus audience and the genus actor will persist. They are one being. Organize them into a single unity, to the end that through them the theatre, wherever it may be, remains alive.

translated by Walter Pach (Garden City, Garden City Publishing Co., Inc., 1937), 354.

6. FROM STOCK TO TELEVISION

Barclay Leathem

"Young man, do I understand that you propose to prostitute the standards of a great university by giving students academic credit for driving nails in wood?"

The speaker was an older professor, the occasion a faculty meeting, the time 1924. In asking approval for the first course in dramatic arts at Western Reserve University, I had explained that students would have the creative experience of producing plays. The course's description included many aspects of practical work in the theatre, but the heresy contained in the words "design and build scenery" was sufficient to defeat the proposal.

Now, some thirty years later, dramatic arts as a separate department at Western Reserve University offers an undergraduate major, and 246 graduate students have received the Master of Arts, the Master of Fine Arts, or the Doctor of Philosophy degree in this subject. Nothing happened overnight. The struggle was fraught with frequent disappointments. I recall the cynical comment of one of my associates after another faculty meeting at which a request for support had been denied. "Remember,

Leathem," he said, "a university moves slowly, if at all."

Opposition to formal instruction in theatre went beyond the normal conservatism of college faculties. Dramatics was tolerated as a rather harmless student activity in most institutions until well into the twenties. Even after applied music and art courses had become part of the curriculum, theatre lacked this academic respectability. Perhaps this attitude stemmed from the belief that actors by and large were unstable or irresponsible members of society. Perhaps it was a long carry-over from the widespread antagonism to theatre in colonial America. It might have resulted from the conservative's resentment of the theatre's popularity with the masses, of the theatre's ability to enchant and excite.

My interest in theatre began early. The first play I remember is *The Old Homestead*. My grandfather took me to see it in Philadelphia, and he took me backstage to meet Denman Thompson, the author and star. Here began my interest in plays and players. It continued through high school. There I rehearsed in plays in the late afternoons and spent many evenings in the neighborhood stock company theatres that preceded the neighborhood movies. At Pennsylvania State College I met Arthur Cloetingh, a young instructor. He had studied theatre with Frederick Koch in South Dakota. As Koch had inspired him, Cloetingh stirred us with visions of what theatre could be in colleges and universities throughout the land. To him it was a way of life, an interpretation of the human adventure.

Another professor at Penn State whose teaching reached beyond the strict limitations of subject matter was Fred Lewis Pattee. He was a pioneer of the academic world, the first to strive effectively for recognition of

American literature as a separate course with stature of its own. He often digressed in class to speak of his fight against the forces that resisted change. He told how during the late nineteenth century the philologists had opposed the first courses in interpretation of English literature: they said is was impossible to give examinations in taste. But when courses in American literature were proposed, the recently established professors of English literature in turn found reasons to argue against change. Years later I remembered Professor Pattee's story whenever the faculty at Western Reserve was reluctant to approve new courses. Liberals often become conservative. And people forget that someone had to win the privileges they now enjoy. Little of value comes without struggle.

After finishing at Penn State, I entered law school at Western Reserve University in the fall of 1921. I was employed to teach classes in English and public speaking, a full schedule of twelve semester hours at Adelbert College of Western Reserve University. I was also engaged to direct the dramatic activities of the Sock and Buskin Club, a group of undergraduates. They spent the first semester arguing whether to do three one-act plays or one three-act play. There being no theatre on the campus, the play finally decided upon, *Stop Thief*, was given in the Masonic Auditorium. The next year, *Tweedles* was staged on an improvised platform in the gymnasium. It was what the advertising agencies now call a "package deal." The play was followed by a dance, the cost of which was included in the price of admission. At least half the audience was more interested in the dance and straggled in during the last act. But the actors had fun, the plays did not tax anyone's mind, and, after all, the university administration's primary concern was that the dramatics club balance its budget.

In 1924, I had to decide between practicing law or staying at the university as instructor in English. I chose the latter—not because the prospect of teaching English and public speaking was inviting, but because Howard Woodward, my immediate superior on the faculty, encouraged my plans for expansion of the dramatics program. So did Sidney Wilson, the university treasurer. For years he made up our deficits. After his retirement I asked him where the money had come from. He said that he had used a surplus in an endowment fund for religious education. In one of his undergraduate courses he had heard about the close relationship between theatre and religion in ancient Greece. Another factor that influenced my decision was my wife's interest in theatre. We had met in a college play; we had worked together to produce plays at Adelbert College. Ruth had designed scenery and helped with direction. A shared interest in a creative activity we both enjoyed seemed to outweigh the possibility of a larger income through law.

In 1921, Frederic McConnell came to Cleveland as director of the Cleveland Play House. I cannot overestimate the value of his friendship and help over the many years of our close association. It was stimulating to see and to act in plays at the Play House. The best of European and British drama was included in a distinguished repertory. I soon realized that a university theatre should set its sights higher than recreational entertainment for tired sophomores. Instead of *Stop Thief*, why not O'Neill's one-act plays of the sea, or Ibsen, or Shaw?

The Play House also experimented with the new theories of Appia, Craig, and other advocates of a new *décor*. I recall the thrill of first seeing shafts of light pierce through the dark to spotlight an actor isolated in space before a black cyclorama. So much of what our students accept today as standard practice was excitingly new in the twenties. The impact of new theories and methods was exhilarating. We were not surprised when Strindberg's *The Spook Sonata* brought more students to our theatre than did *The Bat*.

I stress the Play House and Frederic McConnell's artistic leadership because it soon became apparent to me that an urban university should take advantage of community resources. This concept has been a guiding policy in the development of dramatic arts at Western Reserve University. From the inception of graduate study in theatre in 1931, there has been close co-operation with the Cleveland Play House. Mr. McConnell and members of his professional company are engaged to give instruction in graduate school courses conducted at the Play House. Students are asked to try out for parts and frequently act with the professional company. Especially talented students occasionally earn up to six graduate credits toward advanced degrees by appearing in several plays there. Students enrolled in any course in dramatic arts, undergraduate or graduate, are invited to attend dress rehearsals or are given complimentary tickets to performances during the middle of the week.

Another example of use of community resources is the working arrangement with Karamu Theatre, which provides graduate school fellowships for Negro students. They take twenty-four credits in courses at the university. Six credits of the thirty required for the M. A. degree are given for practical work at Karamu Theatre under the supervision of Mrs. Russell Jelliffe. Because Karamu uses white and Negro talent in all productions, white students sometimes act in or direct plays given either on the Karamu proscenium stage or in their arena theatre.

To return now to the early years of struggle, I recall that when graduate courses first came under consideration, I felt a need for advice from someone with more experience. I had just returned from a convention of the Drama League of America. I had listened to many speeches, but most of them were condescending tirades against the New York professional theatre. Speakers vied with each other in berating the plays and players on "Broadway," a word enunciated with vitriolic scorn. This was not what I had hoped to hear. I wanted constructive approaches to the task of starting a graduate program in theatre. Even at this time, 1930, George Pierce Baker was almost a legendary figure. I wrote to him and asked his opinion of the value of bringing together a few leaders to discuss common problems and objectives. To my amazement, he replied promptly that the idea was sound and that he would come to Cleveland to attend such a meeting. What happened during the two-day conference was a reflection of Baker's personality. His fervor and enthusiasm dominated the sessions. Although nothing specific was decided—Baker warned against attempts to set up arbitrary standards of art—ideas were examined, opinions freely exchanged. What impressed me most was Baker's emphasis on participation in public performance as the core of graduate training in theatre. That Baker should come to such a meeting was typical of the great teacher. He owed nothing to me. I had never been a student in his classes; I had never even met him. But he recognized my need for help in starting a new graduate department in dramatic arts. He believed that the theatre should be strengthened in other universities as well as at Harvard and Yale. His visit impressed the university administration and faculty. Graduate courses were offered the following fall.

Before graduate courses were offered, the undergraduate curriculum in theatre had expanded slowly as faculty fears were allayed. Realizing that nothing would be gained by head-on collision with several older conservative professors whose support was needed, I made special efforts to get them to see our plays. Some dramas were selected from classical literature primarily to attract to the theatre professors, still unconvinced, whose votes were needed. We had to demonstrate the academic value of creative work in the theatre. We had to prove by repeated examples that the experience of staging a play could be even more educational than the traditional study of drama as literature.

In 1929–30, I spent a sabbatical leave in Vienna. The previous year, Max Reinhardt had started a school to train actors and directors for the German professional theatre. I applied for admission to the Regie Seminar and, after taking a written and oral examination, was accepted.

In addition to Reinhardt, there were three directors, each with a different method. Dr. Emil Geyer, the oldest professional theatre man in Vienna, was meticulous and pedantic. He had his own idea of how a line should be read and insisted upon having his way. Some rehearsals would run four hours and cover only two pages of script, because Geyer forced actors to repeat until they used the precise inflection he wanted.

Kalbeck, who directed at the Josephstadt Theatre in Vienna, was the dynamic extrovert. He would leap to the stage and act all the parts, if necessary, to make his point about a scene. He purposely exaggerated; he felt it was easier to tone down overplaying than it was to get an actor to project intense feeling to an audience.

Ivan Smith was the Stanislavsky specialist. Reinhardt had written to Stanislavsky and had told him that he would like to have his method taught. Smith was Stanislavsky's choice. Smith would never read a line or act out a scene for an actor. Instead, hour after hour would be spent in persistent probing for motivation, inner meaning, spine, subtext, and all the other nuances familiar to adherents of the Stanislavsky system. Smith had a contagious intensity of application to the task at hand. No one was allowed to take notes. Every eye had to be fixed upon the scene. One of his typical comments was, "Too many plays have been ruined by the director's cigar."

Reinhardt's approach to a play was both scholarly and instinctive. Himself an actor, he had the rare gift of not only realizing what an actor was trying to do but also being able to show him how best to achieve his goal. Unlike many directors, Reinhardt did not deliver long dissertations about the play. He would plunge into a scene and rely upon impressions given to him by the actors. Unless Reinhardt thought an actor's interpretation inconsistent with the playwright's meaning, he would accept it. He did not believe that there was only one possible correct way to play Hamlet, for example. He thought that each production of a play would differ according to personalities and talents of the cast. Known best in this country for his spectacular production of *The Miracle* and for his unfortunately lavish Hollywood film of *A Midsummer Night's Dream*, Reinhardt, whom I watched at work for over a year, was at his best while working intimately with actors on details. He was imaginative in devising appropriate stage business to enrich a scene. I recall in particular the way he had Malvolio in *Twelfth Night* play with the note—first ignoring it, walking past it, then disdainfully poking at it with his staff, and then holding it far in front of him as though it were contaminated—before reading it.

Despite variety of theories and methods, each of the

four men got excellent results. I have always distrusted individuals who set themselves up as custodians of certitude. In the Reinhardt school I found confirmation of the many-sidedness of the creative process. I believe that students in a university theatre should have the opportunity to work with different directors. The director is more important than the system. So long as he is competent and can enthusiastically communicate his intellectual and emotional reaction to a script, the student will benefit.

Another thing that impressed me about the Reinhardt school was the thoroughness of analysis and preparation by the director before rehearsals. For example, in discussing the preliminary design for a battle scene in a Shakespeare play, Reinhardt pointed out that the opposing armies could not speak the playwright's lines without coming to blows unless they were physically separated. He suggested the use of high platforms for each army on opposite sides of the stage. This thoroughness characterized every detail of production.

In 1940, a grant-in-aid from a national foundation made possible a semester's travel to colleges and community theatres. From February to September, I visited approximately one hundred theatres in forty-six states. Meeting colleagues at conventions is good, but seeing them in action is better. Trudging through a snowstorm in Iowa with Ed Mabie on the way to a rehearsal of an original play written by one of his students, talking with Allardyce Nicoll in his office at Yale, listening to Paul Green pour out his dreams for an indigenous folk drama, attending the opening performance of Glenn Hughes's Penthouse Theatre, and watching many other leaders teach classes and rehearse plays were memorable experiences. But in retrospect the discovery of new leaders stands out above all else. In Houston I asked a local newspaper editor who was doing important work in the theatre. He suggested that I see a young woman who was getting surprisingly effective results directing plays at a settlement house. The young woman was Margo Jones. Those who knew Margo will never forget her dynamic faith in new playwrights, her boundless energy, and her contagious enthusiasm. I last saw her in Cleveland a few years ago. She graciously told a group attending an after-theatre party for Tennessee Williams that I had been the first visitor from the theatre world outside Houston to encourage her to concentrate on doing new manuscripts by playwrights whose names had never appeared in the bright lights of Broadway. Her untimely death was a distinct loss to the American theatre.

Paul Baker was another discovery. He had mobilized the creative resources of Waco, Texas, in a stupendous production of *The American Way*. I arrived in time to see one of the dress rehearsals. Like Margo, Paul was electric. His vitality pervaded the entire theatre. So did his imagination, his strikingly original treatment of the play. This was no pedestrian copy of the New York production, but something appropriately and refreshingly different.

There were too many others to mention without a long listing of present leaders in the American theatre—university, community, and commercial. From everyone I learned something. To stay at home too long is to risk complacency. It is good to get away, to see what others are doing, to re-examine objectives, to avoid confusing mere activity with accomplishment, and to seek deeper values.

Months before Pearl Harbor, the officer who had proposed my travel grant said to me, "Just as sure as we can order ham and eggs for breakfast, this country is going to war. Why don't you go down to Washington and see whether the War Department's recreation program includes theatre?" It did not. Then began the long struggle to convince the decision makers in Washington that for thousands of young men in service the putting on of plays would be as normal and as salutary a recreation as throwing a baseball. We pointed out that since World War I, in schools, settlement houses, grange halls, clubs, lodges, churches, as well as in hundreds of college and community theatres across America, men and women had been rehearsing and performing plays. The familiar reply was, "That may be true, but we're not interested in training actors for Hollywood; we're training men to fight a war —a war for democracy." What did that mean? Could it possibly include the right to use one's leisure time in camp to act in a play? Could it include the right to write a play, a song, even a skit satirizing army life itself? How do you spell out democracy for the man who may die for it? What constitutes combat efficiency? Does it depend solely on muscular co-ordination? Does a man's mental attitude have any bearing on it? It was not easy to get answers.

Frederick Osborn, later General Osborn, as chairman of the Joint Army and Navy Committee on Welfare and Recreation, was the first man in authority who fully understood our purposes. He requested me to join the committee as civilian consultant. Colonel William Draper, later an assistant secretary of the army, was the first officer in a position to help us who did. He agreed to have the National Theatre Conference send a qualified director of amateur shows to two camps that were selected as testing places. The funds to support this, and subsequent projects under the supervision of the National Theatre Conference, were provided by a national foundation. Gordon

Minter went from the University of Texas to Fort Bliss; Joseph Brown from the University of North Carolina to Fort Bragg. These were the pioneers in the struggle to convince the War Department that theatre by and for men in service belonged in training camps in the United States and in bases behind combat areas overseas.

It was General Innis P. Swift of Fort Bliss who finally conceded that it was better to have men stay in camp on their own time to rehearse plays than it was to have them return from binges in Mexico temporarily unfit for combat training.

Then there were the camps from which there was no escape—camps like Huachuca in Arizona, miles from any town in which men might find any recreation, good or bad, and camps too isolated for the regularly routed tours of professional entertainers supplied by U.S.O. camp shows. The men in these camps had to make their own entertainment, or pent-up emotions would find release in other ways. Late one night I had a call from Washington describing conditions at Huachuca. Morale was so low, unrest so widespread that anything could happen. Could I find someone who would help the Negro troops there to put on shows? I told the caller in Washington that I would try. The man who responded to this urgent appeal was Professor Randolph Edmonds, then in charge of dramatics at Dillard University. His success was further proof of the need for a well-directed program of self-entertainment by men in service.

The next step was the extension of the experiment to the nine army areas in this country. With War Department approval, the National Theatre Conference sent trained civilian play directors, mostly from university and community theatres, to organize programs that soon became known as "Soldier Shows." They ranged from the

simplest local talent variety show to the highly professional *This Is the Army*. During the rehearsals of the
latter, Irving Berlin was caught in a cross fire of juris-
dictional dispute among high-ranking army officers, each
of whom wanted credit for what promised to be a spectacular hit. Louis Simon, the National Theatre Conference civilian consultant in that army district, learned from
Ezra Stone, who was helping direct the show, that Irving
Berlin was at the end of his patience in dealing with the
complications of army red tape. He asked me to come to
Camp Upton, where the show was in rehearsal. The three
of us met with Irving Berlin and talked well into the night.
I do not think that many know how much Louis Simon
and especially Ezra Stone, each in a different way, had to
do with the fact that *This Is the Army* finally reached an
audience. They realized that my brief part in the backstage drama was psychological. Irving Berlin wanted to
talk to someone not in uniform, but with an official con-
nection with the War Department, who might be able to
short-cut lines of communication.

The War Department finally took over full administration of the Soldier Shows program. Many of the civilian
consultants were commissioned and continued their work,
under army supervision. To them, to the members of the
National Theatre Conference, to hundreds of college and
community theatre directors, and to theatre people generally who responded to requests for assistance must go
full credit for the Soldier Shows program. Someone was
always ready with help when help was needed. Lee Norvelle also was a civilian consultant to the Joint Army and
Navy Committee on Welfare and Recreation. He was
able on many occasions, through personal contacts, to
penetrate the maze of Washington bureaucracy and reach
a key person at a crucial time. It took the collective effort

of many to make Soldier Shows a success. And what was started by the National Theatre Conference with a few practical demonstrations is now an accepted part of the War Department's recreational policy.[1]

The editor of this collection of essays, knowing of the pioneer efforts of Western Reserve University in television, has asked me to stress the relationship of television to the theatre. My interest began in 1942 when Edward Cole of Yale told me about his experience at WRGB, the General Electric Company's experimental television station in Schenectady. I went there, too, and was convinced that this new medium of mass communication would soon become a powerful force in American life. We built dummy cameras at Western Reserve and converted a room into a television workshop. In 1944, we rehearsed an original play by one of our students and took it to Schenectady. This was the first television program by anyone in Cleveland. Several months before WEWS, Cleveland's first television station, opened in December, 1947, I was invited by James Hanrahan, the general manager, to join the staff as a consultant. I knew little, but no one else knew very much, and we all learned together.

The early days of television were confusing and exciting. I can never forget my first program. Ordinarily the simplest television show to do is an interview. My task was to direct an interview between the president of a kennel club and a dog trainer. I was to have an hour's rehearsal for a fifteen-minute program. I arrived at the station early, hoping to talk to engineers and cameramen before the rehearsal started, but everyone on my crew was

[1] One director, James H. Parke, who had been active in university work and also under the special services branch of the army stayed on in the government branch for hospital care of disabled veterans, to take charge of all dramatic entertainment.

out at dinner. About twenty minutes before the program was to be telecast, the trainer arrived with his wife and two dogs. He explained that they would all appear on the show. I asked what the dogs would do. He said that one was a guard dog. His wife would walk with the dog, the trainer would pretend to be a purse snatcher. "You watch what happens," he said. I raced into the control room, briefed the cameramen quickly, and started the rehearsal. The trainer grabbed the pocketbook and ran. So did the wife and dog. The cameramen frantically swept their cameras around, but all they picked up was empty space. I knew that would not do. Rushing out, I marked off an area with chalk and explained that the action would have to stay within it. The clock showed eight minutes until air time. I asked what the other dog would do. The trainer replied, "He is a search dog and can find concealed objects." We let the dog sniff a key ring and then put it in the belt of the kennel club president, who had just arrived. Back to the control room for camera rehearsal. The dog entered, sniffed, and put his paws on the president's ribs. Being ticklish, he shuddered and the key ring fell to the floor. I knew that that would not do either; so I rushed again to the studio to suggest corrections. I made the mistake of putting my hand on the trainer's shoulder. The first dog, apparently thinking that I was attacking his master, broke away from the floor manager who was holding him on a leash, and lunged toward me. So did the other dog. During the mad scramble that followed, I heard a voice on the public address system say, "Thirty seconds to air time." The show went on. Thanks to the help of the station's efficient personnel—cameramen, floor manager, and engineers—we kept pictures on the screen.

The point of this is that I quickly learned that television, like theatre, is a team effort. Unlike theatre, however, in television the director's active participation does not end with the dress rehearsal. His creative responsibility and his control of results not only continue in the actual performance, they are intensified. Even after that first hectic introduction to television, I realized that here was an exciting extension of theatre—an opportunity to adjust old principles to new forms.

Television, using sight in addition to sound, is not merely visual radio. Neither does it primarily depend on motion-picture technique. But fundamentally it derives its basic principles from theatre. The showmanship that prompted the primitive hunter to act out his kill, the early playwright's interpretation of man's relationship to man and to the forces outside of and greater than himself, the satisfaction of aesthetic needs, the emotional stimulation of new ideas—these are only a few of the elements, essentially dramatic, that have been the theatre's stock-in-trade for centuries. To me, it seemed obvious that training for television should stem from university theatre courses in voice, acting, stagecraft, scene design, directing, and related subjects. The addition of a few courses in television production and policy would suffice to give students necessary specialized information. A university should do more than train in skills; a trade school can do that. A university should emphasize cultural heritage, critical evaluation, original thought, and social responsibility.

In 1948, there were only a few television sets in Cleveland, most of them in saloons. I tried to persuade my faculty colleagues to prepare programs for the weekly half hour of television time given to us by Mr. Hanrahan of WEWS. One astounded professor said, "Leathem, do you seriously suggest that I lecture on biology to bar flies?" Our early struggle to win acceptance of theatre was repeated for television. Because other university departments were not interested in the new medium, we concentrated on drama. Using a grant from a national foundation, we provided fellowships for two graduate students who helped me adapt plays for television.

A cablegram to George Bernard Shaw in January, 1948, brought a prompt reply giving us permission to televise *The Man of Destiny* from the WEWS studio, and *The Devil's Disciple* from the university theatre on the campus. Both were firsts in American television. For *The Man of Destiny* we made the mistake of inviting an audience to the studio and seating them facing a setting designed for a normal theatre production. The cameras were placed between the stage and the audience. We really photographed a stage play in a television studio. Instead of using the creative potentialities of television, we ignored them. This was a common mistake in the early days of televised drama. *The Devil's Disciple* fared no better. Three cameras were set up in the theatre, two down front in the side aisles, one on a platform at the rear of the auditorium. We depended on this third camera for "cover shots" of the entire stage whenever we might have trouble following the action with the other cameras. Halfway through the first act it failed. Thereafter we had only the two aisle cameras. We kept pictures on the air, but to the viewer the results often were bewildering.

Realizing our need for expert assistance, we used what was left of our foundation grant to bring from England Desmond Davis, one of the best directors at the British Broadcasting Corporation. During his three-month visit, he taught us much, climaxing his stay with a television production of *Fortunato*. For the first time, we realized that there was more to television than taking a camera picture of stage action. This was before the coaxial cable brought network television to Cleveland and gave us further insight into the complexities of technical operation. Desmond Davis showed us that television was an art in itself, that, properly used, the new medium could focus attention more exactly, could highlight meaning more effectively than was possible on the stage.

Gradually the number of television sets in the Cleveland area increased. The house with an antenna became the norm rather than the exception. Slowly other departments at the university expressed a willingness to appear on the Sunday half-hour program, which by 1949 was called "University Circle." Surveys in 1950 showed that we were reaching an audience of fifty thousand. By 1952 this had grown to over one hundred thousand. Almost every department, school, or division of the university has now been represented on "University Circle," as have many cultural institutions such as the Museum of Art, the Cleveland Play House, the Public Library, Karamu Theatre, and the Health Museum.

Television policy is determined by a broadcasting council appointed by President John S. Millis of Western Reserve University, who recognized the educational opportunities of television and gave it full administrative support. The presence on the council of Dean Carl F. Wittke of the graduate school and of other deans and departmental chairmen assures broad representation of faculty opinion and general faculty acceptance of the university's television activities.

Once policy is approved, the preparation of formats and the rehearsing and televising of programs are the responsibility of the department of dramatic arts. Assigned to the department as my television assistant is Rand Manning, a graduate of Western Reserve University. He does most of the work developing program ideas, writes scripts, helps with details of production, and shares the directing with me. Scenery is designed by Henry Kurth, who teaches stagecraft and design in our department. Students assist in all aspects of television production. We move into the studio an hour before air time and meet station cameramen and engineering personnel. We have full responsibility for every detail of the telecast, including actual direction of the program as it is sent into the home. In contrast, when educational telecasts are used over most commercial stations, a director from the station puts the program on the air, and students and faculty are limited to appearing as performers.

The close relationship between Western Reserve and WEWS reaches back to January, 1948, when university and station personnel began working together to produce programs. Growing up in television together has been an important factor in our successful co-operation. Another is the attitude of Jim Hanrahan, the general manager of WEWS. His interest in community institutions and welfare is genuine. He believes in public service television and wants it to be as carefully produced as commercial television. If he merely tolerated educational programs as a means to an end—satisfying the Federal Communications Commission's concern for telecasts in the public interest—the station personnel might soon become perfunctory in their assistance. Instead, we have their enthusiastic support. In recognition of Mr. Hanrahan's initiative and imagination in using television for the public good, Western Reserve University in June, 1955, conferred upon him the honorary doctor's degree.

In 1951, Western Reserve University began its daily television of regular college courses for credit toward a university degree. This was another first in American television. Covering a wide range of subjects, this program is now firmly established, and its academic value is no longer questioned.

Television is a natural activity for any department of dramatic arts. Certainly at Western Reserve experience has justified our expectations. Co-operation is essential. Willingness to assist others, to defer to their particular wishes and needs is of paramount importance. Occasionally programs become the special prerogative of departments or schools. For example, *Issues at Stake*, using a courtroom format in which both sides of a controversy are represented by expert witnesses and lawyers, is supervised by the speech department. The law school and the medical school have both developed programs for our series. But the department of dramatic arts, by producing each university telecast, has broadened the base of its instructional offerings and has provided students with varied and practical training for their professional advancement in television.

Television is a contemporary theatre experience. Consuming material, it offers new talent unlimited opportunities. To the precious aesthete, mass appeal, commercialism, and mediocrity are inevitable concomitants. But the real artist need not fear television's popularity. Shakespeare, Lope de Vega, and Molière wrote for a competitive commercial market. From Aeschylus to Arthur Miller, the great plays, with few exceptions, have had the approval of a large audience. Television, because of its insistent demands, has created a climate for distinguished writing. There is an audience for countless Chayefskys. The playwright need not sacrifice his integrity. If he can sensitively interpret the universals of human experience, the largest audience in history awaits his play. The opportunities of television extend in like manner to actors, designers, directors, and other theatrical talents.

In summary, a few things stand out. One is the necessity of overcoming obstacles. Another is the emphasis at Western Reserve upon community concepts of drama. The theatre should be more than an isolated experience for the cultured few. Another is the willingness to experiment with new forms like television. Common to all our activities is the recognition of theatre as a co-operative undertaking. Our staff works as a team. Associated with me for many years is Professor Nadine Miles. She has shared the struggle. So have other members of the staff, past and present. That struggle continues. Complacent acceptance of the *status quo* is the dry rot of academic inertia. It has no place in the theatre. Our objective is to raise our sights to new and constantly challenging horizons.

7. A DREAM ON A DIME

Gilmor Brown

As I LOOK BACK over an exciting career of adventure in theatre development, I realize more and more how grateful I should be to have had the opportunity of living and working in this amazing era of rapid and astounding change in cultural and mechanical progress. How wonderful it was to have been able to see some of the first automobiles, the first airplanes, and the first motion pictures, and to follow the great changes they have made in our social system—and to see the steady development of tolerant understanding between nations and races, gradual though it may be! It is because of that background that I feel I owe the many young students whom I have developed and the many others who are concerned with my particular field of work some account of how a dream can be realized on a shoestring—or on a dime.

All my life has been devoted to theatre. As a child I happened to see a sixteen-sheet poster advertising Minnie Maddern Fiske when she was supported by George Arliss in *Becky Sharp*, the dramatization of Thackeray's *Vanity Fair*. I was so impressed that I begged fifty cents from my parents so that I might sit in the top gallery and watch that magnificent performance. Inspired by it, I felt that I must at once begin a series of productions. I established a theatre in the cellar of our home in Denver and gathered in as many neighborhood children as possible to become a part of my company.

Even then I was an inveterate reader. On the basis of what I had from reading, as material, I decided that I must devote a part of my time to writing fabulous and amazing tragedies for this company—usually in ten or more acts. This proved to be something of a disastrous project, since our adult neighbors began to complain that my company was borrowing far too much of their best furniture to be used in my productions; so, after two years of hectic activity, I was sternly told by my mother that my plays must be discontinued, although I had already had some publicity in the Denver papers. I continued, however, to pursue my histrionic activities under the tolerant encouragement of the sainted Dr. Houghton of St. Mark's Church. Later, through the indulgent permission of Dr. Houghton, I attempted productions in an open-air theatre at St. Mark's in the Mountains; there I again indulged in playwriting, with a tragedy that I thought would put Aeschylus to shame. It certainly did not. Yet, bad though it was, that play brought a complete change of pace for me by bringing me to the attention of a very notable woman. In her honor there still stands, in a corner of the Art Institute of Chicago, a statue inscribed "To Florence James Adams, who was a genius in the evocation of personality." For several years I worked under her guidance, haunting libraries in order to find out more and more about theatre, and attending lecture after lecture at the Art Institute. I was always studying intensively in those years under the direction and inspiration of Mrs. Adams.

She had been sent, as a protégé of James Steele Mac-Kaye, to study abroad. In France, she had been under the instruction of members of the Comédie Française; under the remarkable Marchesi, one of the greatest teachers of vocal technique; and finally an associate of the famous André Antoine, who then was beginning his revolutionary development in drama. Deciding not to attempt a stage career, Mrs. Adams then returned to Chicago and established her own studio. There I heard many notable people lecture on all forms of activity in the arts. Among them were many who were highly successful in the fields of architecture, science, literature, and theatre.

The husband of Mrs. Adams was for many years the manager of the Chicago Auditorium, and, thanks to his interest, I became an usher there. I thus was able to see all the productions of the Metropolitan Opera of that period, with such famous singers as Caruso, Nordica, and Scotti; Sarah Bernhardt, in two weeks of her repertory; and Eleanora Duse in her repertory of the D'Annunzio period. All of these were, of course, a great inspiration to me, as were the famous Melba and the great Chaliapin.

It was in Chicago also that I was enabled to follow the founding and early work of the Drama League of America under Mrs. A. Starr Best and Mrs. Alice C. D. Riley. I came to know the poet Percy MacKaye and his notable book, *The Civic Theatre in Relation to the Redemption of Leisure*. (His remarkable tetralogy, *The Mystery of Hamlet, King of Denmark*, I was to produce many years later at the Pasadena Playhouse.) Another who greatly influenced me in that period was Thomas Wood Stevens, from whom I learned something of drama festivals and pageantry.

Soon thereafter, I began my professional career, with Sir Philip Ben Greet and his Shakespearean company on its second tour out of England. At that time he had many notable actors associated with him. I remember particularly how pleased I was through this association to make the acquaintance of that charming actress Dame Sybil Thorndike. With this Ben Greet company I played everything from extras to bit parts. I next ventured out with a road company on a Canadian tour, with a repertory that included every type of play from Shakespeare to cheap melodrama. I recall that I was paid the phenomenal salary of fifteen dollars a week, from which I was called on to pay my board and room and all incidental expenses.

Those were perilous times for me. Since I needed to earn bread and butter during the summer seasons, I remembered what I had learned from Thomas Wood Stevens and started out to arouse interest in small cities of the Middle West in drama festivals and pageantry. That venture turned out fairly successfully in many places. I remember one of them very well, because through it I was fortunate enough to be associated with the famous Mayo brothers of Rochester, Minnesota. I remember from this period of work and travel my wondering why community theatres could not be established under the same co-operative civic management as the civic pageants, giving a full year of employment and pleasure. I recall, too, the day when I was directing a drama festival at Hutchinson, Kansas, that I had the good fortune to meet a social leader from Pasadena, California, Mrs. J. B. Durand. She remarked that her city was becoming more and more interested in possibilities for drama on the West Coast; she also promised to introduce me to outstanding members of their Drama League, then under the leadership of Miss Eleanor Bissell. I decided then that my next move would be to form a small stock company on my very limited capital and to go to Pasadena.

The one theatre available was an old burlesque house on Fair Oaks Avenue. Our season there was a short and disastrous one, but in the meantime I had managed to win the interest of a few outstanding citizens. I suggested to them that we should establish a community theatre with somewhat the basis of operation that I had used for a limited number of city pageants. In short, I proposed that we incorporate as a civic institution with a board made up of leaders in business, education, social life, civic affairs, and labor unions.

It has always been my good fortune, or possibly my talent, to have the instinct or inspiration to discover exceptional people interested in cultural activities. The greatest aid that I ever have had was from a series of discussions with the famous astronomer, the late Professor George Ellery Hale. He was constantly helpful, not only to me but to the entire city of Pasadena, in advancing its cultural development. It was through his influence that the California Institute of Technology grew in stature and that Professor Robert Millikan, another remarkable leader, came to direct that institution. The entire Millikan family became friends of mine and of the Pasadena Playhouse, as did Professor and Mrs. William B. Munro, Mr. and Mrs. Samuel Hinds, and the Misses Sybil and Alberta Jones. It was under the encouragement of such persons that the newly formed Community Playhouse opened at the old burlesque house on Fair Oaks Avenue, which was soon dubbed the "moth-eaten temple of drama."

Professionally, as socially, that first year had its supporters of notable quality. The season included an appearance of so distinguished a personality as Martha Graham, then beginning her career. I had cheering encouragement from Mary Pickford, Will Rogers, Douglas Fairbanks, Sr., and Charlie Chaplin. For actual production of plays, however, we depended entirely on amateur talent. The only salary that we could pay was my own, as director, on a percentage basis that yielded about five dollars a week. As we then had no capital fund, and never have had since, the success of our venture may prove that even outstanding organizations can be established and can flourish from a shoestring start, provided only that people realize their cultural possibilities.

It was in 1918 that the decision was taken to incorporate the Community Playhouse, with a general board membership such as I have described. I next requested my board to give me an experienced newspaperman to help on publicity, and also an experienced technician to improve our productions. Carl Huxley was chosen as our technician and for many years, until his death, he served us devotedly. H. O. Steckhan, as our first publicity man, soon got country-wide newspaper attention. It was with his help, too, that we developed two notable figures in our activities. One was Charles Prickett, who sacrificed an excellent position in a bank to become Steckhan's assistant. In his long term of service he was a remarkable business counselor of the Playhouse, keeping it in operation at times under most difficult conditions. The other individual developed within the Playhouse was his brother Oliver, who became in turn a fine publicity officer and then an excellent actor. Charles rapidly became a significant participant in the civic life of Pasadena, and his brother Oliver has demonstrated his acute sense of comedy values in films as well as on the live stage.

While we were operating in those years on a wholly volunteer, amateur basis, we kept reaching for professional standards. During those early days, among my greatest friends was that very great man who created the work in drama at Yale University, George Pierce Baker. He usually came to Pasadena in late spring and stayed on into early summer. He became a great personal friend and professional adviser in all my work. Later on I became a member of his National Theatre Conference and succeeded him as its president for a five-year period. As all know, Professor Baker's invaluable knowledge of plays and of theatre were of outstanding significance for the theatre in America.

I now come to the first of almost miraculous events that happened while I was nurturing the slow growth of the Playhouse. During this preliminary period we had existed on a very small box office and occasional small gifts. This was the time of Aline Barnsdall's very promising art theatre in Los Angeles, with its exceptional director and company, and with Norman Bel Geddes as art director. Her company lasted for two eventful seasons, and in that time she occasionally found time to come over to discover what we might be accomplishing at the Playhouse. Then Miss Barnsdall decided to close her theatre and to give me half of her electrical equipment. She also promised fifty dollars as aid in the production of any worthwhile play we might be able to stage, and that was a godsend to us. When she said good-bye and returned to the North, leaving Los Angeles and us as well, she frankly said that she did not believe in our kind of organization, but that she was nonetheless interested in us, and that we might hear from her.

In the meantime, an influenza epidemic hit southern California and no public gatherings were permitted where there might be the danger of the disease's spreading. We even had to wear ridiculous cheesecloth masks over our noses. This situation almost ended the career of the Pasadena Playhouse. The board met with me and sadly said that they feared we must close for good and all; but at that critical moment a letter came to me from Miss Barnsdall that enclosed a check for two thousand dollars. The Playhouse was saved. We were able to carry on. And so we did, steadily improving our standard of plays as well as quality of productions. The city government evinced an active interest in us, by providing two charming open-air theatres in which we were able to have a number of summer productions, especially of Shakespeare's plays. Although these outdoor locations eventually proved unsatisfactory, by reason of weather conditions and the noise from adjoining parks, such encouragement from the city of Pasadena was heartening to us and our audiences.

Meanwhile, I persuaded our board that eventually we must establish a school for the training of younger players, on the ground that such a school would help the general standard of our productions to become still better. We then started our Art Colony, which functioned well enough through two summers to prove the possibilities of the college that we later established. It also was out of that summer effort that I secured two of my finest assistant directors, Eloise Sterling and Lenore Shanewise.

Yet still another crisis was to face us. A splendid new theatre was built on Raymond Avenue, to house an excellent professional company called the "King Stock Company." At first they were so successful that we again feared that we should be compelled to discontinue our work. But now the many loyal citizens who were interested in establishing the Pasadena Playhouse as an enduring organization rallied around us. They proposed building a new theatre for us. Our new president, Paul Perigord, was assisted in this by a wonderful committee, which included Mrs. Robert Millikan, Mrs. George Ellery Hale, the William Reis family, Mr. and Mrs. Frank Sellars, and many others. A drive was started for a new building worthy of such a city as Pasadena. Property was acquired for the site, and, after many setbacks, the drive for funds reached such proportions that the building could be erected. The curious fact in this story is that in a city of millionaires the fund was miraculously raised through generous gifts that ranged from a few of $5,000 each to many of only $0.50. The total gathered in from all sources amounted to $146,295, and the mortgage then assumed was $150,000. Some pessimistic people asserted that the theatre would be closed within six months and the building rebuilt for use as a garage. They were wrong. Regardless of new difficulties ahead, recognized as real by us all, everyone agreed that our new playhouse was one of which any city could be proud.

Then came another of those miracles, for which I shall always be grateful. Mrs. Fannie E. Morrison, a remarkable woman, had come from Boston to Pasadena, and at the suggestion of our committee I approached her several times to ask whether she could assist us with a gift for the new building. Although we became good friends, she steadfastly refused us any aid. This, she said, was because she did not approve of amateur theatre, while I continued to assure her that our steady growth would mean the improvement of standards. Suddenly one day, after watching several of our productions, she decided that possibly she might be wrong. So, to my amazement, she went to the First Trust and Savings Bank and told Mr. T. W. Smith that she wished to pay off the mortgage on the Playhouse that I had started. Unlike many donors of amazing gifts, Mrs. Morrison never interfered with anything in the Playhouse management.

Next came an event that established us as having something of international importance. Eugene O'Neill gave his consent to my making a production of his *Lazarus*

Laughed, a production of such magnitude that the attempt had been given up by the Moscow Art Theatre and also by a well-endowed group in Chicago. The play ran for many weeks to completely sold-out houses and was received with enthusiastic approval by critics as well as by the public. This production, of which I was justifiably proud, was a great stimulus to me. It was followed by a number of others, in due course, that also were great incentives to further progress: *Peer Gynt;* Rolland's *The Wolves;* all the plays of Shakespeare; Rostand's *Cyrano de Bergerac;* a very successful series of plays by George Bernard Shaw that included *Major Barbara* and *The Simpleton of the Unexpected Isles;* and last, but not least, an imaginative production of *Montserrat,* translated by Lillian Hellman.

Recognition from new quarters came out of our series of summer festivals. These began with the chronicle plays of Shakespeare, staged in their historical sequence and produced by generous help from Mrs. Morrison and Cecil B. De Mille. In due time these festivals brought to the stage all the plays of Shakespeare, plays of Maxwell Anderson and Booth Tarkington, many examples of early American drama, and a sequence of well-known works of many other outstanding contemporary writers. The culmination of the festivals was in a great patriotic series, with Robert E. Sherwood's *Abe Lincoln in Illinois* as its climax. For our production of that play we were awarded the plaque of the Freedoms Foundation of Valley Forge, Pennsylvania. I also have been awarded two medals from France for our many productions of outstanding French drama. Our work of the regular seasons, as well as of these summer festivals, has brought its appreciated return in public recognition.

It was in 1924–25 that I established the Playbox. That step was taken because I believed that the next desirable development in theatre technique was to create a greater intimacy between the audience and the player, and between the audience and the play.

About the time when I became interested in the development of the community theatre. I had been talking with a number of European authorities about the current developments in theatre form in other countries. Here, there had been a growing interest in changes structurally and in departures from the old picture-frame stage. Some two years before the founding of the Playbox, two other American observers of theatre had made an extensive European tour. These two, Robert Edmond Jones and Kenneth Macgowan, had published in 1922 their new ideas in *Continental Stagecraft,* discussing such new intimate theatres as the Redoutensaal in Vienna and Copeau's Vieux Colombier in Paris. Also, they had visited the Cirque Medrano in Paris and had suggested that this might be the basis for a new type of theatre. In such indoor circuses the seating arrangement is around a central area that is used for the performance. It was this form that I later suggested to Glenn Hughes as suited to the planning of the intimate theatre that he was to have in a Seattle hotel. This, on completion, Hughes called the "Penthouse Theatre," a name that since has been used to a considerable degree by groups in developing this form of playing approach. Others have called it "center staging," but, if I recall correctly, Jones, Macgowan, and others have used a more advantageous term, namely "theatre-in-the-round."

My own experiment in the new form came seven years after the Pasadena Playhouse opened back in 1917. The

Playbox theatre opened in 1924–25, in an old, unused artists' studio that I had discovered in Pasadena. There we opened with *The Truth About Blayds*, by A. A. Milne. The idea of this intimate theatre (which I have never had quite the necessary capital to develop to its fullest capacity) was that the action of a play would take place in any given area of the particular building being used, and also that from production to production the audience and the playing space might be shifted about. The result was an interesting flexibility and capacity for playing in close relationship with an audience, for the only division between actors and spectators was the lighted area of the playing space. At our first performances, and since then, our audiences have often remarked that they felt as though they were eavesdropping on personal conversations.

This new form of theatre, I soon found out, required an entirely new estimation of the technique of directing and acting. As that first season and later ones passed, we seemed to find this new approach to a play more worthy and, in many instances, more inspiring than the old ways. Audiences discovered new values, very often in plays with which they were quite familiar. Actors suddenly realized many more possibilities of mental, vocal, and physical approaches to a part. There was no elaborate production formula to hamper them or the play. Limited properties and slight indications of locale were enough to suggest different settings.

The techniques developed by us at the Playbox have had their parallels elsewhere. To a great extent they have been found in the productions of the Circle Players in Hollywood and by the late Margo Jones in her much-discussed Theatre '47, and in its annually named succeeding seasons up to this present one, Theatre '56, in Dallas, Texas. These are among the major sources of new technique in what has become a fully marked kind of American theatre, with its own traditions of staging, acting, and directing.

From the repertory of our own first season it is possible to discover how varied the Playbox productions can be over a wide variety of theatre possibilities. After *The Truth About Blayds*, we next did *Pelléas et Mélisande*, by Maeterlinck. The eighteen scenes of this play captured, by the simplest means, all that "other world" quality of the Maeterlinck poetry, which you find also in the opera that Debussy composed from the play. This was followed by two new and original scripts—one called *Woman's Honor*, and the other *The Song with Wings*, by Marjorie Driscoll. *March Hares*, the famous, slightly screwy comedy by Harry Gribble, and John Masefield's profoundly moving play, *The Tragedy of Nan*, were followed by Willard Robertson's *Desire*, and then by that astonishing and provocative comedy, by W. J. Turner, *The Man Who Ate the Popomack*. Here was a series of productions that demanded and also created new approaches to the possibilities of theatre-in-the-round. Advances in technique since that first season have been constant and significant for audience and for actor, as well as for the director.

My feeling about the Playbox is that an audience must try to become an integral part of the action and thereby enter into its spirit in a wholly new manner. Therefore, in our first program (reprinted many times to inform new members coming into the Playbox audience) this announcement appeared.

Please remember that the Playbox is a unique experiment along many new lines and that we—audience and players— are taking our first timid steps tonight. This is the laboratory of the Community Playhouse, the Drama League, and the

Tuesday Drama Circle. Here, under the most intimate conditions we shall experiment in many new ways with new and old plays of the type usually known as "highbrow," though we trust that we shall not become unduly serious for all that. Remember that we do away with the conventional stage, footlights, proscenium arch, and all things which make a division between the player and the auditor. Perhaps we shall both be a little self-conscious of this at first. But eventually we feel sure that the unusual intimacy will bring out values in play, auditor, and player that will prove interesting and instructive. Suppose you try applauding only at the end of the performance and then only, of course, if you care to. Stay and discuss the play if you like—keep the Playhouse spirit of meeting the player for a friendly confab, and please consider this an introduction to everyone else in the audience.

Other features of the Playbox have been the production of the kinds of play that possibly have their special audience but no wide appeal, and also the staging of plays that we might know very well but which might have an entirely new value from a more intimate style of production. Our second season, for instance, gives again an idea of how wide a variety can be utilized in a Playbox repertory. The list included *The Discovery*, by Frances Sheridan, mother of Richard Brinsley Sheridan; *Bernice*, by Susan Glaspell; Alfred Sutro's *The Two Virtues*; a cycle of one-act plays by George Bernard Shaw; *The Mollusc*, by Hubert Henry Davies and what is still one of the greatest plays of our time, *The Great Galeoto*, by José Echegaray; and then *The Dragon*, by Lady Gregory, which I am glad to say has lately been produced once more by the Actors' Lab in Hollywood.

A break in such activity came when the building of the new Playhouse involved everyone on the staff in a tremendous amount of activity. We decided to discontinue the old Playbox after the 1926–27 season. Even so, we carried on special performances in the same manner— first in the Recital Hall of the new Playhouse, then in the Cheesewright Studio, and next in the most interesting experiment with intimate theatre techniques in the Serendipity Gardens. Since I have always been interested in the development of open-air theatre, this third location gave us another phase of Playbox development. Of similar nature were the series of matinees staged in the Playhouse. These included *The Wild Duck*, by Ibsen; a revival of *The Truth About Blayds*; John Kemp's *Wager*, with all its English folk dancing; and *The Vegetable*, a little-known but very amazing play by F. Scott Fitzgerald.

For many years an interesting feature of the Playbox was to give during the Christmas season—at midnight, mind you—a series of the old mystery and miracle plays. We have constantly produced new plays, too. New incentives to experiment and fresh encouragement from the successes of other workers in theatre have spurred us on in this endeavor. For example, during 1936, when I visited Russia, I found the same approach that we had been working out in the Playbox being used in Nikolai Okhlopkov's Moscow Realistic Theatre. Although he kept more closely to the practices of central staging, he did so with greater variety than is usually attempted in that form. To quote what Mordecai Gorelik says of him in his *New Theatres for Old*:

He attacked an old problem with new determination and ingenuity. It was the question of direct audience contact: how to abolish the proscenium, how to bring the stage into the audience. Okhlopkov quite literally carried his stage into the center of a hall where no proscenium stage existed, varying the shape of his central stage platform from one bill to the next, along with the seating arrangement around it.[1]

First and last, I am remarkably proud of the program of plays that we have been able to offer our Playbox audiences: plays by Ibsen, Strindberg, St. John Ervine, Galsworthy, Hugh Walpole, Schnitzler, Browning, Noël Coward, Ashley Dukes, Shakespeare, Chesterton, Rostand, Chekhov, Euripides, Beaumarchais, Sheridan, Upton Sinclair, Stephen Phillips, Eugene O'Neill, Emlyn Williams, Bruno Frank, Frank Vosper, Pirandello, Witter Bynner, Philip Barry, Heijermans, Saroyan, Clare Kummer, George Bernard Shaw, and Albert Bein. There have been two famous old East Indian plays, *The Fatal Ring*, by Kālidāsa, and *The Little Clay Cart*, by King Shudraka; also, several new plays by Tennessee Williams, particularly the first production of his very charming play *Stairs to the Roof.*

Returning to the College of Theatre Arts for the moment, I wish to note some of the changes that have come since it was founded. The arts of communication in our particular field have become increasingly important— something that I had foreseen concerning their relevance to everyone intending to become active in the theatrical profession. First, in considering radio, I knew that to participate in its advance, a student must first be made aware of the technical side of this difficult art; and, second, I knew that as a player he must realize the great importance of well-placed and intelligent voice production in projecting engaging personalities to the auditor. So, in this par-

[1]Mordecai Gorelik, *New Theatres for Old* (New York, Samuel French, 1940), 347.

ticular field I was successful, through the help of the famous voice expert in London, Elsie Fogerty, in bringing to our staff a remarkable voice coach, Belle Kennedy, to evolve her special course in the speech arts. Next, there was the ever expanding importance of television. For that medium the Playbox has been effective in impressing the student with the fact that without a huge stage and a stupendous production he can still achieve quality of acting within a very limited space. One consequence has been that our Playbox training has been especially recommended by Albert McCleery of the National Broadcasting Company and by any number of other experts in the television field, as well as by particular studios of production. In fact, our Playbox techniques and television techniques are similar, as McCleery, executive producer of "Matinee Theatre," and many other experts in this field have demonstrated. Of this truth the great Réjane first made me aware in a lecture delivered at Mrs. Adams' studio, where she demonstrated the possibilities of an entire drama when staged on a tiny square platform.

These are among the reasons for my constant belief that any real theatre should function with the aid of a college of theatre arts devoted to every phase of the drama. I begged the board that one should be established; but again they doubted the advisability of doing so, since we lacked the free capital or endowment and so depended almost wholly on box-office receipts. Fortunately, our president, Mr. Morin, was able to interest a beneficent lady from Washington, Mrs. Harriet Hurst, in the matter. She provided us with enough capital to begin work on February 4, 1928, and, with help from many fine theatre people, I defined the courses to be given in theatre education. Since then I have continued my practice of visiting other countries to study the theatre. Although at times war has intervened to prevent it, I have followed this program ever since I founded the Playhouse; and it was from England, on one journey, that I brought word to our board that television was the most important force developing in the theatre world.

Today, our school enrollment has grown from a small, more or less local group to an international representation. We have been training scholars from all over the world— from Europe, South America, the Middle East, the Far East, even from South Africa. This is, to me, one of our most important functions: in promoting international understanding, as well as in teaching theatre, we have an opportunity for service. One of the best examples of this reality came through a recent visit of the prime minister of Burma, whose play, *The People Win Through*, I produced under the direction of Bobker Ben Ali. The play created interest in many countries of Asia, thanks to the broadcasts by the Voice of America and to showings of the motion picture made at the time. The most amusing comment to reach me regarding our production was that some persons out there were glad to realize that "there might be some culture in the United States."

Thus, at home and abroad the Playhouse has had a place in the creation of a greater regard for the arts of America. All this growth from drama on a dime to national and international service, to better understanding among nations as well as to the advancing of theatre in our time, is gratifying. It proves that others can do as much and more in the future. Yet these gains in values here outlined are but a small part of the total change that we have seen here in Pasadena since my Playhouse was opened in 1917. It has been one of the pioneers, and the one among our many community theatres to have had the longest uninterrupted life. The people of the Playhouse have witnessed a slow and wonderful advance of those arts within the United States, within the theatre, uniting to make this country mature in creative self-expression. Today our proponents of theatre are many and are very influential. They are proving what was always advocated by our great actress Minnie Maddern Fiske, what constantly has been the purpose of the boards of our American National Theatre and Academy and of the members of the National Theatre Conference. Other national organizations have similar aims at other levels of action. We have, too, as final proof of the new vitality of our American theatre, the symbol of participation and of leadership that Hallie Flanagan Davis left for us all in the Federal Theatre. That demonstration, among many others less quick to emerge, proved that the American theatre will become a possession of national significance in the minds of all our people.

NEW GROWTH

8. THEATRE FOR ART'S SAKE

Leslie Cheek, Jr.

THAT THEATRE is a completely independent art form has, of course, been realized for centuries. But I have found it particularly useful as an art leading to the enjoyment of other, less dynamic arts, while still being quite wonderful in its own right.

Many of us in the United States, despite our apparent success at home and influence abroad, harbor an inferiority complex about the arts. Perhaps the chief reason for this is to be found in the not-too-remote colonial status, first in relation to England, and later to our own East Coast, as our country has constantly expanded westward. The colonist, of necessity removed from his cultural center, instinctively wonders about his artistic judgment and, because of this concern, tends to overdo or underdo his cultural interests. In this manner many Americans take the arts too seriously for true enjoyment, and some self-consciously deny even the existence of the arts.

Although the latter situation is, fortunately, now disappearing, it is not uncommon still, especially in the American male, to find an open suspicion of and disrespect for all things artistic. The necessary emphasis on masculine strength for felling forests, harvesting crops, and killing Indians in pioneer days has a strange continuation into this era of increasing automation. In some regions men who express any interest in the arts are still branded as "sissy," as if such a preoccupation were taking them from their proper duties as the physical protectors of a primitive society.

Parallel to colonialism, and continuing into our day, are the aesthetic problems of industrialism. The simple aristocratic cultural evolution of our colonial society was upset in the early nineteenth century, and its place was taken by a competitive industrial society with uncertain standards of all types, artistic and otherwise. Americans became, and still are becoming, rich quickly, using various misunderstood outer trappings of culture to cover their more humble origins. The machines meanwhile have produced in constantly greater, and usually aesthetically unguided, quantities for this huge market of national poor taste.

But despite colonialism and industrialism, a touching desire for personal improvement fortunately still runs strong in the majority of Americans, and the arts are very definitely included in their aspirations. When one considers the truly short time that elapsed between colony and nation, the aesthetic progress of all, not merely the very wealthy, people of the United States is prodigious. Such a rapid development probably cannot be matched elsewhere in social history.

Though varying types of patronage of the arts have continued throughout our national growth, the largest support has come from our aesthetic organizations and educational systems. In the decades of peace and increasing prosperity following the Civil War, cultural leaders appeared in practically all the then major cities of the country and gathered about them citizens of similar interests to form and support a remarkable number of organizations—symphony societies, art museums, and a host of other large and small institutions devoted to one or more of the arts. Thanks in some measure to the influence of these groups, the universities and colleges slowly began to add the arts to their curriculums, and later the idea gradually spread to the primary and secondary school systems of the nation.

Today, almost every American community has one or more well-established cultural organizations at work, and practically every school, college, and university is teaching the arts. With so much time, effort, and money being given to aesthetics in our life, one might very easily jump to the conclusion that our cultural problems are now solved. But, alas, such is not the case. Despite the symphony societies, museums, and educational systems, the arts still have a superficial relation to most Americans. Most of the leaders of our cultural facilities know this and are trying manfully to improve their techniques of communication at all levels.

As an average American, I have experienced our art teaching at school, college, and university and have been exposed to a typical number of our cultural organizations. By chance, my career has been devoted to teaching art and operating museums, and I have individually wondered much about how these jobs could be done better. I have been fortunate enough to be allowed to try different methods, and of all the so-called new means, none has proved as effective as the ancient art of the theatre.

In 1935, at the very bottom of the depression in the construction business, I was graduated from the Yale department of architecture. It soon became obvious that I was to find no work as an architect. Finally, through an acquaintance with a Yale architect turned curator of Colonial Williamsburg, James Cogar, I was taken on by the College of William and Mary as an "Instructor in the History of Art."

In Virginia at that time I was perhaps the only employee of any educational institution assigned full time to art history. There were no full departments of fine arts in any of the colleges, and the very few courses in art history were given almost as extracurricular activities by a few dedicated instructors, who invariably were regarded as rather queer. This situation in Virginia I found repeated elsewhere in the South, where the arts were considered a kind of foreign whipped cream on top of the more nourishing native educational layer cake. The long, lean years after the Civil War had provided no funds for such extravagance. Thus, to the national aesthetic complications of colonialism and industrialism, the South had been required to add the debilitation of poverty.

Since my academic title had the word "history" in it, I was handed over to the head of William and Mary's history department, David Morton. To my relief and delight, this gentleman did not regard me as an exotic; rather, he welcomed the opportunity thus offered to broaden the view of his students and did much to help me. In fact, I found no real opposition on the part of any member of the faculty, once each knew what I actually proposed to do. The chemistry department let me use its lab in after hours to make my slides, the buildings and grounds people put in shades to darken my lecture room, and the librarian ordered art books at my request.

But it was the greatest of good fortune that the president of the college, John Stewart Bryan, understood by nature and education what the arts were about and aided me in every possible way. Toward the end of my first year, I happened to say to him that I thought the college should have a full-fledged department of fine arts, and, to my astonishment, he immediately agreed, asking me to write down what I thought would be needed and to draw up plans for renovating an old building on the campus as headquarters for the proposed new department. All this I worked on during the summer of 1936, and by January of 1937 the building was complete and the new staff began teaching.

The concept of the department was new in the South, and perhaps in the nation, at that time. A very conscious attempt was made to balance the history of the arts with some knowledge of their practice, and, most important of all, with the basic, ultimate purpose of illustrating their potential use and enjoyment in contemporary life.

My undergraduate courses in the arts at Harvard, although later wonderfully useful to me professionally because of their academic intensiveness, had shown me how uninspiring a one-sided emphasis on history can be to many students. On the other hand, my summer courses at Peabody College had suggested the vacuity that a preponderance of how-to-do-it art instruction can provide. At Yale, thanks to Dean Everett V. Meeks's dispensation, I was the first architectural student to be allowed to take courses in the drama department, and the excitement and understanding that this comparison of the arts offered left me with a latent desire to attempt to bring such a rewarding experience to others.

From this assorted background came the initial framework of the new department at William and Mary. Five of the major arts were to be represented by five instructors, each of whom was able effectively to teach the history and practice of his particular discipline. Thus, the arts of architecture, sculpture, painting, music, and theatre were brought together in a single undergraduate teaching unit. Fortunately, a remarkable lady, Althea Hunt, had already been doing a pioneer one-woman job for a number of years in the field of the theatre, and, to a lesser degree, some instruction in music had been in progress. Both of these activities were assigned to the new department and expanded.

The underlying purpose of the department, although not formally stated, was to illustrate in every way possible the place and pleasure of the arts in daily life. A large number of students concentrating in the art field was not sought, but rather a large number of students taking elective art courses. Beyond this, however, was the desire to have the arts actually at work in undergraduate affairs, as a normal and necessary part of fine human existence. Thus, the department's instructors and more skilled students constantly designed, supervised, or executed simple architectural projects about the campus, layouts for college posters and stationery, decorations for major ceremonies and parties, installations for loan exhibitions, and, above all, theatrical productions.

In the struggle to make the arts actually function in undergraduate life, rather than become merely another field of academic knowledge, the theatre soon became by far the best medium. The arts of architecture, painting, sculpture, and music, by their less dynamic and relatively individual creative processes, impressed relatively few persons by their practice on the campus. But theatre, demanding that all the artistic skills be combined in a final dramatic unity, seemed to infect in one way or another all who came to the productions. Also, the theatre is nonacademic by nature and is certainly the most glamorous of the arts, if properly practiced.

The problems of proper practice—of adequate auditorium and stage, of rehearsal rooms, shops, and equipment of all types—seemed as insurmountable at William and Mary as they must have seemed everywhere else. But theatre is truly not theatre without its dramatic trappings. Fortunately, this art has a way with people who have tasted it even slightly, and small successes can quickly be converted into larger ones. Thus, it was not too difficult to get the plaster ceiling over the "speaker's platform" type of stage removed and simple sets of rope lines installed, and to get various college divisions with extra space to lend it for scenery, costume, and prop construction. The most expensive needs—historical and technical books, and lighting and sound equipment—were given by two national foundations, after properly documented appeals and proof of past and future effective effort had been presented.

As the theatre at William and Mary rapidly improved, so did the size and variety of its audiences. Going to each production soon became the thing to do for undergraduates, faculty, and rarest of all, townsfolk. Almost without their knowing it, the arts had entered the lives of these people through their attendance at the theatre. Tactful suggestions about the relationships of all the arts were always made by loan exhibitions displayed in adjacent galleries and described in the theatre programs.

It was the hope of William and Mary's president and of the fine arts department staff that the arts had been made so much an enjoyable part of living for all students during their four undergraduate years that these young people would support or create a similar cultural pattern for the communities in which they would live out their adult lives. Obviously, it will take many art departments in many colleges throughout the land to achieve this goal. But the experiment at Williamsburg seems to have worked beyond expectation. If it has, I believe that the art of the theatre is at the heart of the matter.

For reasons that have never seemed very logical to me, I was offered the directorship of the Baltimore Museum of Art. When I went to work there in the fall of 1939, I found a city with three museums: the Peale, with its literally hereditary right to all the local culture; the Walters, with its obviously unequaled collections; and the museum that I was destined to head, with no truly established position in the local scene.

The only real opening left in the cultural picture was that of contemporary art from a collecting point of view, of a broad variety of well-organized loan exhibitions from an intellectual point of view, and of extensive leisure-time activities for all ages from an educational point of view. The essence of the situation seemed action, to get people to participate in the arts, since the other institutions had long possessed the attributes of more static cultural usefulness. This goal was made more difficult, however, in that the idea of a museum visit was associated with dull inaction, with something that might be "good for you," like dentistry, but certainly not much fun.

Although Baltimore was more or less on the tryout circuit for theatre en route to Broadway, as well as for road companies of Broadway successes, and although it supported several established and active little theatre groups and a near-by summer theatre, there apparently were many people still unsurfeited with drama as an art form. Thus, when the Baltimore Museum decided to start using

theatre as a component of its changing exhibition program, there was no problem in obtaining volunteer actors
and crew, and, most important of all, interested audiences
—despite the fact that the museum's theatrical fare was
admittedly only a facet of a cultural theme, not an end
in itself.

Theatre, perhaps because of the fact that it must have
living actors to exist, tends to give life to cultural ideas
or periods that otherwise would remain uninteresting to
many. For example, in Baltimore we used theatre as a
planned part of programs devoted to:

City Planning: by presenting the W. P. A.-spawned melodrama *One-Third of a Nation,* to spotlight the need for
better housing.

Art of the Medici: by staging a locally written pageant-
drama based on the life of Lorenzo, to humanize this awesome artistic family.

Romanticism in America: by giving on alternate nights
a "Musical Evening," composed of the popular songs and
poems of the period between 1815 and 1865, and *The Six
Degrees of Crime,* the sentimental period's favorite melodrama—with, of course, the proper between-the-acts curtain speech by an earnest lady on the evils of strong drink
and the "foul weed."

Scenery for Cinema: by comparing the film and stage
versions of O'Neill's *Anna Christie,* to point up the technical scenic differences in these two means of dramatic
presentation.

Georgian England: by restaging in the manner of the
times Britain's eighteenth century musical hit, *The Beggar's Opera,* to show how Gay and Hogarth were both
surprisingly saying the same thing in different media.

The Baltimore Museum possessed a four-hundred-seat
auditorium and a wide but low stage with some shop

space; however, surprisingly effective productions were possible. To aid the museum staff in the second year of this theatre activity, a generous foundation made possible the salary of a truly dedicated theatre director, Katherine Rivett, plus some additional lighting equipment. Unfortunately, when the project truly seemed to be getting into gear, World War II overtook the country, and within six months most of the museum's theatre workers were in the armed services, including myself.

The experience served to reinforce my previous conviction that theatre was a magnificent ally of its sister arts, that Americans everywhere were hungry for it, that aid in theatrical production was forthcoming with heartening readiness, but that any serious contemporary theatre needed adequate plant and equipment.

After World War II and editorial work in New York, I returned to Virginia in 1948 to become director of that state's Museum of Fine Arts in Richmond. The job appealed to me in that I could continue in the field and region where I had begun my career seventeen years before, and in that the Virginia Museum of Fine Arts was the nation's first state-wide cultural institution, with a mandate to bring knowledge and enjoyment of the arts to as many Virginians as possible.

But the opportunities were even greater than I had envisioned. Here was an entire region on the verge of vigorous interest in the arts. Poverty following the Civil War had prevented the growth of overlapping and conflicting cultural institutions, and burgeoning prosperity following World War II now made rapid progress possible—provided leadership was forthcoming. Advances could be, and needed to be, made in all the arts, static and dynamic, for they did not exist in quality or quantity anywhere in the state.

The static arts—architecture, painting, sculpture, and so on—being the accepted role of museums in the established culture centers to the north and west, were obviously the ones to approach first, and over sixty exhibitions, covering this artistic field and carefully designed for travel, were soon made available for circulating about the commonwealth by express. A little later, a complete gallery-on-wheels, the "Artmobile," began taking fine original examples of the visual arts into the remotest Blue Ridge or Eastern Shore towns of Virginia.

At the museum's headquarters building in Richmond, a typical municipal museum operation needed to be conducted for that city, simultaneously with the state-wide activities. Since the permanent collections were insufficient and insignificant, a constant series of exhibitions of art generously lent by more fortunate communities was the most useful pattern. These temporary possessions, and the permanent ones that the museum gradually acquired, needed the best presentation, and my previous experiences in theatre work gave me most valuable and unexpected aid at this particular turn in my career.

I discovered the rather obvious fact that an art object can far better play its role to the beholder, particularly to one who has little or no cultural background, if the setting is interpretive. Usually this meant using the characteristic physical proportions and shapes of a particular period, in combination with appropriate mood established by color and light. But these precepts were also those of stage design and lighting that I had studied and practiced in creating scenery for the Dramatic and Hasty Pudding clubs at Harvard, for the University Players Guild on Cape Cod, for the drama school at Yale, and for the art department at William and Mary. The proper installation of art objects is rapidly becoming an important aspect of modern museum operation, and the theatre scenic arts are the basic disciplines from which this long-needed improvement must come.

It gradually became clear to me that the Virginia Museum of Fine Arts was presenting only part of the art field, and that many of the other parts were not available at all to the community. This was especially true in the dynamic arts—those requiring human participation, like drama, music, and ballet. Yet these very arts, because of their immediate human communication, were the ones the public could, and would, most willingly love and support if such were available. It seemed to me that our museum would benefit all the arts, static and dynamic, if it could but add the dynamic ones to its regular program.

However, the great cost of a properly complete stage and auditorium, especially in a region where the joys of the theatre were relatively so unknown, seemed to create an immediate, insurmountable block. But, as I had discovered before, a truly needed facility seems to have an inherent appeal, and to my joy—and surprise—the funds for an excellent, fully equipped theatre were forthcoming through combined aid from state, foundation, and individual sources.

Before rushing into construction, we wisely consulted a series of advisers on the various technical aspects of our proposed theatre, carefully co-ordinating their counsels. In this manner Yale contributed Edward Cole for the stage and auditorium layout and equipment, Stanley McCandless for lighting, and George Izenour for light control. Other generous technical advisers were Leo F. Mulqueen, acoustics; Albert Heschong, shops; Joseph

Vasconcellos, rigging; Donald Oenslager, scenic requirements; Willard A. Yoder, film and slide projection; and
Walker Cottrell, sound and communication system.

With the theatre building under way, the next pressing
problem was its actual operation. Distinguished small professional groups to present music and ballet could be
brought to Richmond, and, of course, interesting films
were available. But truly professional theatre did not, and
would not, come to the community, and local amateur
and summer theatre groups were small and uncertain.
Therefore, if the important art of drama was to become
part of the Virginia Museum's program, the museum
itself would have to be the producer.

A little figuring soon indicated that the cost of a resident company of true professionals would make ticket
prices beyond the purse of the citizens for whom the
drama productions were intended. Thus, some plan that
would keep standards as nearly professional as possible,
yet keep costs within the means of the community, had
to be found. I went to see Frederic McConnell in Cleveland, Maurice Gnesin in Chicago, Gilmor Brown in Pasadena, Norris Houghton in New York, and Boyd Smith
in New Haven. I wrote details of the problem to Fred
Burleigh and Henry Boettcher in Pittsburgh, and Curtis
Canfield came fresh from Amherst to look over the actual
situation in Virginia.

With the advice and aid of these generous and experienced gentlemen, a professional staff of six, who would
train and direct volunteers from the region, was agreed
upon. The first such staff consisted of Vincent Bowditch,
director-producer (and associate director of the museum
in charge of theatre activities); Ariel Ballif, designer (sets
and costumes); James Nicholson, assistant director; Joseph Carner, technical director; Edward Devany, techni-

cal assistant; and Judith Perdue, clerk. Of course, the museum's administrative division staff aided this group in money, promotion, and housekeeping matters, and I served as liaison with the trustees.

Assuming that this combination of professional and volunteer workers would, indeed, give the high-quality theatre the museum desired, the great problem of how to underwrite the salaries and expenses until the public would take over full support had to be solved, for a distinguished staff could not be recruited on promises alone. Finally, with great good fortune, a foundation agreed to make up the losses for three years, starting with the fall of 1955.

At the time of this writing, January, 1956, we have produced only two plays, but it is already my feeling that the project is a success. The chief difficulties seem to have been in the choice of the plays and in securing and training technical volunteers for the tight, month-apart schedule. Perhaps lighter plays than *High Tor* and *Liliom* would have had more immediate popular appeal, and plays with fewer sets and costumes could have made production easier. But ticket sales are increasing and enthusiasm for the entire undertaking is gathering force.

Particularly pleasing to me is the doubling of total attendance at the museum since our theatre began operations, and the equally remarkable advance in museum memberships. This can only be interpreted as a benefit the dynamic arts are conferring on their equally important, but less immediately attractive, static cousins. The use of the museum by the general public is already becoming a less self-conscious, more natural, and needed *part of life*. By inference, all the arts, not merely those of the theatre, have gained in prestige.

It is my profound hope that this enlargement of the

smaller museum program to include a complete circle of the arts will be so beneficial to Virginia that it may serve as the pilot for similar cultural projects elsewhere in our country. Also, I believe that parallel gallery and theatre staffs have a vast future potential in working together with film technicians to record series television programs for state and, if successful, national broadcasting. Television is an ideal medium for presenting and discussing all the arts, but it is still a daughter of the theatre and must be a dramatic product if it is to be effective. The museum that has a staff trained in *all* the arts should be truly useful as we rush headlong into the latter half of our hectic twentieth century.

To me, *theatre for art's sake* is desirable and inevitable.

9. SCIENCE AND THE
CONTEMPORARY THEATRE

George C. Izenour

"In your work and in your research there must always be passion."
—Ivan Pavlov

THIS ESSAY will attempt to recount certain happenings that resulted from a combination of forces exerted from both within and without the individual that in due time brought about the forming of scientific opinions concerning certain discontinuous mechanical processes in our contemporary theatre. It tells how this led to the fulfillment of a desire to set up a research laboratory wherein these phenomena could be studied in a more fundamental sense, and where engineering development could be done on instrumentation needed to solve these technical problems.

In any attempt at self-analysis, especially before one reaches the age when self-criticism no longer matters nor can affect in any way one's egotistical impulses, it is nevertheless impossible, no matter how pure the motive, to escape entirely the most human impulse to merge one's thoughts and actions into a compact whole, instead of depicting them as the more or less discontinuous things that they really are. Perhaps this effort is similar to one's having to accept both the wave theory and the quantum theory in order to form a better understanding of the phenomenon of light, even though at times they are antagonistic. One man who succeeded admirably in merging his thought and action was the eminent American architect, Louis H. Sullivan. *The Autobiography of an Idea*[1] is a penetrating self-analysis written in the third person. Sullivan was more than an architect; he was a poet-philosopher and as such could express himself symbolically. He was able through development of a unique literary style, manifested first in the earlier *Kindergarten Chats on Architecture, Education and Democracy* and brought to full flower in *The Autobiography of an Idea* to propel the reader into thinking in the abstract about "the idea." As a result, the reader senses that Sullivan and the idea are an organic whole. The thought and the action have become one.

I am not suggesting that Sullivan was consciously trying to be a literary stylist. He would not have sought the comparative safety of a dependence on style.

As one who possesses neither the gift of style nor the gift of wit—always safe ground—I shall try to explain how dramatic art and a mind with a scientific bent met head on and how they have been living together ever since. The fostering and nurturing of seemingly diverse and opposite interests may at a glance seem unusual, but upon reflection they no longer appear so. To appreciate and to enjoy the similarity between the music of Mozart and the calculus of differentials, or to see a symmetrical likeness between some of the poetry of Emily Dickinson and some of the mathematical aspects of the new physics, is, I think, not at all strange. The fact that an excellent mathematician could also be a poet, or an insurance salesman a

[1] Louis H. Sullivan, *The Autobiography of an Idea* (New York, W. W. Norton and Co., Inc., 1934).

successful composer of music, does not seem unusual if one considers that most intricate mechanism, the human brain. Likewise, it is no more unusual for the "mathematician-engineer" to devise an analogue mechanism in order to facilitate mathematical expression than for the "musician-engineer" to make a violin in order to provide the means by which it is possible to make audible the abstract notation of a page of music.

This unity is simply invention, which is the inevitable outgrowth of ideas put to work on existing phenomena. There is always the urge to form a better analogue than those that now exist. There were vibrating strings long before the invention of the violin. The abacus preceded by many centuries the invention of the electronic computer. No one can name the prehistoric inventor of the wheel. He might have been a singer of songs, and perhaps a slave at that. Only this is certain: He was first an observer, second a creator, and third a communicator. Are not the scientist and the artist alike concerned with these things? Wherein lies the difference?

I would put it this way. Science is based primarily on judgments of fact, art on judgments of value. And how are these judgments formed? By the use of artifice—except in science we prefer to call it "hypothesis." And what of passion, which Pavlov spoke of? Is it necessary? If man could acquire complete knowledge concerning anything that he might choose to accomplish, passion would never be necessary. Neither would theatres, nor laboratories.

As is true of almost everything in life, with the possible exception of pure thought process, theatre is a composite of opposites. The highly spiritual must unite with the basely mechanical. And that epoch which best understood this achieved the most satisfying union of artistic and scientific expression, for herein *is* the artifice. Just as science is not the whole of life, so theatre is not wholly of the spirit. If this were so, there could be no communication, nor any shared experience. Whether we participate actively or passively in a theatre experience, we must be able both to be seen and to be heard as well as to see and to hear. This requires a mechanism. The theatre building that facilitates the communication between actor and audience is here our analogue. Although we do not go to the theatre to hear the reciting of poetry, or to be subjected to amazing lighting effects, or to be dumfounded by clever mechanism, yet each of these has its important place in the totality of the experience. They all contribute to the atmosphere of theatre, which is fundamentally physical.

It is this atmosphere, once established, that is taken over by the actor who performs in a play. It is he who causes our spirits to soar or sink. It is he for whom the playwright, the designer, and the technician function. Otherwise, the theatre would need only to concern itself with the publishing of dialogue. This empathy, if it is alive, requires that certain relationships be established. This was true on a hillside in ancient Athens; it is equally true today. This magic phenomenon comes under the broad heading of what today we call "*instrumentation.*" There is no form of communicative art or science that does not require it. From simple sticks of charcoal and paper to atom smashers, the delicate alchemy of instrumentation goes on.

Our problem in the theatre, and for that matter everywhere else, is to relate the carbon of the charcoal to the smasher of the atom. To do so requires a certain boldness and breadth of concept that moves above reliance on technique alone. It is first a state of mind that will take hold and cause our mental prejudices to wither away. Art and science have always depended upon one another, and it is strange to find that in human existence they ever have been in contention. Theatre is one crucible that yields this truth.

I think that our failure in this age to see this interdependence has come about more by chance than by design, probably because science has received the lion's share of support—economic as well as popular. It used to be possible for a man to be equally well informed, although not necessarily expert, in natural science, philosophy, mathematics, and art. But today, since science has given us so many answers and, at the same time, posed so many additional questions, it has become impossible for one man's scope to encompass so much factual knowledge in such diverse fields. How this came about is in the history of the past two centuries. Since the theatre was a part of this, it could not escape the effect.

It is my thesis that the artist must unflinchingly face up to science and recognize it, primarily not for what it is but, more important, for what it does. Once he understands this, it will follow that instinctively he will know what it means. I believe that such comprehension and appreciation of his world has always been the problem and the excitement for the artist. It is when he becomes fearful that he is in trouble. At such times he does not lead; he follows. If the artist fails to grasp the use and power of the machine in a creative sense, he and his art are lost.

The life and work of Frank Lloyd Wright is our finest contemporary example of one man who as an artist understands that prodigious child of science, the machine. It is Wright who said: "Grasp and use the power of scientific automatons in this *creative sense* and their terrible forces are not antagonistic to any fine individualistic quality in man. He will find their collective mechanistic forces capable of bringing to the individual a more adequate life, and the outward expression of the inner man as seen in his environment will be genuine revelation of his inner life and higher purpose."[2]

There are only a few such as Wright who speak to us in the direct, symbolic language of the poet. Adolphe Appia, a great theatre artist, was another. His work gives us a conception of new and truly contemporary theatre, which, like Wright's architecture, is dependent not upon technique but on function. Appia's concept of dramatic art is still confined largely to drawings and word pictures, which have yet to be translated into a living actuality. As a scientist would say, the analogues of these ideas have yet to be built. For it is not enough to give birth to ideas either in architecture or theatre. Ideas must function. Therefore, they must be turned into the realities of stone, wood, metals, yes, and electrons—all paraphernalia of the physical world!

I have never forgotten the concluding sentence of an essay on the art of Adolphe Appia written by Lee Simonson and published in *Theatre Arts Monthly* in August, 1932. It reads, "For the time being the forces that can contribute to the growth of play giving as a modern art lie outside the theatre's walls."[3] I had a high regard for this statement then and still do now. The desire to bring these phenomena, in a suitable form, within the walls of the theatre and by so doing eventually to change the very walls—that is my work.

When I first read this statement, which struck me as prophetic, I was a young lad, a sophomore in college. I was fighting not only the *status quo* in a small Midwestern

---

[2] Frank Lloyd Wright, *The Future of Architecture* (New York, Horizon Press, 1953), 89.

[3] Lee Simonson, "Appia's Contribution to the Modern Stage," *Theatre Arts Monthly*, Vol. XVI, No. 8 (August, 1932), 644.

college theatre but the Depression as well. Sometimes it takes the poet's language to kindle mental fire. In this instance it was the words of Appia, Simonson, and Jones that provided the flint. I so wanted to be the steel.

Often comes the question, "What brought you into the theatre?" And, as always, there is not a clear-cut, simple answer. There were no theatrical folk among my friends, nor any such tradition within my family. But the opportunities offered through drama education in the public schools and then in college provided the incentive. Since the community was small and the general interest limited, the opportunity for me was extensive. By the time I had been graduated from college, I had had full rein to do what I chose. I had run the gamut of acting, directing, designing, lighting, stage managing, and even adapting material for the stage. Quite often I had played all these roles in a single production! I hasten to add that all this was accomplished only in amateur fashion. Professional awareness had not yet taken hold to develop a more mature point of view, which evolves but slowly out of the search and struggle for expression. It is an outgrowth of youth's ideal of perfection. The ideal of perfection, which to mature minds is occasionally the goal of ambition, sometimes becomes an impossible abyss. More often, it is but a *vision fugitive*. Yet its power to create internal human change is constant.

It was during the latter half of my college days that I began to think seriously about the theatre as a life work. I cannot recall that then any particular phase held a special attraction. There were certain definite patterns of thought and discipline, however, which were the foundation stones for my later activity; these I can now attribute to the influence of certain professors. These men were all gentlemen of the old school and the flower of this college faculty.

There was my Latin teacher, Professor Ness, whose chief language interest was Sanskrit. With him I studied Livy, Horace, Martial, Plautus, and Terence. He was a taciturn Norwegian with twinkling eyes who, long before I sat at his feet, had memorized all the Latin he was teaching. I remember especially the courses in Horace and Plautus, where I alone was the class. For half of the period we would read Latin, and then we would discuss whatever subject came to mind. Professor Ness was tough-minded. He sincerely believed in the cussedness of man, in hard work, and in the ancient poets. And he shared with me his opinions, he who as a boy of twelve went to sea in a sailing ship from his native Norway and eventually landed in America and at the Johns Hopkins University.

My other Johns Hopkins teacher was Professor Schneider, with whom I studied comparative literature, notably Shakespeare, the modern dramatists, Dante, Milton, and Chaucer in the original. Whereas Professor Ness was tough-minded, Professor Schneider was expansive. His readings of Shakespeare, Dante, Milton—much of it from memory—were a revelation to me. Even more impressive were the insertions, observations, and footnotes that were pure Schneider.

The other members of what I have always referred to as the "culture quartet" were my professors of philosophy, Greek, and the history of art. Professor Birch, the philosopher, was an authority on medieval abbreviated Latin, with a passion for the philosophies of that period. He was a benign man who was an undergraduate's ideal of a typical philosopher. This man I admired for his scholarship. Professor Hiller, the fourth in this quartet, whom Professor Ness called "our blue bird," was a most gentle and kind person. He guided me through Greek drama and the history of art, also in classes small enough to allow informality.

With Professors Weaver and Thomas I studied physics and subjects relating to engineering. These kind men allowed me the use of the well-equipped model machine shop. It was there that I built my first mechanical and electrical models. To these men I owe deep gratitude. They were all inspired teachers.

In contrast, the work in drama was linked to the public-speaking department, which, as is usual in small denominational colleges, emphasized debate and oratory. It was left to any enterprising students to make up the lack of interest with their own enthusiasm for work in the theatre. We had a studio theatre seating two hundred—if some were standees!—and a mammoth field house that offered a combination gymnasium and auditorium, the hybrid that satisfies neither the athletes nor the aesthetes.

Some of you will remember that our country was still in a state of depression during 1934. There was nothing to graduate to; so, I decided to work for a master's degree while teaching to earn my daily bread. My first interest was in producing five full-length plays each year. In addition, I was the fencing coach, the maintenance electrician for the college, and occasionally its steam fitter. In my spare time I undertook to serve as designer and technical director for the Ohio Town Players, organized by a graduate of George Pierce Baker's 47 Workshop and Yale University. To me, stories of the Yale drama school were the Arabian Nights of the drama. They were well told by Harold Igo, playwright-director of this community group. As the college schedule demanded my presence at rehearsal five nights each week, and since the week-end evenings were devoted to the Ohio Town Players, one can see that little time was left for sleep.

The home of the Ohio Town Players was the old opera house above the firehouse. At ten o'clock each night the fire engine would be started and allowed to run for exactly ten minutes, rehearsal or performance notwithstanding, by reason of town regulations. In time the Ohio Town Players failed, not for the lack of enthusiasm, but when we finally ran out of ready cash—mostly Mr. Igo's. This was for me an enriching experience. From Harold Igo I gleaned a point of view. Many were our talks long and far into the night. Here I had my first insight into what is a professional point of view of the theatre as an art and as a business. Here was a man who had experienced having his own plays produced. To me this was exciting and real.

My program of study included special work in Greek drama, modern drama, and psychology. Now I began in earnest to read and study the work of Adolphe Appia, Gordon Craig, Robert Edmond Jones, and Lee Simonson. It seemed to me then, as now, that the designers had a truer vision of what contemporary theatre should be than did any other people. This stimulated my interest in lighting, which Appia called "the unifying force." My studies in experimental psychology took this bent. Using apparatus that I designed and built in the physics machine shop and using undergraduate students as guinea pigs, I attempted in a most crude way to correlate color and form in light with emotion. I got nowhere.

I learned then the first hard facts about controlled experiments. First the problem must be defined, or the data is meaningless. Mine was. I went back to the laboratory, where I tackled the problem from another angle, that of the design of electronically controlled, tuned circuits for color control in light. Here I made some progress. Working with inanimate things, I found that my results were more concrete and also more predictable.

This experimental work was undertaken on my own initiative and was eventually to get me involved with the graduate committee. One member of my examining committee was a lady professor of English. Her attitude toward graduate research at this level was that it should be of a scholarly nature always pursued in the library. This was her stand, and there she stood. With typical youthful vigor, I objected and eloquently stated that if my experimental laboratory work could not be acceptable, I had no interest in the degree. Fortunately, I was rescued from the lady's firm resolve and saved from myself by my sympathetic quartet. An academic compromise was arrived at, to the effect that I should do half of the work for my thesis in the library in the conventional manner, and the other half could be an essay describing my laboratory experiments. One lady plunged me into this trouble; quite another extricated me from it. The latter, whom I later persuaded to become my wife, did my library research, for I never shall have the aptitude or patience required for that kind of work.

These two years of study toward the master's degree gave me a rich experience and offered me rare opportunity. I had great leeway in all my work. I mapped my course of study and chose the plays that were to be produced. After designing sets and costumes and directing the play, I also counted up the box-office receipts at the end of the run. It was imperative that we pay our way. We did. Our productions ranged from Ibsen to medieval drama, propaganda plays, and Broadway successes. This varied and concentrated activity got out of my system once and for all any yen for acting that I may have harbored. All my world had been nothing but a stage. I now knew that I preferred to do a walk-on part behind the scene.

Two years of teaching and a degree to my credit brought

me to that time when I was entitled to some remunerative reward, or so I reasoned. Boldly I asked for a salary of one hundred dollars a month. It was refused. Food and shelter being an insistent and ever present problem, I started to work in an industrial plant on the night shift. It proved a fortunate choice, since daytime hours I could call my own. I was living in the home of one of my former college professors. Mr. Thomas permitted me to have a small electronics laboratory in the basement. There I continued my work with lighting control, and into that I poured every cent that I could not possibly afford. It had by now become clear to me that if the theatre was ever to possess better instrumentation, this could be developed only in a laboratory detailed to study and experiment with this problem, unique in this limited field.

To further this dream, I wrote letters, many letters. I wrote to prominent people, to organizations and universities, to corporations with research facilities, and to the broadcasting companies then conducting limited experiments in television. In return came letters of encouragement, but no offers of laboratory space for experiment. I was not ready. I was not yet able to define the problem. I knew it as an instinctive thing, to a youth a far more precious possession than mere work, so long as he is able to keep it alive through concentrated thinking.

All familiar avenues seemed closed. As so often happens, this crisis marked a turning point. Economic necessity forced me finally to sell all my hard-won laboratory equipment, in order to have the hand of a chosen lady. All bridges were burned and soon thereafter we arrived in Los Angeles. The first stops were at motion-picture studios. I tried them all. I had sketches, blue prints, and designs for instruments. Most people were kind, but there was the union. One could not be hired unless one belonged, nor could one belong unless one was hired. Stalemate. Yes, and frustration.

Generally speaking, meaningful experiences are accompanied by poignant emotional and intellectual activity. They are very personal and exert a powerful influence. For a youth the sympathetic ear of an understanding adult can sometimes supply the stimulus so needed at the low ebb of desperation. It was at this time, with my spirits and aspirations at lowest ebb, that I met Gilmor Brown of the Pasadena Playhouse. He found time in a busy schedule to listen to another hopeful. Gilmor Brown has always typified for me a steadfastness of spirit that is unique. If there is one man of the theatre who was responsible for keeping me thinking and working, it was he. Not that he could be of immediate assistance in securing a job for me in his or anyone else's theatre, but he rekindled in me a self-respect for my own work, immature though it was. This helped me to find within myself the courage to persist. Such an experience opens the deep wellspring of faith that one draws on for spiritual sustenance. Perhaps one is not aware that he is providing such a stimulus; but it is that selfless quality that is at the core of one individual's power to help another.

Having listened, Mr. Brown was soon able to do more for me. It so happened that Hallie Flanagan Davis of the Federal Theatre Project was making one of her periodic visits to California in her capacity of the project's national director. Gilmor Brown arranged for me to meet her. I went to this meeting with a certain sense of futility. I knew that to be employed on the project one had to go on relief and had to have been a resident of the state for at least one year. But I was eager to meet Hallie Flanagan, since I was familiar with her work at Vassar's experimental theatre. This gallant lady also listened to me. She inquired whether I had put into writing my ideas on lighting control techniques and on the technical devices that I had mentioned. I left with her my thesis, which contained the embodiment of my ideas.

To my astonishment, shortly thereafter I was informed by the local office of the Federal Theatre Project that I was to be lighting supervisor for the Los Angeles project. As anyone who was ever a member of the Federal Theatre Project can testify, the next eighteen months were staggering. At one time there were six theatres going in Los Angeles and traveling companies on tour. Musicals, straight drama, modern dance, puppetry, and vaudeville were all represented. It was truly the "arena" so well described in Hallie Flanagan's book of that name. There was an ever present sense of crisis, not only of the usual production-to-production variety, but a day-to-day concern that the project could go out of business. When pay checks were late and did not appear on the date due, each of us found himself with a personal crisis as well. Then there was always the army in the person of the colonel who directed central W.P.A., through whose hands all requests for expenditure had to pass. I remember one of mine for optical equipment that was submitted each month and was turned down each month. It never was granted.

The frustration for young supervisors who wished to do a workmanlike job but who had to cope with old-time professionals stranded in movie land was sometimes pathetic, sometimes comic. Here, I was speedily educated in the ways and means of theatrical trade-unionism. It was my first experience of working with men who wore ignorance as a badge of courage. As a young supervisor, I needed the respect of these men in order to function. From the first, I realized that I must operate from memory and with an absolute minimum of work sheets in evidence. In most instances, anyone who worked in "juice," as lighting is called by a stage electrician, did so from experience alone, without the aid of layouts of any sort whatever. Sometimes that lack became a drag on the memory, since it was not unusual for the project to have as many as eight shows in various stages of production. I grew up quickly in terms of practical theatre. Production problems both human and technical were daily grist for the mill. These were lessons no school could teach, since technique was hammered out in the white heat of urgency, with a budget large in man-hours but slim in equipment.

I recollect that at this time I began a series of exercises directed toward the mathematical reduction of some of the more troublesome problems inherent in lighting. This turned out to be more than just an exercise; it is now a part of my permanent mental equipment. Now when I investigate a given problem to consider whether it is timeworthy, I can by this method quickly size up proposed solutions by using tools that are not a part of the problem. I do not mean to imply that this was a discovery of something quite new, but rather only new to me. (I am reminded of just such a method, now in general use, that is a striking solution for the torsion-bar problem, which was found in the unrelated field of the study of soap bubbles. This testing yielded a solution far more graphic and usable than that arrived at by manipulation of complex mathematical functions.)

Again I had arrived at a "landing stage" in my concepts of theatrical functions. The using of such interesting paradoxes for solving problems has become almost daily fare in many fields. But the theatre has not assumed a sophisticated attitude toward its problems. The lack of a mature approach to these problems is evidenced by graduates of drama schools as well as by their brothers of the professional theatre. This is a curious thing, but perhaps the answer is obvious. For me, at least, the answer lies in haste. The student and the professional alike hasten to cultivate a sophistication of attitude toward their work and their profession, instead of first acquiring a fine intellectual attitude toward the cultivation of the reasoning power and the use of knowledge, which is the true sophistication of the mind. In theatre, much is made of tradition. Traditional methods rule virtually supreme in every field— writing, acting, directing, design, and technical production. If we are to remain alert, these traditional approaches should be at all times under attack.

Think of design in the American theatre before Jones and Simonson! Yet we fail to realize that their innovations have taken place in a playhouse that has changed but little in two hundred years. On all sides one hears talk of a new form. How can there possibly be a new form without an organic change in the mechanisms, upon which its execution depends? Anything less amounts to nothing but a changing of the façade and not to a changing of the function that must precede the change in form. I do not wish to imply that a change of method or machinery will automatically change everything else; but, to be sure, form cannot possibly be changed unless the analogues of production are also changed. Certainly the ideas and the work of men like Jones and Simonson were restricted because of the crude mechanisms that they had to depend upon.

We can point to an example in an allied field. The buildings of Sullivan and Wright could not have been constructed by using the engineering methods of the eighteenth and early nineteenth centuries. They required the application of methods and materials that contemporary science has made available. Fortunately for both Sullivan and Wright, they could serve their creations equally well as engineers and as architects. But such talent is exceptional. It is not usual to find a designer or a playwright who can solve his technical problems. He must be shown by demonstrating with a full-scale analogue or working instrument, not, I hasten to add, by confronting him with a solution in the abstract, although it be a valid and honest mathematical exposition. Certainly a theatrical designer is more likely to appreciate a lighting control instrument as a working machine than as an extensive mathematical treatment of the lighting problem. To him, what is vital is not what machinery is, but what it can do.

What we are saying is that both the analytic mind and the artistic mind are essential, but that artistic answers based on value alone never, never can be productive of instrumentation. Often they can suggest it, but they can never solve the problems. This confusion is compounded when the artist tries to give other than symbolic answers to these questions and becomes dogmatic in the area of technology, where he is apt to lose his identity along with his integrity.

It was while I was on this Federal Theatre Project that I learned to divide my time between that by which I earned my livelihood and the precious part that freed me for the mental stimulation of research. How to make better use of both, and eventually how to make the latter provide for the former, was the happy result I so wanted to realize.

In the summer of 1938, the Golden Gate International Exposition on Treasure Island in San Francisco Bay was in its planning stage. The national office of the Federal

Theatre Project decided that the Los Angeles project should be represented at the exposition and that we should have a theatre of our own design. The building itself was included in the budget for the federal building as outlined by the Department of Interior. It was rare good fortune that our successes so far had filled our coffers, which meant for us funds available for equipping our theatre. Excitement and enthusiasm overflowed. Jerome Coray, Ralph Freud, and I met with the well-known San Francisco architect Timothy Pfleuger to work out the details of our playhouse. I was appointed design consultant for the structure and its equipment. It was agreed that this theatre should accommodate eight fifty-minute shows each day, with ten minutes between shows, plus possible full-length musical productions in the evening.

We met in August and were to open in January. To carry on all the work in Los Angeles while designing this theatre, I needed help. I asked for a draftsman, preferably one who could do both mechanical and architectural drafting. That request brought one of the great good fortunes of my life. I was sent a mechanical designer and engineer who had had a most interesting and varied career. He had been a soldier, weapons designer, inventor, pioneer aviator, self-taught scholar, and a sugar mill engineer. He was obviously a man of the world, this Scottish-American named Robert Macfie. Mac revealed a new world to me. His store of factual knowledge was incredible, but it was his method of thinking out problems of design that became stimulating and engrossing. There was no problem that Mac could not reduce to a mechanical analogue, whether it had been presented in the abstract or as a practical statement of a chain of events. Our long discussions I now consider a postgraduate seminar in engineering. Of things fundamental and lasting I learned more than I contributed. Through his broad outlook, gained by diversity of experience, he revealed to me the true boundaries of the worlds of engineering and invention, and showed me that they are poles apart.

Together we did the job. When I moved to San Francisco for the opening of the exposition, Mac followed. During its short life this project was a fine experience in operating a theatre that was designed for such a flexible program. It had not reached its goal of eight productions a day, but the musical *The Swing Mikado* had been running a short while when the project was ordered closed in June of 1939. I had lost twenty-five pounds in those mad months, but I had gained in experience. Indeed, richer was I than my financial status seemed to indicate. But I still had no laboratory to begin experimental work in earnest. This was one more time when a pivotal decision had to be made. Again it was made for me. I was informed that I had been granted a fellowship by one of the large philanthropic foundations. In a few short months I found myself at the Yale University drama school, happily sitting in an unused squash court, alone with my thoughts.

Many months of intense work resulted in a small working design model for the electronic control of stage lighting. On the basis of this modest work I was granted funds to build a full-scale system, which, if it proved successful, was to be installed in the Yale University Theatre for the use of the drama school.

The ever faithful Mac soon followed me to New Haven and for another year made available to me his rich store of knowledge and his unique point of view. How he sustained me through times of doubt and discouragement he never knew. Or did he? Work on the full-scale model was begun in June, 1940, and for the next three years I was at last living with the ups and downs, the hopes and despairs of research. I found that the laboratory, on a day-to-day, year-to-year schedule, can be a lonely but exciting place, where one's knowledge and imagination become as quanta along with the inanimate machinery and instruments. At times the seeming finality of negative experimental re-sults, which often hold up for months the orderly pro-gression of thought, requires a mental adjustment having little in common with the producing theatre and far from the urgencies of the market place. I found myself turning more and more to the subjective. Great music became a faithful companion and often released me from the men-tal tension of the laboratory.

Early in 1943 it became increasingly difficult to obtain materials, and in April the laboratory was closed, as the cold reality of war made all else seem unimportant. No positive result had been reached.

After this period of isolation, I joined the scientific staff of a laboratory devoted to war research, operated by Columbia University under the Office of Scientific Re-search and Development. I found myself with engineers, mathematicians, and physicists who had been recruited from the industrial and institutional laboratories and the broadcasting networks. We were a motley crew, and the work was absorbing, with time always of the essence, re-quiring that improvisation and ingenuity be our chief commodities.

I remained at this work for a year after the war was de-clared over. Then I returned to my laboratory at Yale with renewed vigor. Within six months a lighting control sys-tem was ready for installation and public demonstration. At last here was the positive result of four years of work, during all of which time both the laboratory and I were philanthropically supported.

Now my problem was no different from that of all

workers in the theatre. A new playwright who has just had his first play produced by an off-Broadway group, or a young scenic designer who has just enjoyed the first critical acceptance of his work, finds that his problem is to make a living from that which he enjoys most to do. There are many practical considerations, and from past experience I knew that work of such advanced technical nature would require more financial backing if it was to continue beyond the single research model that was now installed in the Yale University Theatre. I was aware that my only hope would be that either the institutional or the community theatre would be interested in continuing this work. I understood that the commercial theatre was not at this time interested in pursuing such work. Nor was I, for that matter, in a position to discuss it with such interests. Long since I had learned that an individual, if relatively unknown, finds his talent and himself carrying little weight if he is unable to negotiate from a position of strength equal to that of those people sitting across the table from him. This is as true of theatres as of any other business. My work being of a technical nature, this meant patents, if such were possible. The procuring of a patent, however, requires much time, patience, and again capital. But in the meantime what? Teach? Practice engineering?

I had no heart for either, because I realized full well that if I was ever to succeed in getting the laboratory to pay its way, it would have to be now. Rarely is one able to return to this kind of endeavor after having turned to some other pursuit. Once effort and thought are transferred elsewhere, it becomes increasingly difficult to retrace one's steps and begin again where one left off. To leave the theatre would be a fatal mistake. To teach in a college drama department would for a time mitigate the situation somewhat. To enter into a producing theatre, either community or commercial, would put me in a situation not unlike the metallurgist who is forced to work in a rolling mill. New steel alloys cannot be developed in a mill, nor can new instrumentation be developed in a producing theatre. In both instances the relative seclusion of the laboratory is needed. Here, in its own peculiar atmosphere, suspended judgments are not only eagerly sought after but cherished. It is this ephemeral thing, neither pure theory nor workable analogue, that is the bane of producers—of steel or of theatre. To be sure, many large modern industries do support this kind of laboratory activity. Steel does; theatre could but does not.

Only a quantitative difference operates here. Whereas the steel industry reckons its economic status in billions, the theatre involves itself with but a few millions. Some will come to its defense and point out that the commercial theatre is overall an experiment. In a sense, this is true, at least in so far as the professional playwright is concerned. But once one turns away from writing and possibly some aspects of directing and design, one is confronted with a monolithic mass of outworn and obsolete buildings, equipment, and archaic methods that are virtually the exclusive province of the theatrical craft unions. This condition is further aggravated by the hard fact that the commercial theatre does not own its home. On the other hand, the situation, in a technical sense at least, is healthier in that theatre which is either part of an endowed institution or which has become a thriving community enterprise, for here there is a degree of freedom to try out new ideas.

In this great country, since 1930 these people of the noncommercial theatre are the ones who have built theatres. These are the theatres that have pioneered, in so far as buildings are concerned, every technical advance since Robert Edmond Jones and Lee Simonson began practicing the new stagecraft that they, as young men, learned in the theatres of Western Europe.

The director of one such theatre, Maurice Gnesin of the Goodman Memorial Theatre of the Art Institute of Chicago, commissioned me to build the second console system, thus allowing the laboratory to continue for another year. In rapid succession, similar commissions were forthcoming through the enterprise of Henry Boettcher of the Carnegie Institute of Technology and Robert Kase of the University of Delaware. These men virtually bought for me the time needed to allow the laboratory to grow into its adolescence. It was during this period that patents were granted, which protected the work now established. Soon thereafter, solicitation of commercial interest resulted in the licensing of the patents for commercial exploitation. Thereupon, a better than hand-to-mouth existence for the laboratory, and my dream of making the work self-supporting, came a step nearer to reality. Fortunately for all concerned, the demands of a vigorous television industry accelerated the reduction of the technique of building these systems to the methods of limited mass production and so made the equipment less costly for all. But the major stimulus for its use in the theatre still came from the nonprofessionals. Within five years the system had an acceptance that saw it installed in theatres from coast to coast.

Since its establishment, about ninety per cent of all the work of the laboratory has been in the lighting field. It is not my intention so to limit its scope. Work has been done on scenery-handling systems, flexible floor control, automatic drive and control systems, servo-control systems, mechanical control of light sources, and an analysis of the application of computer techniques to the control problems of the theatre. The pressure of commitments and the scarcity of money for continuing these projects have been the chief deterrents to building full-scale, acceptable solutions for these varied problems.

From such dreams is the laboratory made. At this point I should like to comment on two practical aspects of this laboratory without which it could not have survived. It could never have continued had not the Yale school of drama given it a permanent home. The personnel who have worked with me, in most instances, have come from the student body of the drama school. They have been research fellows, full-time graduate assistants, or part-time student assistants who often have worked out thesis problems in practical model form, using the facilities of this laboratory. In citing these facts, I wish to point out that if the modest endeavor here at Yale could be duplicated in graduate drama departments of other schools, the reduction to practice of the many urgent technical problems could be accelerated. Over the next decade our theatres and their technical competence could be vastly improved.

This is assuming that a better way can be found to integrate endeavors that by nature must be highly individualistic with the teaching program within the schools and with current practices in the producing theatre. There is, however, an ever present danger to be guarded against when considering the needs and goal of education and training for the professional theatre. Its function must not be allowed to slip into the mere routine of training for the technical competence of the trade school. Not watched, this routine can be deadly and can make of technique the *raison d'être* rather than the means, which should be loftier than its method. Technique is, after all, but a human invention, and its only constant is change.

It is this attribute of change that I hold to be the keystone of all thought and activity beyond the necessary rudimentary dogma, and it should be the true challenge to the graduate professional school.

It is true that creation can be neither taught nor learned. But it can be recognized and encouraged by good training and incentive. At the technical level this might require that a promising student be advised and even encouraged to avail himself of training in fields other than drama. In the long run, this might well do more for the theatre and for the exceptional, scientific-minded student. In addition to his instinctive feel for theatre, he can then equip himself with a more abstract approach to these problems. The fundamentals underlying these problems would then appear in nontheatrical trappings and devoid of their artistic prejudices. The intellectual rough and tumble of the seminar can help to bring the student who shows such promise to the attention of his teachers. More conventional classroom procedure often antagonizes and finally alienates such people.

This is a complex problem that demands of a faculty great imagination and greater integrity. Often, unorthodox methods and uncommon sense must be tried. Just as events in the life of a single electron cannot be predicted, so events in the working of a single mind might defy classification. This is education for the individual. It is only this kind of talent that can both create and solve problems. To discover and to help in the training of this needed talent is the duty and the privilege of education. It is this human investment that pays off with the ideas and the ingenuity required to construct the analogues without which reduction to practice is impossible. Machines can but produce their own kind. It requires the creative mind to begin anew.

This may seem idealistic in the extreme and far re-moved from professional theatre practice. But it seems to me that it is thus that the synthesis of art and science will surely again be made. How intelligently we are able to ac-complish this synthesis will, to a large extent, determine the vitality as well as the form of the theatre of tomorrow.

10. SYMPHONIC DRAMA:
A NARRATIVE OF REMINISCENCE

Paul Green

BACK IN THE WINTER OF 1916, Professor Norman
Foerster and I stood in his classroom there in the old
Alumni Building in Chapel Hill and talked about the
mysterious matter of writing a play—he a young associate professor of English at that time, and I a student
only a few years younger. After many a plan and hope
deferred, I had finally come up from a farm in eastern
North Carolina to go to school at the university—come
up from years of plowing, cleaning new grounds in the
winter, chopping and picking cotton, pitching baseball,
and writing shy and useless verses while sitting on a log
in the woods on many a wide and soundless Sunday afternoon. I had taught country school, too, for two years to
save up money enough for a try at college.

The Senior Class had decided to put on an outdoor
play at the little hillside theatre just off the campus. A
contest had been announced and the prize-winning script
would be honored with a production at commencement
time. A script of some thirty or forty minutes in length
was needed.

"Why don't you try for it?" Professor Foerster said.

"I wish I could," I answered.

"This is your first year here, but that doesn't matter. It's open to anybody."

"I don't know anything about playwriting," I said. "I don't know how to begin. I've never even seen a play."

"You get yourself some characters and put them to talking, to acting, to doing things."

"Yes, sir, but what sort of characters and what things?"

"That's what you have to decide—that's what your plot, your subject matter will be—what they talk about and what they do. Since this is to be produced by the Senior Class, the contest terms suggest that something to do with the university life would be preferable. Why don't you read Dr. Battle's history, and perhaps you'll come on some incident or character that would interest you?"

So I got Professor Battle's two-volume history of the university and read its total of seventeen hundred pages, statistics, alumni roll calls and all. It was unbearably dull, as such books perhaps must be, but one of the happenings recounted in it interested me. It had to do with the occupation of Chapel Hill by the Federal soldiers in 1865. A young brigadier general was in charge of these Yankee occupation troops, and to the shame and horror of the bitter and defeated townspeople, he fell in love with the daughter of the university president, and she with him. The courtship of these two young people was a scandal, and the scandal grew greater when the wedding was finally held in the little chapel there under the wide oak trees. Prayers of vengeance were raised against President Swain, and apparently some of them were heard. For shortly after this, the horse he had received as a gift from the young general ran away with him, overturned the buggy, and fatally injured him.

I wrote my play about this love affair, entitled it A *Surrender to the Enemy*, and it won first prize. I have suspected since that it was the only script the committee received. I shall never forget that spring afternoon when it was produced and I sat on the bare hillside among the audience and sweated streams down my face and under my clothes. I felt the eyes of everybody on me. But they weren't. There was enough talking and moving and mixing of costumes and color down on the popping plank stage to keep them interested—where a garrulous old colored woman was serving as a go-between for the young lovers, and the irate father was fulminating in windy blasts against the North; and where the mother was trying to keep peace and help love on to its normal conclusion; and the young general, with his homemade uniform and his shining, scabbarded sword, was keeping up his intent to win his sweet and lovely Southern belle; and she in turn was encouraging him on with a lot of longing, eyelashed looks and expressive workings of her little heirloom fan.

In the end, of course, love won over politics and war, and everybody seemed happy; at least on the stage they did.

The European war was now thickening over the Western world and enshrouding the United States. And inspired by the idealism of Woodrow Wilson, I enlisted to go to France and help make the world safe for democracy. And, too, I had already decided to be a poet, and from what I had read and heard, I knew that a poet must have experience—experience in hardship, pain, and struggle. And what better place to get them than in a war where there was plenty of bleeding and death?

226

Then in the long hours of digging ditches and marching and drilling in several army camps in this country, I
grew depressed, discouraged, and frustrated. I began reading philosophy and religion furiously in my spare hours—
Tolstoy, the New Testament, Buddhism, Nietzsche, Kant,
and Hegel. And I wrote a lot of poetry. It was no good,
but it eased me some. I selected two or three dozen poems
from the hundreds that I had written and had them published by a local printer in near-by Greenville, South Carolina. It occurred to me that I might be killed in France,
and this little book would be something of a sign to tell
how I wanted to go in the world.

So finally I sailed away and landed in France, and ulti-
mately in the muddy and death-rotted trenches of Fland-
ers. Sitting deep in the oozy, dripping earth at night, with
the mumble and angry growling of the guns above me, I
kept on writing poetry and sending it out to be mailed to
magazines back home. But so far as I know, not a single
piece of it was ever published, except a short one in *The
Ladies' Home Journal*. I finally realized that raw and
actual experience did not necessarily always help free the
imagination into glory. It too often destroyed it. And I
thought a lot about this.

Then as the months went by, and I saw more and more
of the wastage of death and decay, of the red tooth and
claw of survival, the perishing away of all the finer instincts and purposes of the men and boys about me, as
they tried to kill and keep from being killed, I realized
that peace would never come through violence, love
would never come through hate, and brotherhood of
brother could not survive the killing of the other brother.
At least I thought so. And I determined that some day
and in some way I would write about these things. Maybe

I could not do it in poetry, but perhaps in stories, in novels, or in plays even.

And all the while I was saving what money I could. And when I moved up from private to sergeant and then at last to second lieutenant, I saved more. And with the war ended, I had enough to go back to the University of North Carolina.

Meanwhile I had grown more and more interested in religion and philosophy. Only in these could I find some sort of answer to the troubles that tortured me—the meaning of my life and what I was here for, and what others like me were here for. And back at the university I won a sixty-dollar philosophy prize, and that encouraged me in that subject. About this time Professor Edwin Greenlaw, head of the English department at the university, brought Frederick H. Koch in from North Dakota to teach playwriting and tap the rich stores of North Carolina folklore, legend, and song. And Koch was the man needed. He believed that everybody was a playwright more or less, and the amazing thing was that he got the folks around him to believe it. And a great stew of playmaking soon got started.

I joined the playwriting class somewhat on the side and began turning out one-act plays along with Tom Wolfe, Hubert Heffner, Elizabeth Lay, George Denny, John Terry, Harold Williamson, and many others. My main purpose still was philosophy, and I looked forward to getting my doctorate and teaching in that field. But at odd hours I wrote a lot of plays, and a number of them were produced at Chapel Hill. Then I won a fifteen-hundred-dollar fellowship in philosophy, and that determined me. Elizabeth Lay and I got married, and we set off to Cornell, where I was to do graduate work.

But I couldn't quit writing plays. And during my stay

at that university I wrote dozens of them, all short ones. It was great fun. And many a night I hammered my typewriter through the long hours and joyfully saw the sun come up—writing about the Negroes and the poor whites of my boyhood remembering in eastern North Carolina, and pouring out on page after page my indignation at their piteous and doleful lot. Then a call came for me to return to Chapel Hill to teach philosophy. And there I kept at it for many years. But all the while I had a typewriter in my office, and between classes and conferences with students I would get in short spasms of work. I sent a couple of short Negro folk plays off to *Poet-lore*, and they were published. Then I sent one to *Theatre Arts Monthly*. Mrs. Isaacs, the editor, wrote me an encouraging letter and published it. Then the next year the Dallas Little Theatre of Texas entered this play, *The No'Count Boy*, in the contest for the Belasco Cup in New York. The group won the cup, and a few days later I had a wire from Henry Holt offering me a contract for a book of one-act pieces, with a sizable financial advance. And the birds sang to me from every bush on the campus as I walked home in the evening. I had had a play done on Broadway. True, a short play but still done on Broadway.

Holt published my book, *The Lord's Will and Other Plays*, and then Robert McBride brought out six short Negro plays; and the next year, 1928, Samuel French published another volume, *In the Valley and Other Carolina Folk Plays*. Meanwhile, I was working on longer things. In 1926, I sent two full-length plays up to New York, and they were both produced in that season. one of them, *In Abraham's Bosom*, winning the Pulitzer Prize. I attended some of the rehearsals of *The Field God* and made my first acquaintance with the professional New York theatre. I saw a number of Broadway shows, and with the exception of O'Neill's *The Emperor Jones* and the wonderful Jewish folk drama *The Dybbuk*, I was disappointed in what I saw. Maybe these two dramas should have satisfied me for all the sorry ones. But they didn't. Perhaps I was expecting too much from Broadway. I met a lot of theatre people and shared in a number of high-cackling cocktail parties, and I grew more and more unhappy. I had to do these things mostly at week ends and at holidays, for I was carrying on my full-time work in philosophy at the university.

I learned about the star system, unions, and contracts, and rents, and guilds, and agents' commissions. These I realized were necessary, but the lack seemed to me to be in the dramas themselves. Something I wanted wasn't there. In my frustration, I struck out with some experiments and wrote a few bitter plays, among them *Tread the Green Grass* and *Shroud My Body Down*. They were sick, wild things and pretty formless. *Tread the Green Grass* went into rehearsal at the Greenwich Village Theatre under the direction of Jimmy Light, but it was too much for even that hardened theatreman and was given up a week or so before it was to open.

Pretty soon I was tired of the Broadway theatre. Even my own plays tired me, and after the final dress rehearsals, I couldn't sit through them again. I had never had this trouble with certain motion pictures that I liked, for example *The Birth of a Nation* and the German picture *Variety*. And certainly never could I get enough of Charlie Chaplin's work. I saw *The Gold Rush* fourteen times. There was something missing in the so-called legitimate drama—missing for me and missing in me.

I had read a lot of Shakespeare, of course, and could not dare hope to find any comparable richness of imagery and beauty in the language of any of the Broadway and

modern plays. I didn't expect that. I also read a lot of
the Greek dramas and books on them, and I had imagined
their wonderful productions and thought that I would
have liked them had I been alive in those days—and I
knew that I would like them now if they could be repro-
duced with the chanting, the flute and the harp, the choreography, and the imaginative movements of the actors in
those ancient times. I went to musical comedies, and they
seemed empty and worthless, too. Gradually I began to
realize that the Broadway theatre was the theatre of mass
entertainment and was meant to indulge the passing
crowd and to make money. No doubt, as I say, in my ignorance and high-mindedness I had come expecting too
much. I banged off a piece about it all as an introduction
to a theatre anthology in which I said, with youthful
fervency:

I found, it seemed to me, that the American professional stage
—and that is to say the New York stage—is an industry and
not an art as I had dreamed; that it is a business run to the
pattern of supply and demand, with its standards of excellence
derived from the general wants of the buyers. Such a method
may not be so bad as it concerns matters of sentiment, slapstick, and farcical vaudeville, for these take their rise from and
prosper in a milieu of mediocrity and standardized emotions.
They make no absurd claims. They are the theatre of entertainment, and in their honesty we can enjoy them. But this
is not enough. The serious theatre—the higher professional
drama—appears to be neither the one nor the other. I went to
it again and again. I went behind the scenes, I talked with
stage hands and saw the workings of the unions, heard the
complaints of tired actors, arguments and interpretations from
the directors and impresarios, saw fights and quarrelings of
peevish stars as to the size of their names in electric lights,
jealousies and backbitings, listened to the 'how will that go?'

the 'what will she gross?' and 'they won't stand for that'; saw publicity and its methods, read facts and figures on salaries, rents, contracts, censorship and equity, investments, overhead, receipts, the box-office—and all these spoke of dog eat dog and look to your suspenders.[1]

A New York theatre friend of mine, who spent much time traveling out into the land lecturing on the American drama, told me that I need never expect to find my kind of high-minded theatre on Broadway. "What you are looking for," he said, "is what might be called the 'New Theatre,' the theatre of the imagination—is that right?"

"Yes, I guess that's right," I said.

"Well then, there is such a theatre—not out in the provinces, not in the schools and universities and civic centers—no—but right here in New York."

"Where in New York?"

"Among the independent groups," he said, "and there are many of them."

"Well, if there are such groups—like the old perished Provincetown—funny I haven't heard of them."

"Most of them are small, obscure, but they are trying. Go and see."

So I did—hunting for the theatre of splendid creation, of imagination and the dream. And I got acquainted with what might be called the "arty theatres." I found them living in squalor and misery in the dark places of the great city. And there I found the symbol for the thing, the pose for the content, attitudinizing and gesturing, and talk, talk, talk—talk of a vorticist and cubistic kind, and always with plenty of social philosophizing about the weird and

[1] The views of the writer appear in greater detail in his book of collected essays, *Dramatic Heritage* (New York, Samuel French, 1953).

decadent state of the world, including our own America—
talk about how Freud had been born to set man free in
his insides. These devotees were the sleepless, unbathed,
and disheveled ones, young people who mostly had come
from all parts of the country into the bright metropolis to
find expression for their souls, the space to stretch their
wider-reaching arms, not finding room enough in the
thousand-mile prairies or in the big, broad fields of the
South. And here they had spun downward into this quag-
mire of confusion and frustration.

But they were brave and determined, these young people, and they comforted one another in the certainty of
their pure devotion to the ideal of art. And I listened to
their proud aesthetic, which they had developed mainly
from hearsay and secondhand out of Europe, out of Russia, and with a mixture of our own American creed of
psychological behaviorism thrown in. They pooh-poohed
the idea of money. And there were long and dawn-break-
ing after-performance discussions in some cheerless apartment about soul and spiritual form, about inner releases
and outward expressions, about the curves of desire and
turgid glots and spouts of significance, and about ecstacy
and the great unconscious. And there was much quoting
from Isadora Duncan, Gordon Craig, and from Freud
again, and the then popular John B. Watson.

And on their little stages that I visited I found an ever
increasing din of carpentry and constructivism, of strange
contraptions to make clear the dramatic meaning sought.
I remember one little run-down studio where I was shown
the setup for a piece entitled *Man Is Man*, with credit for
the idea to Gertrude Stein. And sticking up in front of
the color-smeared, outlandish backdrop was a huge hand,
tall as my head.

"That's the hand of God you see there," said the enthusiastic and grimy young director. "It stays there through every scene."

"But doesn't the constant sight of the hand distract from the action of the play itself? I believe I'd be looking at the hand all the time."

"That's what we want you to do."

"But shouldn't I watch the actors?"

"You'll watch them both—for the meaning of the action is emphasized as it were, made significantly symbolic by the hand itself."

"I'd rather see the hand in my imagination, let it be referred to in the script maybe, and—"

"No, no. You are wrong. You should just go read the last issue of *The Mask* magazine."

"I read it, and I remember it says," I answered a little coldly, "that Shakespeare was not a good playwright—said he was too long-winded, diffuse, poetical, and the like."

"Yes, and I think he is."

"Then what about Goethe, Hebbel, the earlier and the later Ibsen? What about Racine, and what about Ansky who wrote *The Dybbuk?* And what about J. M. Synge and his *Playboy of the Western World*, William Butler Yeats and *Cathleen ni Houlihan*, and Paul Claudel with his *Tidings Brought to Mary?*"

"I don't know all of them, but if *The Mask* says they're not good, then I agree."

"But their works are representative of the 'New Theatre' you talk about," I went on, and a little sharply now, "the theatre of the imagination. They don't find it necessary to provide all this carpentry work. They use language to suggest, to connote, to lead the imagination, as it were, through the walls of the theatre out into spaces of freedom and beyond. Their theatre is for me *the* theatre of the imagination—using for the dress and facts of environment just enough of actuality to suggest and help the imagination in the course of its flight. It seems you would kill the imagination. Take Shakespeare. His greatness lies in the very words you seek to delete. Don't novels, poems, the great plays of the past—the Book of Job, The Ancient Mariner—don't they prove the superiority of the mind over the factualities of the eye and the ear?"

"Now you're talking about books, about literature; well, I tell you the theatre is not a literary art."

"That's the very point. You try to make it a literary art by trying to force it to take the place of literature. And I should think that to be the great falsity of the new theatre's measure and use of such strangely contrary souls as the constructivist Meyerhold, the lurid and visionary Strindberg, Freud with his sex dreams, and the allegorical William Blake—these the patron saints of the new theatre. This is false mysticism, it seems to me, if ever there was such. What I find here is much like a scene in the movie version of *Pilgrim's Progress*, where Christian's soul is taken up to heaven. And this soul was shown as an object. And that is really your watchword and election sure, isn't it?—everything an object—whether the need is for mood and impression, a splendor of shining poetry, or digging dialogue of ideas—like God's hand there? Well, this soul was an object some two feet long, wrapped in white, and was carried up the mountainside by some dozen women dressed supposedly like angels. How dull and factual it all was! Let the children, let the grownups read the book. Let their minds fill and throb and reach to all the simple but rich poetry of old Bunyan himself—with his description of the higher clouds and the pilgrims sweetly talking of the celestial city where the heavenly shining ones, riding on the wings of the wind, met their mighty Lord of Glory with trumpets and songs of praise. The dramatists of the *Oresteia, Faust, Lear,* and *A Midsummer Night's Dream* knew enough. They have shown us the way. No, the truth is, lacking the power of words, we've taken refuge in mechanics, haven't we?"

"Then I can see you won't want any tickets for our play," said the young director with a weary, pitying smile.

"I'm afraid not," I said. "I've only seen the hand of the play, and when I think of the God who scooped out the seas, piled up the mountains, and with his finger marked the course of great rivers down in my country, the God who hurls thunderbolts and rends the heavens asunder with sheets of water and flame, who turns the planets in their courses and stirs the whirling nebulae in eternal time and infinite space—when I consider this, then this constructed hand becomes puny, dead, lifeless and cheap."

"All right, all right," he burst out.

I had a charge on, and I went off and wrote my feelings down in my notebook, saying: "And so I came back from there—back where the elements of the new theatre I believed in—the theatre of the imagination—were to be experienced scattered and apart, for there they long had been—back to the true make-believe of the marionettes, up to the cathedral with its mystic chant and ritual pantomime, back to the art gallery, or the circus, or concert, or athletic field, or to my room with a copy of Apuleius, Aeschylus, or Sophocles, or Haigh's *Attic Theatre,* or to the university library for another book wherein to revision Beelzebub squatted on a wave in hell and the drunken crew of Greece raging in the woods, or to the movies where Emil Jannings wakes in his sour bed the morning after and Charlie Chaplin walks so exquisitely between two worlds. For in all these, now existing somewhat apart —marionettes, painting, sculpture, and architecture, the dance, music, folk song, and ballad, legend, music, religious ritual, and the dance, circus and stadium spectacle, the written and spoken word, the sleeper's dream, the movies, the world of work and machinery even—in all these are to be found those elements which could be drawn on, elements which someday will receive their proper fusion in the new theatre, the theatre of imagination, of lofty common sense."

And I began to work on another play for Broadway, in which I hoped to use some of those elements.

I was on my way to New York one day to meet with a producer and talk things over, and I struck up acquaintance with a man on the train. He and I were sitting on the rear platform of the lounge car as we rode through the hills of Pennsylvania. He introduced himself as a civil engineer, and I to him as a schoolteacher and writer. He began talking about this vast and powerful land of ours.

"Why don't the literary men in this country," he went on, "interpret it, really speak what America is? When I was younger I loved to read American novels, loved to go to the theatre. But after getting out into the world and helping build such things as these," and here he indicated the great river bridge we were gliding over, "I began to lose interest in most of the printed tripe as well as the stuff I saw on the stage. Of course, I go to the movies now and then, or even to a light musical comedy, but for easy entertainment, nothing more, certainly not for any great inspiration of truth or meaning. And I go to the theatre still, now and then. But the characters in the plays are usually pretty sorry folks—sick, confused, bellyaching about this and that. They usually go to pieces before the curtain comes down and run off with somebody's wife, or kill somebody, or maybe kill themselves. Well, the men and women that built this country didn't go to pieces. They were tough; they lasted. Why don't you writers tell about them—show them struggling and fighting against all kinds of difficulties and coming out on top? Take this train we're riding on. Take that airplane that just passed us in the sky. The fellows that built them kept on working, thinking, planning, never giving up. And the great skyscrapers there in New York and in the big cities from the Atlantic to the Pacific! Talk about wonders and marvels—well, here is plenty of material to use. I've been all over this country many times. I always get a thrill at its power, its strength, and its glory. I never feel any power or any glory in the books I read or the plays I see. Something's all wrong with these writers. Go out in the Middle West at harvest time. Take a look at the tremendous irrigation projects in the Southwest. Look at the mighty highways crossing and crisscrossing this continent, the trains pushing and pulling. It lifts you up, makes you want to do even bigger and better things—makes you want to get in there and do your best—get in there and pitch a good game—a no-hitter if you can. Yes, like religion the feeling comes over you. And the huge river dams—think of them—the Roosevelt, the Coolidge, the O'Shaughnessey, and the one they're planning to build on the Columbia River. And what a mighty thing the Empire State Building is. My business is as a builder—the making of things—and I never get over the wonder of them. The other day I was standing by the Empire State Building and looking up the corner of the structure as it pushed its way more than a thousand feet in the air, seeming to hang out over me, so high it was. Scared me, made me want to sort of shout or something, like being in a great church and the organ sounding—if you get my meaning. Yeh, men, that's what they were, these builders, strong men, and none of 'em sitting off to themselves studying their navel and moaning about the misery of the world."

"Maybe you ought to write plays yourself," I said.

"Oh no, not me."

"You've got the words for it."

"I don't know about the words, but I know how I feel. And there are plenty of others feel the same way I do. We fellows riding back and forth and doing our work in the country, we talk about it at times, in the smoking cars, at dinner, in hotel rooms. The truth is we don't think much of you artist fellows."

"I guess I don't blame you," I said.

"And it could be different," he said. "It could be. If the fellows that write and paint and compose music and do what I call dabble in the arts really knew and felt what America is—it could be. But they're ignorant. Most of 'em don't know any history for instance, don't know what Washington and Jefferson and men like them stood for. Most of them stay shut up in a room or congregate around Times Square at night, and they don't know anything— no past history and little or nothing of what is being done in the present. Take the men building the George Washington Bridge over the Hudson. I've had a bit to do with it. There's one of the big things of the Western world. Show me any book or any play or piece of music—anything in American art to compare with it."

"All right then," I said, "how would you go about getting this kind of writing and music, the kind of art you talk about?"

"Lord, I don't know," he said, throwing away the stub of his cigar and rising. "That's up to all you fellows."

And he went back into the lounge car.

About this time a good critic-friend suggested that I try for a Guggenheim Fellowship to go to Europe and have a look at the theatre there. "You'll learn a lot there," he said. And so when the prized award came through, I got a leave of absence from philosophy teaching at Carolina and, with my wife and two children, set out. I landed in Berlin, where the best theatre in the world was supposed to be at that time. I saw a lot of shows and opera. And true, I learned a lot. And I kept filling my notebooks with comments all the time.

I went to many plays at different theatres—at the Schauspielhaus, the Schiller, the Lessing, the Berliner, the Deutsches, the Volksbühne, the Metropol, the Renaissance, and others. Three opera houses were running, and I saw much opera, too. And there were playwrights everywhere—192 practicing professional ones in Germany at that time—according to a literary yearbook I read. And actors, singers, designers, and technicians were everywhere. The plays ranged from Tolstoy's *The Living Corpse* to *Abie's Irish Rose,* and there was much emphasis on homosexual and neurotic themes in between. For all its activity, I found the German theatre a pretty sick one. The frustration and defeat of World War I were heavy on the people, and inflation was running wild. The future looked harsh and drear, and the name of Adolf Hitler, the man with hope in his raging voice, was beginning to be heard. Perhaps it was no wonder that a subjective expressionism and a personal idiom of self-analysis were so evident in the drama being produced.

"Maybe you just don't like the theatre," my wife said to me one night as we returned home over the crunched snow. We had just been to see a depressing piece about sex aberrations among German youth. "Maybe you ought to go back home and write stories and novels."

"Maybe I ought," I said.

"You rather liked the *Dreigroschenoper* by Weill and Brecht."

"Yes. The people were a sorry lot, but there was something about the way the music and the story mixed together that I liked."

"Why don't you try to get more music in your plays, more dance?"

"Yes, I always like good music in plays, especially folk music and dancing too, some kind of dancing. They can be very beautiful—like the weird beggars' dance in *The Dybbuk*. But I seem to be bad as anybody else when I sit down to write my folk pieces—it's always ugliness and violence, and somebody killing somebody, and this person or that going crazy. Words seem to come easier when I write about terrible and pathetic things. I don't understand it."

"You've written some good comic things too, *The No'Count Boy*, *Quare Medicine*, and — and —" she spoke up loyally.

One night I was invited to a party given by a German newspaper editor to honor the American millionaire and art-sponsor Otto Kahn. I had met Mr. Kahn back in New York the year before. He had asked me to have lunch with him down in his palatial Wall Street office. And there, while he ate his milk and mush, and I ham and eggs, he had talked encouragingly to me about the theatre. He was a fine, sympathetic man and was always ready to help beginners in the arts, whatever the field. "Get out of North Carolina," he said, "get out and broaden yourself. Find new subject matter to write about. Folk things are all right, maybe, to begin with. But they're too narrow, too provincial. If you're going to be a real playwright, you must write about things that count."

We renewed our acquaintance at the party, and he said he was glad that I had taken his advice and got out to see what was being done in Europe.

"But I'm still writing folk plays," I said.

"In time, in time," he answered with a smile. "There's another folk theatre man here," he went on, "just come from Russia with his Yiddish repertory troupe—Alexis Granowsky."

"I've been reading about him in the papers," I answered eagerly. "I'd like to meet him."

He took me over and introduced me, and Granowsky and I had a good talk. From the first I was keenly interested in his ideas. "In my theatre there are three things I emphasize—music, pantomime, and the word," he said.

"You put music first then?" I queried.

"Perhaps I do. I hope you'll come and see some of our plays. We are opening next week at the Theater des Westens on Kantstrasse."

I went and was delighted. I went again and again, and I decided that if I had seen nothing else in Europe, this Moscow Jewish Academy Theatre would have been worth my coming. True, here again was much of the symbolism and constructivism of the confused new theatre followers back home. But there was more. Except for that impassioned and wonderful story of religious ecstasy and human love, *The Dybbuk*, I had never seen any modern plays that were more lyrical and intense in their productions. Such use of music, pantomime, acrobatics, masks even, and energized properties! And such rhythmic harmony of ensemble acting! It seemed as if the director had deliberately meant to fuse all the elements of theatre art into one. And later I learned that that was just what he was attempting. One of the plays I saw, *A Night in the Old Marketplace*, was a sort of grotesque, tragic carnival, with

hardly any dialogue or spoken words, nearly all pantomime, dance, and musicalized action. It, too, dealt with
decay and death, but with such verve and even comic
satire that a sense of liveliness and zest spilled over from
the footlights. The old market in the center of a small
Jewish town was made a sort of symbol of a failing and
degenerate world. The characters in the play—members
of the synagogue, visitors to the brothel, all kinds and
types—were confused and frustrated enough, but hanging tenaciously on to life. Finally the dead were raised out
of their graves, and the living found to their astonishment
that there was no difference between these dead and
themselves. As part of the new Russian creed, the play
seemed to declare that the old world and its times were
perished, and those who believed in them were as good
as perished, too. Distorted masks, a ghastly stage setting,
queer, outlandish dances added to the gripping effect
of the play.

And then there was an eccentric piece, *The Travels of
Benjamin III*. Granowsky had taken an old Jewish folk
tale and adapted it in his free theatre manner. He showed
two Jewish friends who set out adventuring through the
world in search of some of the ancient glory of their Jewish
heritage. Actually, the play was a sort of dream in which
all kinds of miraculous things happened. One of the Jews
married the daughter of the Mogul of India and adopted
the title of Benjamin III, king of the Jews. Later, the two
comrades came to their senses and returned home to their
little village, better and wiser men. They now realized and
declared that the reality of life was to be found in their
everyday village work and living, and not in fancies and
dream escapism.

There was no hang-over of ancient Jewish pessimism
or sorrow in these plays. The actors were buoyant, strong,

and vital even in scenes of despair. Here was the will to live, to create, to be strong and build, build for the future, to build the Russian socialist republic. Apart from all politics, I felt the power and freshness of Granowsky's theatre. And I was eager to talk with him again.

He received me in his apartment, glum and downcast for some reason. But my high praise and enthusiasm for his plays evidently cheered him up a bit.

"I am glad you liked us," he said. "What pleased you most about our productions?"

"I don't know. I liked it all—the acting, the dances, and, I guess, especially the music."

"Ah, the music," he spoke up eagerly, "that is it. Mine is first a musical theatre, last a musical theatre."

"But not musical comedy."

"Oh no, not that, not musical comedy as in America. Our plays are real, full of life; they say something."

"A social message."

"Yes, but always in terms of the theatre. I am more interested in the theatre than politics."

"I wish you could bring your group to America. It would mean a lot to us. We need to see the sort of thing you are doing."

"Ah, America. I want to go there. Mr. Otto Kahn has offered to guarantee us a few weeks in New York. I have appealed to Moscow for permission. I am waiting."

"Wonderful. And then you think you will go?"

"There is much strong feeling between the two countries. Still, I have asked permission. And I may tell you that I may not be wise in asking this permission."

"Why not?"

"These politics—I am waiting the answer, as I told you." And he smiled a little wan smile, his gaze indrawn as if some inner apprehension or dolefulness bothered him. Then he shook his head and went on. "I am glad you liked our—music drama."

"I remember Wagner called his operas 'music dramas.'"

"But they were operas. Music swallowed up the words, submerged them, changed their real and actual meaning. I use music—and the same for dance, pantomime, costume, properties, and setting—to interpret the words, to give them a richer meaning. I have been working in this type of drama now for ten years, and every day convinces me that I have just begun to glimpse the possibilities. Here is the truly free theatre—I mean it is ahead. For instance, musicalized pantomime, speech, facial expressions, and bodily movements can liberate all those imaginative human meanings which straight realism or even the most poetic language itself can never completely do. Yes, music is the word. With music and stylization of the proper sort, one can obtain short cuts in scenery, properties, and in moving the story forward. It is easier to get right down to business, go right to the heart of your dramatic matter, to reach the inner meaning and symbolism even of the story you have to tell, to make it immediately available to the audience—with music. If I should ever be forced to leave Russia," and once more that wan smile and indrawn, empty look were in his face for an instant, "America is the place I'd want to go to begin my theatre over again. Your nation has everything to make a great theatre movement possible. You are the richest of all countries in dramatic material. You are a country of conflicts. And I don't mean those that result in physical violence necessarily. I mean spiritual conflicts, conflicts of ideas, of individual feelings, of points of view, of mass groupings, of types, of individuals, and of organizations. And always energy, energy. Your country is boundless in that. And think of your many nationalities with their own inheritances of speech and custom. Surely at this hour yours is the most creative nation on the globe. I know something about your theatrical history—I have heard of a few of your pioneer workers—William Vaughn Moody, Percy MacKaye, and, of recent years, Eugene O'Neill. And then there was another man—he wrote some one-act Negro plays."

"Ridgely Torrence."

"Yes, Torrence, that's right. Who else have you?"

"Maxwell Anderson is writing poetic drama now. You may remember his and Laurence Stallings' great success, *What Price Glory?*"

"Yes."

"Some of us are hoping Anderson is beating down a path which will lead toward a new expression of American genius. And there are Sidney Howard, Robert Sherwood, Philip Barry, Marc Connelly, George Kelly, Elmer Rice, Lynn Riggs . . . ."

"Do any of them make a great use of music?"

"Not much. But Connelly in his play *The Green Pastures*, created from a series of religious folk tales by a southern writer, Roark Bradford, used a lot of Negro spirituals."

"Do you use music in your plays?"

"I try to now and then—folk things. And I plan to use a lot of music in the future."

"I hope you will," and he nodded his head encouragingly. "I can't understand why America hasn't developed music drama,"—throwing out his hands nervously. "Well, that is one of these mysteries of art. The impulse and the creation come when they will come. But I prophesy before the real genius of your country can be expressed, can find its statement on the stage, music vitally integrated into the drama itself must be used. For instance, why hasn't America ever created a great Negro theatre? More than once in recent days and under the present regime in my homeland of Russia, I have seriously considered migrating to America to try to build a Negro musical drama there. Think of the singing, the religious rituals and practices, the superstitions, the vivid folk speech, folklore, and tall tales, the dramatic conditions surrounding that submerged yet marvelously gifted people."

"Some beginnings are being made," I said. "When I spoke of Marc Connelly's and Roark Bradford's *Green Pastures*, I should have mentioned DuBose and Dorothy Heyward's Negro folk play *Porgy*, which uses a lot of music. And then there are Negro drama groups in Harlem, New York, Cleveland, Ohio, in Chicago, and in some of the larger cities. But they are only beginnings."

"I have talked to Mr. Kahn about this too, about such an idea as a Negro theatre in America. And he said he would consider subsidizing it if I would come and organize it. Well, it is a thing to think about, and there is much, much to be done, and let us hope we shall have time and a chance to do it."

I saw Alexis Granowsky once or twice more. I was present at a meeting with him and a few others on the tragic night he reported that his theatre had been dissolved by a command of the Soviet authorities, and his actors had been ordered back to Moscow. This was perhaps the answer he got for his request to take his troupe to America.

He did not return to Russia. Maybe he didn't dare. He moved to Paris, and not long after I heard that he had died there. I never knew why he did not come to America in accordance with this dream he had, instead of going to France.

I stayed on in Berlin through the spring and then moved to England for several months, with a short excursion into

France to visit some of the old Paris scenes that I had known during and after the war. The theatre in those two countries was much the same as it had been for generations, and I saw nothing that got hold of me, except parts of Sean O'Casey's *The Silver Tassie* and an English production of Strindberg's cruel and bitter tragedy, *The Father*.

Of course, there was Bernard Shaw. I had a chance to spend an evening with that remarkable man, and we—rather he—talked theatre for hours. "Speech is the thing," he said, "not music, masks, pantomime, or dance. Speech is glorious." He repeated it more than once. "That's all you need in the theatre—a voice with something to say, with ideas that have meaning. All the rest is furbelows and fancies. Words, words, fine and powerful words saying something people need to hear. And if they need it, they'll like it—provided, of course, the playwright knows how to say it interestingly. Shakespeare depended on words, and he did rather well as a playwright now and then in using them. Don't you think so?"

When I got back home, I took time off to work with the newly formed Group Theatre in putting on a play that I had written sometime before, *The House of Connelly*, a drama of the old and the new South. It had some critical success and a fairly decent run at the Martin Beck Theatre but made no money. By this time, my family was in need of something more substantial than dramatic theories. So I got a leave of absence from the university and set out for Hollywood. I worked there for many months and ran into plenty of grief as well as money, but that story lies outside this narrative.

When I got back to Chapel Hill, and with my bills paid, I started planning another play for Broadway.

During my student days at the university, I had often walked out in the evening to the west of the town where the Negroes lived. For generations they had lived here, camped, as it were, under the very eaves of the great gray and red brick buildings of the campus and with little intellectual or spiritual profit from the nearness, so far as I could tell. In and around their poor houses they gathered in the evening, sang their songs, cracked their jokes, carried on their love-making, and now and then fell into fights and killings. And each morning they rose to work for the white man—some as cooks and washerwomen, others as janitors at the university, others as bricklayers, yard boys, and waiters in the boardinghouses. I decided to try to write a play about this Negro settlement, with its teeming, upboiling life, its intense emotions, superstitions, frustrations, hopes, and accomplishments, its grievings and dark humilities. I would write not about a single protagonist and antagonist, but about the whole village.

What about a gathering place for my characters? A church would not do, for only the religious life of the people would come to the fore there. I needed a place in which all facets and turns of their habits and actions could be displayed. A boardinghouse seemed the best place then. And as for room to give these people purpose and place to move in, I conceived that a sort of street roadway ran in front of the house, and before the house a yard. Then as for the house itself, I needed different rooms and levels for the spilling of the action. So I put a porch on the front of the house, where some of the characters now and then could gather and say their say. Then behind the porch, a step higher, the eating room interior, and still another step higher at the back a lean-to bedroom. Thus, I had four levels of action—the street and yard, the porch, the eating room, and the lean-to. Then at the left of the eating room I joined on a shed bedroom, and out in the yard at the left a little brick barbershop shack, where action going and coming and moseying about could take place. At the right of the boardinghouse was another narrow street down which people could come now and then. And behind the house I imagined a rising bluff along which a distant and miniature train could pass, with its shrilling whistle and sparks and smoke, and the Negroes giving their wild, longing cry of "Hot damn, hot damn, there she goes!" In and around this boardinghouse with its playing areas I collected my characters—some seventy-five or one hundred of them, all representative of a cross section of Negro life in the South—a voodoo worker, a preacher, a granny woman, several convicts, a harlot, a beautician, a feeble-minded lad, several day laborers, a singing blind beggar, a sport, cooks, an undertaker, a folk philosopher, a salesman of death insurance, a barber— and men, women, and children. These last were in the main atmosphere and chorus figures.

What about the time? I must choose a day and hour in which it would be natural for this sprawl of Negro life to come together in such a setting. A Saturday night or afternoon would do. And it must not be in winter, for then my numerous characters wouldn't have the free play of the outdoors to move around and sit about in, and my different acting areas would have no meaning. So it would have to be in summer—and rightly a warm summer evening or night when the hard work of the week had ended, and Sunday with its anthems and sermons and sinners' warnings had not come, and the blue workday Monday was still another day away. At such a sweaty, oozing, and dewy eveningtime, then, the story germ would sprout naturally and grow its pushing way along to the final bloom of explosive fulfillment—after which the Negroes' normal life would return to its deep tide of rest and the play be over.

As I worked at this drama, I felt myself sitting in a high chair or on a high stump in the middle of the road in front of the house, watching the events take place, seeing the characters coming in here and there as the story required, saying their say, doing their do, and retiring as their inclination and need pulled them off. And I was sitting there with a notebook on my hand writing it all down. And of course there was a sense of will-at-work on my part too, a creative energizing into being all that was happening before my eyes. There was this double dialectic all the while then—the happenings of things and people of themselves and at the same time their being caused to happen consciously and purposely on my part, each a separate and individual reality—concerning personality, appearance, dress, behavior, and speech, all separate and individual souls—among them old Quiviene Lockley, the boardinghouse keeper; Willie Lockley, her youngish and feeble-minded husband; Bantam Wilson, a convict broke loose from the roads; Ed Uzzell, the philosopher, with his inner moan of "Under the tight pot I hear you calling, and oh, seas—rivers of brick and mortar and iron—open the way—let it flow on"; Bad Eye Smith, the drayman, dreaming of money and a new truck to come; Doodle Wilson, the boy preacher, with his song of "Death, oh Death, spare me over another day"; Murdoch, the bad man, seeking regeneration and a new name through love and steady work; the black stranger John Henry, the mighty steel-driving man, croaking up from the deep caverns of his breast the awesome statement, "I done sold my soul to the devil and my heart it's turned into stone"; and many, many others.

And often I would leave my chair or stump and find myself up on the porch or in the bedroom right among my characters, close enough to hear them breathing and smell the odor of their bodies. In controlling and handling these many characters as they played out their story, I felt that I was in something of the same position as a composer driving forward his composition for some eighty or one hundred instruments, or even as the conductor directing the orchestra which played that composition after it was written. The entire body of the piece must be kept moving itself along, by means of the individual instrumentations that came forward to personal fulfillment, turned, retired, and gave place to others, and they in succession likewise. Character and story motifs must be developed, thematic statements made and exploited, and an upboiling and stewing of symphonic creativity kept going toward a dynamic finale.

And a stern control over the material must be kept all the while. And that control lay in the story line. Whatever failed to advance the story must be left out. For, after all, drama—whether it deals with five people or one hundred —is storytelling, storytelling through speech and action. Of course, some splurge of language and lyrical area display could be indulged in, but only for heightened effect. And the fixed idea, as in a Beethoven or Berlioz symphony, the sensed and felt and consciously shaped inner natural form, call it the plot or even melodic line, whether submerged or coming boldly now and then to the surface —as it always must—this fixed idea and intent must control matters.

I kept searching for a term of definition and interpretation to describe my play and to help in its unification as I worked along.

In trying to express the inner lives and their meanings

in my Negro community, I found that I was having to call upon about every element available in modern theatrical art. Folk song and poetry were needed, also dance, pantomime, and chorus voices—and dreams and visions, too, and the grisly microphone for the voice of the white man's law or fearsome God speaking from the sky to his people. Moments of horrification would require masks, and always there must be the liquefication of light to accompany the human behavior at work—light that would illuminate an ever advancing story point. And in that illumination the mind of the spectator could read the message clear. The fabled fire in the Scriptures was like this light, the furnace fire in which the Hebrew children once stood all bright and glorified. So it seemed to me.

And always there was music—music!

"Music drama" didn't seem the right term for the play. For there was more than music. "Ballad opera" it could not be, nor "opera." "Festival drama" was too loose and "misnoming." "Lyric drama" lacked entirety. Finally, "symphonic drama" seemed right. Yes, a "sounding-together" in the true meaning of the Greek word. And so I adopted the form and have used it for a number of other like dramas that I have written since.

I found in writing this Negro drama that by the symphonic use of the various elements of the theatre, especially music, there came a freedom and fullness of possible story and character statement not otherwise to be had in dealing with large groups of people in action. As Granowsky had said, I found that with the use of music, short cuts and intensifications could be quickly indulged in which the audience would accept without questioning. Conventions could be quickly established or other conventions dispensed with, and the story beginning, say, could be hatched out of an obstructive matrix without much ado.

And in this kind of theatre, time could be telescoped through a symbol, even could become that symbol, and space could be compressed like the breathing of some huge and delicate accordion of the mind. Tomorrow is already here. A voice of the inner chorus commentator out of my Negro village could say so. And in the thickened moody and musically charged environment, in the climate of credibility established, the audience would agree.

There was a nemesis in this Negro play. A huge and oncoming highway was being built across the earth by the white man and was aimed straight at the Negro settlement. The deep reverberations of dynamite exploding in the hills, clearing the way for this road, sounded ominously and constantly nearer as the drama proceeded.

Passions and hates and loves and fears and whorings were fecundating in this village. During the play murder was committed in the boardinghouse. Then came the wham-wham of a policeman's stick, and the hoarse great voice of the Law was heard bellowing like Behemoth through the valley. Culprits and innocent ones ran this way and that in fear. The Golem tread of justice and retribution came nearer. The reverberations on the distant road sounded closer, louder. Nature herself became sick, upset, violent. A fierce wind whoomed and whistled among the shacks in the valley and around our particular boardinghouse. The limbs of the shade tree in the yard twisted and swung like a gesticulating maniac. A final and terrific explosion occurred in the street at the right. A pandemonium of shrieking and lamentations of the people rose in the valley. The moon dropped down the sky like a shot. And then, with the echoes falling away, the tumult and the terror died. The scene faded gently and musically out. From the darkness came a low and fervent chanted prayer of the persecuted and disordered people. A

few heartbeats of time and no more, and the light swam
up again.

The iron-snouted, machine-age road had arrived. The
nemesis was there. It had plowed its revengeful way
through the settlement like a cruel steel colter through an
anthill. The old boardinghouse had been pushed aside.
The entrails of furniture and pieces of bedding spilled out
along the earth. Because of the depravity, the sinfulness,
the causeless misery of these sorrowful ones, the road had
taken its toll.

A dozen or more striped convicts were working, digging
away on this road now, slinging their picks and bringing
them down, and ever bringing them down in the white
blazing sun. The heat of August shimmered across the
land. "Lazy Lawrence" danced his fiendish monkey dance
in the sun. The sweat poured down, the only cooling
dampness in the world for the mourners on that road. On
a stump to the left a guard squatted, drowsy, vapid, like a
toad. The rifle in the crook of his arm kept alert; its muzzle
warned like an eye; it threatened. The convicts dug on
and on, their faces set down the infinite stretch of cruel
road that reached from the rising to the setting sun. And
as their picks came down against the earth with a thud, a
husky, desperate, groaning chant burst from their baked
lips, carrying on and carrying on over the long deadening
hours of pain.

> *They call their Jesus—hanh—*
> *They say their Jesus—hanh—*
> *They mean their Jesus—hanh—*
> *Eigh Lord!*

In this form of symphonic drama the convicts and the
digging had become the road.

The form seemed right then for the expression of such group life, of setting forth the relationships of individuals and their fellows, of masses and crowds affected, energized and motivated as they would be by some centripetal idea and dramatic intent—some story of tradition, of folk inheritance and legend, some famous native character or group of characters splurging themselves forth out of their heritage.

Under the title of *Roll, Sweet Chariot,* the drama opened at the Cort Theatre in New York in the autumn of 1934. A brave-hearted woman, Margaret Hewes, was the producer and Em Jo Bassche and Stanley Pratt the directors. It was a sad occasion for all of us. The audience was confused with our experiments. I had insisted that the play run without intermission. And in the pit we had a Negro chorus of twenty-two voices, flanked by timpani and a clarinet, which expressed the joy and grief of the drama in notated wordless vocables. Dolfe Martin had written what I thought and still think was a beautiful score for the chorus. At a crucial moment a fuse blew out in a loud-speaker in the loft with a banshee wail, and our Law and our God became comic. The audience was embarrassed and then rarely tickled.

Out in the lobby I paced up and down during the performance. About midway, Robert Benchley came bursting out of the auditorium and several others with him.

"Intermission or not," he said to me angrily, "I'm going to smoke. What's it all about, anyhow?"

The play closed at the end of the first week and to a half-empty house. The reviews were violently mixed, although a day later I got a wire from the *New York Times* critic commending me for my use of language, and the valiant Edith Isaacs, editor of *Theatre Arts Monthly,* wrote strongly in the play's defense.

I went back to my teaching and to writing one-act pieces and a couple of volumes of short stories. Then I wrote two folk novels and occasionally took a hurried trip to Hollywood to get money to pay for my house. But I couldn't give up my idea of symphonic drama. I thought to myself that if I had some place other than Broadway to try my theory out—some place where unions and rents and the implacable demand for profits could wait its season—maybe there I could possibly succeed.

Kurt Weill landed in this country about this time, a refugee from Hitler's fanaticism, and in 1936, with the encouragement of the directors of the Group Theatre—Harold Clurman, Cheryl Crawford, and Lee Strasberg—he and I got together on a musical drama to be produced by the Group. I introduced some symphonic elements into my script, but it was in the main a straight music drama. Weill's score was splendid, but the public did not like the play. Perhaps the story line was faulty, and I suspect the subject matter was too. I had put into it a lot of my abhorrence of war and made Johnny Johnson, the leading character, a kindly common-sense man against whom and through whom I might measure the madness of violence and hate. Lee Strasberg did a good job of directing, and in the asylum scene especially, where Johnny had organized the League of World Republics on the pattern of the United States Senate, his work was sheer genius. Russell Collins played the lead, and among the cast were Robert Lewis, Roman Bohnen, Lee J. Cobb, Art Smith, Albert Van Dekker, Elia Kazan, John Garfield, Ruth Nelson, Paula Miller, Luther Adler, Morris Carnovsky, Tony Kraber, and others. The play limped along for three or four months and then closed.

Once more I went back to my teaching. The university had been patient with me, giving me more than my share of leaves of absence over the years. And I kept writing stories and articles on the side. But still in my mind were the plan and hope to try out my ideas in a symphonic drama somewhere and somehow.

Such an opportunity came down in North Carolina the next year, when a group of local people decided to put on a celebration commemorating the three hundred and fiftieth anniversary of Sir Walter Raleigh's tragic attempts at a settlement on Roanoke Island down on the coast in the eastern part of the state. I got in with the group, and a play was planned. But we had little or no money. It was still the Depression and W. P. A. days, and finally the federal government helped us out. We got some funds, and contributions of labor and materials were made locally. So work began on an amphitheatre in which to produce the play. It was built on the exact spot by the sound's edge where Sir Walter Raleigh's colony had lived and died, and I set about writing the script.

This time, let me hold true again, no matter what be the stimulation of my subject matter. Let me keep ever before me the sense and image of this group of tragic, suffering people—more than 120 of them—men, women, and children—who had fared forth from England on that fatal day in 1587 to brave the turmoil and terror of the vast and raging sea in search of their destiny, these the keepers of a dream—the yearning and the hunger that were in them. Away with all secondhand sources— let it come prime, let it come raw.

And I would forget the famous baby, Virginia Dare, except as one of the items in the whole dramatic symphony. No need to worry either because the father's name "Ananias" must cause a dramatic emphasis different from that of history. These didn't matter. The main thing was the people. For these were the folk of England, the folk of our race—these who now must labor with their hands to wrest from cryptic nature her goods and stores of sustenance—or die—these who now must live with their feet in the earth and their heads bare to the storms, the wind and sleet and the falling fire from heaven. Flood and drought and hunger were to be their lot, their minds and spirits a prey to the nightmare fear and horror of the dark and impenetrable wilderness around them.

And yet, out of this testing, this straining and tension here on these lonely shores, this being hammered on an anvil, oh, God! there must emerge the faith that lies native in them as workers, as believers, as spiritual beings who lift their eyes in awe to the great Presence riding the lightning flashes down the sky, the Power that breathes in earthquakes and in the bellowing of the storm, or sweetly sings His pleasure in the birds of spring and smiles His joy in the flowers by the forest's edge. Yea, out of this play must come a sustaining faith, their faith, a purified statement of aim and intent, of human purpose for our heritage, or all was waste and sacrifice made vain.

And so here on these yellow muted sands of Roanoke Island, let my hero, John Borden Everyman, speak out in the play on the night he and his companions are to disappear into the vast unknown, out of our sight forever— let him speak the words that are his credo and our credo as self-reliant and valiant men: "Hear that once Sir Walter said, the victory lieth in the struggle, not the city won. To all free men it standeth so, he said. And by the death of our friends and companions and those who lie buried in this ground, let us swear our consecration to the best that is in us. Let the wilderness drive us forth as wanderers across the earth, scatter our broken bones upon these sands, it shall not kill the purpose that brought us here! And down the centuries that wait ahead there'll be some whisper of our name, some mention and devotion to the dream that brought us here."

And as always let there be music, music on which the story might ride.

And then, before we could begin rehearsals our money ran out. With Frederick H. Koch, who was a sort of inspiring guardian over the project, I went to a foundation in New York City for help—and got it.

We opened *The Lost Colony* on July 4, 1937, with Samuel Selden as director and Frederick H. Koch as advisory director, and although the nearest city was ninety miles away, it was a success from the start. We had some twelve or fifteen Federal Theatre Project actors in the main parts, many local actors in smaller parts, a chorus from the famous Westminster Choir College, and a swarm of C. C. C. camp boys as Indians. So the financial burden was relatively light. But everyone was paid something for his work. Our admission price was one dollar for adults and fifty cents for children, and with good crowds in an outdoor theatre seating thirty-two hundred we were able to pay our way. We got good write-ups from the leading critics. Atkinson, Garland, Kronenberger, and many others came down and gave us a boost. And the Cavalcade of America program carried a condensed nationwide hour-long radio broadcast. Then President Roosevelt came, and later Mrs. Roosevelt. The night the President saw the show we had to give two performances to accommodate the crowds. People were literally hanging in the old sprawled live-oak trees that surrounded the amphitheatre

At last, I felt my theory of symphonic drama was vindicated. And with the exception of the blackout war years, the play has run a summer season of ten weeks each year since. Last summer marked its twentieth season, and soon it will pass its one thousandth performance. Hundreds of thousands of people have come to see this project of communal theatre—there on the yellow sands of Roanoke Island—come to hear the old English music, the folk songs and hymn tunes of our musical tradition, and to see the native Indian dances—all part of the symphonic drama that tells the story of a brave group of people, who in their struggle and death vindicated and made more living the ideals in which they believed and on which our nation is founded.

With *The Lost Colony* established, I looked around for other chances for symphonic outdoor productions. For by this time I had already decided that this sort of drama was exactly fitted to the needs and dramatic genius of the American people. There seemed to be something, too, about the outdoors that was native to our hearts and feelings. For we are a muscular, lithe, and bounding-footed people. Maybe it is the pioneer field, prairie, and forest influence still on us. And sitting under the stars at night and witnessing again plays that had to do with the making of this country maybe brought a sense of man and God and nature into one. Our richness of tradition, our imaginative folk life, our springing enthusiasm and health and drive, our singing and dancing and poetry, our lifted hearts and active feet and hands, even our outpourings of mechanical creations and things for self-expression—maybe in the outdoors and not in the professional and killingly expensive confines of the big cities these could flourish and have their place.

And so I went to work with a will in writing other symphonic outdoor dramas to be produced in different parts of America—among them, *Big John* for South Carolina and *The Highland Call* for the Cape Fear River Scots. Then World War II came on, and all was stopped. I continued to teach, visit Hollywood now and then, and work on a novel. I wrote a straight play about education too, *The Enchanted Maze,* and with Richard Wright dramatized his intense novel *Native Son,* which Orson Welles directed and produced in New York with much success.

After the war, Virginia decided she would like to have a play also. And under the leadership of the former governor, Colgate W. Darden, money was raised, and a beautiful brick amphitheatre was built on the edge of the lake in the woods of the William and Mary campus at Williamsburg for the production of *The Common Glory.* In this play I told the story of Thomas Jefferson's struggles in helping to establish democratic government in the United States during the years 1775–81. Again I used with a free hand any and all elements of theatre art that I needed—music, dance, dreams, mental speech, battlefield scenes, warships in the river, and narration to drive the story along. Once more the same philanthropic organization up north encouraged us with a timely grant-in-aid. In spite of rain and storm and katydids in the trees, the play opened successfully in 1947 under the direction of Althea Hunt. Howard Scammon took over as director after Miss Hunt, and with Allen Matthews as manager, Myra Kinch as choreographer, Roger Sherman as technical director, and Sue Sherman as costumer, he has improved the production summer after summer. Last season was the tenth, and I hope it will be running many years more.

Then Washington, D. C., decided to celebrate the one hundred and fiftieth anniversary of the setting up of the Federal Government there in 1800, and I began writing a drama for it. Immediately we ran into politics. The President of the United States came to our rescue with talks in our behalf, but politics continued. I spent more time lobbying and trying to raise funds from the Congress than

I did on the play. At last, the huge amphitheatre in Rock Creek Park was completed at a cost of several hundred thousand dollars. We had everything one could ask for in lighting equipment, sound, dressing rooms, machinery, and shops. But the production didn't get across. I worked and sweated to do for George Washington what I had done for Sir Walter Raleigh's colony and for Jefferson, and the drama students from George Washington and Catholic universities did their valiant best for the play; but still our city audiences remained pretty skeptical and aloof. They were not impressed with my interpretation of the Father of Our Country, nor with the shadow-drama scenes and dream visions in the sky. However, I remember that Washington's crossing of the Delaware got a hand every night. We raised such a racket, too, in the Battle of Lexington scene that near-by irate householders flooded the papers with letters and even got out injunctions. After two seasons we closed up, and the multitude of lameduck souls and pie counter habitués who had been foisted on our payroll by the yea-saying congressmen and politicians had to seek sustenance elsewhere. It was all very sad, and for quite a while the thought of "symphonic drama" gave me the shudders. The only thing that eased my regrets was the knowledge that the city had received a fine civic outdoor theatre for band and symphony concerts, musical productions, Boy Scout gatherings, sunrise Easter services, and other public uses.

In 1951, the foundation that had twice helped my own plans asked me to go to Asia to lecture about art and literature in the United States. I welcomed the chance. Not only would I be able to say to many groups and organizations that there was more in America than Yankee imperialism and scrambling for the dollar, but also I would have a chance to look at the theatre and dance drama in different lands. It was a tough assignment, although I did not know how tough when I accepted. And so with my grant from the foundation and the blessings of U.N.E.S.C.O. and the State Department, I set out. I managed to survive, and so did my wife, and I learned a lot. I first visited Honolulu and saw the indoor and outdoor theatres there and the great university collection of oriental drama. Then I went on to Japan, and no doubt that was the most fruitful part of my trip.

I do not have time in this account to tell much about the great Japanese theatre. It is already becoming well known in the United States through the recent writings of Faubion Bowers, Earle Ernst, James Michener, Joshua Logan, A. C. Scott, and others, and through such fine Japanese motion pictures as *Rashomon*, *Gate of Hell*, and *Ugetsu*, and through the visits of the Azuma dancers. But I found that in both the Noh and Kabuki dramas the Japanese were doing things on the stage—and had been doing them for one hundred years—that we were just beginning to do. Here indeed was the truly lyric and imaginative theatre so many of us yearning American playwrights had dreamed about. Here was the theatre in which were finally interwoven in proper proportions the various elements of dramatic imagination—music, dance, athletics, pantomime, choral chants, poetic narration and commentary, light and sound, and the impassioned actor's speech—all clothed in colorful costumes, settings, and the habiliments of the poet's dream.

I visited many other countries, made my lectures, and saw theatre in the Philippines, Malaya, Thailand, Burma, India, Turkey, Greece, and Italy, but nowhere did I see anything to equal what I saw in Japan.

It is my belief that in Kabuki, Japan has the finest theatre in the world.

264

Back home I took up the symphonic drama idea again. Ohio was busy making plans for celebrating the one hundred and fiftieth anniversary of its statehood, and I was asked to write a play for that. I began work, and bills were introduced in the legislature to provide money for the production and for building an amphitheatre. The governor took a personal interest in it. One hundred thousand dollars was appropriated for the production, but the bill for the amphitheatre was killed. So we had to put the play on at the fairgrounds, and that meant it had to be changed into more of a dramatic spectacle, a pageant, than a play. The areas were too vast, the distances too great for much straight storytelling. We used some five hundred actors in the production, two hundred dancers, a multitude of wagons and carts, horses and automobiles, choruses, an amplified orchestra, six narrators, Indians and soldiers, and in the finale a parade of the machine age as Ohio had contributed to it. As a "curtain" to end the spectacle, a coal-burning locomotive moved in along the race track from the right and a diesel locomotive in from the left to meet in front of the grandstand, while a huge chorus on the wide stage across the track sang Isaac Van Grove's patriotic anthem and a tremendous Ohio State flag descended from wires in the sky with spotlights flaring on it. We had audiences up to eleven thousand during the two-week run. The production was under the direction of Helen Geraghty.

In 1953, Berea College in the Kentucky foothills made plans for celebrating its 1955 centennial, and after getting off a little volume of essays about our dramatic heritage, I set to work on a symphonic drama for the event. The project was a challenging one from the very beginning. In the first place, I admired the kind of democratic education Berea College stood for, and in the second, I welcomed the chance to get at some of the beautiful, stored-up Appalachian folklore—ballad, folk song, and dance—to put in my play. I finally decided to try to dramatize Berea's educational philosophy itself, using as a sort of collateral model for my main character the person of John G. Fee, one of the founders of the school. I soaked myself in the history of the Appalachian country and the Scotch-Irish people who had settled there. At last the imagined characters of the drama and their relationships were pulled into being, coming reluctantly forward to the stern demand of the drama's theme—creative education.

I made my imaginary hero, John Freeman, a blazing idealist and considered him inspired by John G. Fee and his associates. He had got himself some training at Berea and then at Oberlin College and finally come back into the mountains hoping to start a school among his people founded on the Berea ideal—an ideal expressed in the motto of that college—"For God hath made of one blood all nations of men for to dwell on all the face of the earth." His Scotch-Irish people lived in a narrow mountain valley and had lived there for two or three generations. Feuds were common among them. And many a young man in desperado activity had landed himself in an early grave or behind penitentiary bars, when with less ignorance and a little more learning he might have become a useful citizen. John Freeman had decided that education was the answer, and he went to work to prove it.

When he was a little boy, his father, a kindly mountain preacher, had been killed, say, by an exchange of shots when he stepped in between two angry groups of mountaineers in an effort to make peace. This tragedy had a profound effect on John. It helped him even in his early days to see the evil, the cruelty and waste of hate and bloodspilling, and it determined him in his heart never to take up a gun against his fellow man.

And there in his little mountain cabin he worked away at night, the fire flickering, worked at his books, his dreams, and his plans, studying and reading from his father's Bible, from American history, *Pilgrim's Progress*, and from many a book of sermons and poetry that he borrowed from the Berea library.

And he went forth preaching education and dedication of spirit in its name. He found some help in the mountain girl he loved, and he was always encouraged by his strong-hearted mother. Perhaps the task John Freeman set himself could not be accomplished, for it was nothing short of trying to teach and put into practice the Christian faith in which he believed.

As ye know, so shall we do, he said; and as a man thinketh in his heart, so is he.

He soon ran into difficulties. Old ways do not change easily. Old beliefs are not broken in a day, and the Scotch-Irish people in that valley were a hardy, stubborn lot. And John was stubborn too. Like St. Paul, he had seen the vision. He would not give over.

Then murmurings and suspicions began to rise against him. The threat of the Civil War grew darker over the land, and his pro-Southern neighbors found themselves more and more outraged by his beliefs. He was against slavery and said so. He was for the Union, and he declared it. He was against guns and killings, whatever the cause, and he kept speaking this conviction. And then, perhaps worst of all, he advocated education of the Negroes and giving them a chance to grow and develop their lives. And day after day in his little school he stood up and taught these beliefs to his students.

The threats against him finally became a fact, and the brutish feet of force swept over him and his work. But he was a fighter, too—not with swords and bayonets and bullets, but with words and ideas and with love. And although his neighbors came in the night and burned down his school, he would not strike back with his fist, he would not hate the misguided hand that had furnished the torch. But he would go on preaching his ideas—preaching from the church, from the crossroads, the country store, whereever he could find a listener. And when he was dragged out and beaten, he still kept his faith, his determination. And while the blood ran down his stricken shoulders, he cried out, "I'll never give in to them. In God's name my flesh will be stronger than their steel."

Then when the Confederate forces overran Kentucky, and he saw the nation he loved about to break in two and slavery and oppression continue, he was faced with the dilemma of remaining a follower of his pacifist religion or taking up his gun and fighting for the cause he believed in. He prayed and agonized over this decision, and in a scene at night on the mountain top he communed with the spirit of his dead father. From the void beyond the crags the voice of old Luke Freeman spoke again to him the ancient and homely mysterious doctrine of a man saving his life by losing it.

Out of his Golgotha experience John Freeman thought that he glimpsed the nature of sacrifice—the implacable demand that an ideal always makes of its followers in the crisis hour—and the crisis hour must always come if the ideal is to live—a demand that he, the believer, must offer up what he holds dearest and most precious to prove his faith, prove it not only to himself but to those who must to their human eyes have that proof. And laying aside his Bible, he picked up his gun and marched away to war.

And there in the smoke and yelling fury of battle he led his Federal troops against his Southern neighbors, among whom was his own brother—led them to victory and to his own death.

At the end of the play, with the fighting done and the Blue and Gray united in a common sorrow, the people in the valley brought John Freeman's body home again and above his open grave promised one another to build his school.

John Freeman's teachings would go on.

Under the leadership of Dr. W. D. Weatherford of the Berea board of trustees and President Francis S. Hutchins, a charming amphitheatre of native stone was built for the play there among the Kentucky hills some three miles from the campus. It was decided to limit the seating capacity to some eighteen hundred, as compared with twenty-five hundred or three thousand in the others. For I had found it hard to put across vivid and intimate scenes in the larger ones. And more often than not pageantry and crowd gatherings had been necessary to subdue the outdoor environment when the uncluttered story itself was what counted most. Gestures had to be broad and definite, exaggeratedly so, and the speech more often of a declamatory kind than not. The individualization of the characters had to be done in a few broad strokes, and most often a narrator or interpretative voice was required to keep the story cleaned up and running to the point so that the audience could receive the full impact of the play without too much waste on explanatory matters. In this smaller theatre I was able to remedy some of these defects and realize a more intense drama than before. The results proved the wisdom of our decision, and with an average ticket price of $1.80, a seating capacity of this size could still support a weekly payroll of several thousand dollars and leave something over for a sustaining fund.

With Samuel Selden directing, *Wilderness Road* opened on June 29, 1955, for its first summer season. The reviews were good in all the local papers, as well as in the New York *Times* and *Herald Tribune*, although some of the critics made a point of "the inflammable nature of the play." The people liked the folk singing and dancing, the flags and waving banners, bugles and drums and marching feet—all an integral part of the story—but they liked most the inner drama of John Freeman's struggle to make the ideas he believed in prevail. The play now seems set for a run of many years.

This type of drama, which I have elected to call "symphonic," seems to be catching on throughout the country, especially when the productions are outdoors and the subject matter is historical. Samuel Selden, head of the drama department at the University of North Carolina, has been one of the most consistent workers in it. Also Kermit Hunter, Harry Davis, John Parker, Foster Fitz-Simons, Kai Jurgenson, and Irene Smart—all of that university— are helping to spread it into a movement. They have cooperated on such projects not only in North Carolina and Kentucky but in Illinois, Tennessee, and Florida. And other similar undertakings are now in the making in Georgia, Indiana, California, Pennsylvania, and Massachusetts. Kermit Hunter's play *Unto These Hills*, which he calls a "saga" drama and not "symphonic," is one of the most popular of them all. It plays every summer at Cherokee, North Carolina, in a lofty mountainside amphitheatre built for its production in 1951, and has an annual attendance of around one hundred and fifty thousand. Hunter has written a number of these plays, and his *Horn in the West* also is acted annually at Boone,

North Carolina. During the year 1956, he opened two more, one in Tennessee and one in Florida.

So great is the demand becoming for this type of play that new playwrights, directors, and technicians now need to be recruited. I think the drama departments in the different colleges and universities could well turn their attention to training their young people for this work—as well as for Broadway. It is still in its infancy. And I do not think that it is too much to hope that other playwrights, directors, actors, and workers to come someday will somehow perfect this form, and every American city of any size will have its neighboring amphitheatre, where plays derived out of the people's lives and their history will have continuing productions. Then, who knows, we may have created an American dramatic art comparable with that of the ancient Greeks, when Aeschylus and Sophocles walked the earth and spoke lifting words for all to hear.

It is now long past time to break off this narrative. In conclusion, I will add that I am at present working on still another symphonic drama, dealing with the love story of the Indian girl Pocahontas and John Rolfe and the first English settlement at Jamestown. It will be produced in 1957 for Virginia's three hundred and fiftieth anniversary celebration, and it is my aim to introduce into it some new experimental ideas that I have been working at. There is no room or time to talk about them here, though, and no doubt it is safer to wait and see how they prove out in the production.

Well, as Granowsky said, there is much, much to be done.

BIOGRAPHICAL SKETCHES

ROBERT E. GARD has entered upon several missions that he himself discovered to be in need of doing and then made original plans for their fulfillment. All called for research in archives and in the field, a gathering of folk material, and talking with people. No two have been alike in form or outcome, but all have on them the hallmark of their maker. Three such projects having lasting results have been in western New York State, western Canada, and in the state of Wisconsin.

Preliminary to these was the project of completing his own formal education. Some lines of that can be traced in the pages of Mr. Gard's book *Grassroots Theater*, recently published for him by the University of Wisconsin Press. That book is built out of the essential substance in all his work, namely an aptitude for discovery of people. Gaining his final degree was incidental; it was a bench mark in time rather than of formal completion of studies. The merging of theory and practice has been with him a continuous process.

Only one significant gain came out of graduate studies

in drama at Cornell University. That was the formulation, under Professor Alexander Drummond, of ways to apply at once the theories gathered in study by working with people. In this balance of studies and field experiences Mr. Gard established the pattern of all later work with his own students, and like the other nine writers for the present book he has illustrated in doing so what lasting power can come out of the influence of a single teacher.

In his folk tales, stage plays, and shorter pieces for television or broadcast, Mr. Gard has demonstrated his originality in seeing and in expressing what he sees, in reality or in imagination. He likewise demonstrates in expository writing how he can make other people see, hear, and appreciate through his oral discourse. For these reasons, the University of Wisconsin wisely chose him as professor of drama in its extension division, to serve the entire state. From that point of vantage he does his original writing and gives out his ideas on the theatre. These ideas now reach groups ranging in age from childhood through adult maturity, and the writings are being read beyond state and national borders.

PAUL BAKER is one of many who carried away an impulse toward excellence from his studies under George Pierce Baker. A native of Texas, he first was a student in that state at Trinity University, and then at the University of Wisconsin before taking his final degree at Yale University. His two chief accomplishments thus far are important as demonstrations of what is possible for other talented, energetic individuals. He began work with nothing more than opportunity in a college then unaware of the potential values in theatre for education as well as for entertainment. He went on to bring drama into the living experiences of young people. In these circumstances he has approached the goal that Leslie Cheek aimed toward at William and Mary College—to make week ends in the arts as attractive to college crowds as week ends of football.

At Baylor University, Mr. Baker has developed new forms of staging within newly designed buildings suited to the full range of theatre expression. He has established his own patterns in production, and his own methods of training for directors and actors. During World War II he had unusual experience overseas in administration and in production; later, in Texas, beyond the formal work in his university, he has brought animated interest among religious and community groups by his direction and by the plays of his traveling companies.

ALAN SCHNEIDER began his love of theatre in a foreign country. He had lived a childhood seeing plays in the theatres of Russia. His parents had then brought drama into his life more critically by their appreciation of the Moscow Art Theatre in talks at home. They also had opened to him the world of books and films. Finally, and opportunely, they had brought him to the United States at the best time for essential experiences in American schools. Here, as unconsciously as he had absorbed the idiom of Russian drama, he built up his stock of English and American idioms in language. Higher studies and other experiences in this country have not changed his youthful conviction that theatre is a universal and that he is a part of it.

Mr. Schneider's contribution to this book can show a neophyte in theatre what to expect when he lives in two theatrical worlds almost simultaneously. It shows how determination and talent join to give an individual steady development and to create among others the belief that

275

he can do the next harder task. His narrative proves too how significantly encouragement influences a person toward a particular plan of living and working; it demonstrates how word and example play their parts in the growth of any individual.

The manner in which this present story was written illustrates something else of value to the beginner in theatre. The demands put on anyone who is caught completely in the operations of the American theatre show through the incidents that are here reported. They were brought into form for printing during three months of movement between his two cities, with the interruption of a journey to Madison, Wisconsin, and a final move of several days over to London and back home. The last page was turned down as his steamer docked at the end of the return voyage. Alongside this marginal note is another that gives a reader an understanding of the success of this writer: he wrote that the story had been done "for Vicki, Jean, Rebecka, and Leo." The spirit of his narrative proves that his future stage productions will be prepared with the same sense of obligation personally toward his audiences.

In 1956, Mr. Schneider was awarded a Guggenheim Fellowship as aid toward a comprehensive, historical study of the open stage.

MARGO JONES, by her every act and word, gave a characterization of herself. She was alive with theatre. No one, after the first moment of meeting, could doubt her undivided purpose. It was to make a finer theatre here and everywhere, and rapidly. Her passion for drama began in childhood and was undimmed up to the day of her death, July 24, 1955. Unawares, she once packed that life story into two sentences that stand as last words in the following paragraphs from the *New York Times* of July 26, 1955.

One Aim in Life—Theatre

From early childhood in her native Livingston, Tex., Margo Jones had a singleness of purpose; a career in the theatre.

This led her to read Shakespeare at the age of 10 in the pastures behind the modest Jones home. It was this attitude that achieved for her prominence as a director-producer. She produced more than 100 plays in her famed Theatre in the Round in Dallas.

Broadway theatregoers knew her best for her production and staging of Tennessee Williams' play, "Summer and Smoke," in 1948, and her role as associate producer with Herman Shumlin of "Inherit the Wind" in 1955.

The theatre was the dominant theme in the life of Miss Jones. At one time, someone ventured the observation that most persons considered the theatre "a minor part of living." Quickly, she retorted, "Everything in life is theatre."

In addition to reading Shakespeare as a child, she managed to achieve such high grades that she entered Texas State College for Women at the age of 14 and earned an M.A. degree for a thesis in psychology.

Equipped with that academic background, Miss Jones entered upon a theatrical career. She studied every phase of the theatre at the Southwestern School of the Theatre in Dallas. She worked with the Ojai Community Players, found time to travel around the world and then worked at the Pasadena Playhouse in California.

The year 1939 found her in Houston, Tex. A woman of tremendous vitality, she persuaded the guiding fathers of the Recreation Department of Houston to permit her to stage plays as the head of the Community Players. Moreover, she sold tickets to her productions, thus saving the city the expense of subsidizing the project.

Then followed an association with the faculty of the University of Texas, where she worked on an experimental theatre. Miss Jones also managed to work in trips to the Pasadena and the Cleveland Playhouses in an active role as producer and director.

Her first association with Mr. Williams came in 1943 in Cleveland. She staged his play, "You Touched Me." Two years later she was back in Dallas and establishing the Theatre in the Round that became her shrine and workshop. But this had a prelude.

Miss Jones obtained use of a theatre in Dallas, but it was condemned as a fire hazard. Then she gained possession of an air-conditioned building owned by the Gulf Oil Corporation. The structure once was part of an exposition. She borrowed 300 seats from a movie chain. The name, Theatre in the Round was selected because the audience surrounded the stage.

Thus began her crusade of championing the works of unknown American playwrights and espousing radical departures in theatrical production.

Her production of new and classical plays had critics beating a path to Dallas.

Miss Jones came to New York in 1945, when she co-staged Mr. Williams' "The Glass Menagerie" with Eddie Dowling. The next year, she staged Maxine Wood's "On Whitman Avenue" and Maxwell Anderson's "Joan of Lorraine," with Ingrid Bergman. In 1950 she directed and co-produced Owen Crump's "Southern Exposure."

Although her approach to life was marked by vigor, Miss Jones imparted a lightness and delicacy of touch to her theatrical productions. Time and again, she was critical of what she termed the archaic character of Broadway theatres and of those who would not experiment in new ways and devices.

In speaking of her love for the theatre, she once remarked, "The theatre has given me a chance not only to live my own life but a million others. In every play there is a chance for one great moment, experience or understanding."[1]

On December 2, 1954, she wrote as always about what was ahead. Her new name of the coming season was up over her Dallas playhouse and in all printings of programs for the oncoming season. As always, there were three new scripts among the ten for production between November and June. Theatre '55 was already on the move. In the same letter she recalled a first night of the previous season, when *Oracle Junction* brought down from Oklahoma a group that knew intimately the physician who had made medical history and so had become the central figure in the new play. That night she called "kind of special," and it was. The same remark describes her entire career. Also, this unfinished narrative is, in its incompleteness, a symbol of her unfinished adventure through theatre into the surrounding world.

FREDERIC MCCONNELL, by making the Cleveland Play House what it is today, has done more than contribute to local history. He has made his city known wherever the drama is a part of living rather than merely occasional entertainment. It is unlikely, however, that this thought has occurred to him; the past has slight interest for his mind except as background in experience for what lies ahead.

The Play House began to grow in well-cultivated soil. In 1921, the city of Cleveland had a strong community interest in higher education and in all the arts. Western Reserve University was then nearly one hundred years old, its influence steadily increasing. It soon was to follow the lead of the Play House, although in its own pattern of graduate studies, by establishing parallel activities in dra-

[1] Used with permission of the *New York Times*. The most significant statement of the work of Margo Jones, in point of her theories and methods, is in her book *Theatre-in-the-Round*, published in 1951 by Rinehart and Co., Inc.

matic arts. The directors of the two centers have worked together with unfailing harmony. As officers of the National Theatre Conference, they also have been responsible for much of the improvement in quality of American theatre on a national level, another reason why their city has distinction widely for its cultivation of stage plays and the building of theatres across the nation for their adequate presentation.

For thirty-five years, trustees, audiences, actors, and students have now followed the lead of Frederic McConnell. In that time the reason has been a belief in the future of what he does and plans. The scale and direction of his intentions are shown in these two sentences: "In the coming new world, let the principal university and community theatres organize within themselves the nucleus of a permanent and fixed theatre company of actors, directors, designers, and technicians on some kind of professional basis. Five hundred of these professionally organized nonprofit theatres scattered throughout the country will give us a truly national theatre, democratic and universal in its appeal and influence."[1]

BARCLAY LEATHEM is undoubtedly the one best able to tell what has happened in the American theatre since 1939, for, in a paraphrase of a television expression, "he was there." While creating a graduate school of drama, he served, and still serves, the National Theatre Conference as its secretary. Over the years this has meant something more than onerous office routines. It had called for circuit journeys into all parts of the country, convincing Government authorities that plays were a part of wartime living for servicemen everywhere, and managing such com-

[1] *Bulletin*, National Theatre Conference, Vol. VI, No. 4 (October, 1944), 20.

plex assignments as choice of fellows for advanced study and of teachers for all levels of work from school through university. Leathem has had many careers in one, while at all times developing new ones for his students and followers. No one has equaled, or now can equal, his pioneer work in television. No one, surely, can do more than illustrate the variety of his talents and constancy in performance of duties.

One quotation, from an article written by him in 1940, will illustrate a number of these broad assertions. The year before he had been on the road helping other theatre people, while his own staff worked along back in Cleveland. He wrote of one stop, "Last January in Kalamazoo, Michigan, I saw a production of *Julius Caesar*. Back stage before the performance I watched a doctor prepare to play Cassius. Near him in Brutus' costume was the president of a local bank. At the switchboard making last minute tests of the stage lighting was the general manager of Consumers' Power. The girl who had had the leading role in a previous play, *Susan and God*, was sewing a button on the uniform worn by a young man in the mob scene. This was a community theatre in action. Here was a city that took pride in having one of the finest theatre buildings in America. . . . The theatre is a synthesis of the arts. It reaches *more people* in *more ways* than any other form of community expression in art. . . . In cities large and small all over America men and women turn to drama because it satisfies a basic urgent need. In Wisconsin 100,000 farmers write, produce, and attend their own plays. From kindergarten to graduate school, dramatics is a part of the curriculum. Far from being a frill, the theatre is a vital necessity in American life."[1]

[1] *Quarterly Bulletin*, National Theatre Conference, Vol. II, No. 3 (August, 1940), 3.

GILMOR BROWN lately was described in a newspaper story as being founder, president, and producing director of the Pasadena Playhouse. These are solid words, but they fail to carry the more significant truths regarding this visibly inspiring worker in the stuffs of theatre. This man has brought the myriad values of theatre into union and has held them in an effective relationship. His staff now trains an individual in voice control, music, ballet, and acting. Before walking on stage, the typical graduate of his school may even realize what are the secondary sources of his anticipated success—the financial and administrative controls of a theatre. These secondary needs are primary ones, in point of timely foresight, if a director is to hold to his purpose of opening every autumn and staying open in a state of solvency.

The Playhouse reached its twenty-fifth year of productions in 1943, eighteen years after the new building was opened and thirteen years after it had been freed from debt. During that quarter-century Gilmor Brown brought to Pasadena his own designs of staging and acting. Beyond his home base of operation, he now has reached by proxy other actors and directors over the country through the active graduates of his school. On the records of thirty-eight years are the names of some three thousand persons, with three hundred more now enrolled to be the graduates of existing class groups.

The temper of the man who opened his first curtain in Pasadena back in 1917 appears in a remark that in their most frugal existence he and his people trusted "a wind of inspiration to fill our sails," and that in early years there was "never enough room, enough money or enough of anything except loyalty and devotion at the old Playhouse."[1] Any who know Gilmor Brown can hear these words spoken in the quiet clarity of his tone and in a mind's eye can see the spontaneous smile with all his speaking. Few persons have done so easily, from outward signs, so many difficult tasks in the theatre. It is a natural consequence that he has excelled in creating diversified values for the acting stage which can be carried over into broadcasting and television, to bring personality into characters through the lively arts of the theatre.

LESLIE CHEEK, JR., is today director of the Virginia Museum of Fine Arts, a position that he has held since 1948, when he gave over his duties as associate editor of *Architectural Forum*. In the eight years since that change, he has made this one of the foremost smaller museums in the country. He has done this by bringing the visual and active arts into a new unity. This unity is never forced or obvious, but a natural one. The interpenetration of one form by another is demonstrated most recently in the conduct of the new theatre. With the resources of the museum in personnel and material objects, the stage is focus for productions in many styles, with flexible margins for new types of staging as well as for film and telecast.

It was after studies in architecture and in the arts generally that Mr. Cheek began joining theory and practice in an institution for higher education. In 1937, at William and Mary College, he developed the first well-balanced program in liberal arts that brought historical perspective and experience equally to bear on drama, film, painting, and sculpture. Later, in the Baltimore Museum of Art and during war years in Washington, he carried further his ideas for undergraduates to applied uses with the public and in the camouflages of conflict.

Out of these varied opportunities and proofs of origi-

[1] *Quarterly Bulletin*, National Theatre Conference, Vol. V, No. 1 (January, 1943), 5–6.

nality have come generous support from the state of Virginia. Among the returns to the people is the yearly visit to all parts of the state by the artmobile, with its exhibit of fine original objects. Touring all sections of the commonwealth, it is a demonstration of art in life. The artmobile has been one medium of contact to bring persons to the museum. It has done this through the schools, in isolated communities, and in larger centers. What is of more concern, for the present purpose of this book, is that staged plays uniting art with life, and in new settings, are being brought before people as something to live with rather than to experience incidentally.

GEORGE IZENOUR is a research associate at Yale University, where his teaching in the school of drama is subordinated to research in electrical and mechanical aspects of stage management. Within a few years he has brought into use new principles of light control that can make staged plays appear in the varied and changing moods of author and actors. This fundamental achievement is widely known through useful application in American theatres. Other works of Mr. Izenour, as his design and building of an operating "world globe" some twenty-eight feet in diameter, are less commonly mentioned outside engineering circles but are similarly significant.

His contributions to the contemporary theatre are well stated in a recent history of drama having the following conclusions on Mr. Izenour's importance in opening new sources of artistic value: "Lighting reform has gone much further in the universities than on Broadway. To be sure, Belasco abolished footlights and Granville-Barker installed the lights on the face of the balcony that are now in general use. University and community theatres, however, have developed ceiling lights and used a good deal of projected scenery. The theatre at Yale, with the aid of the Rockefeller Foundation, installed the first of the highly versatile pre-set and remote-control dimmers, devised by George C. Izenour, that make use of electronic tubes."[1] To this clear statement might be added another, that Izenour installations in time will give economical and flexible controls of light to the most modest stages in schools, grange halls, and wherever people gather to make acted drama a part of daily living.

PAUL GREEN has lived the life of a writer. In his home town of Chapel Hill, North Carolina, he is also teacher in the university and participant in affairs. He may by now have put off his professorial role of philosopher in formal discourse for the last time, but he always will teach. This he does through all that he writes, does, or says. His learners will be writers, theatre folk, and audiences before screen and stage. By print his meanings go to others. As a worker for U. N. E. S. C. O., the Federal Theatre Project, and the National Theatre Conference, he has made the artist a full member of society at home and overseas.

Above all else, Paul Green is American in origin and material. His plays, poems, essays, prose fiction, and lyrics unceasingly express the spirit of his country. Some would wish to have written his short story "Fine Wagon," others the symphonic drama *Lost Colony*, or the plays *In Abraham's Bosom* and *Johnny Johnson*. These all are out of his life and thought, as distinctively his own as his manner of speech. Commercial successes have helped him to maintain intellectual freedom, but they never have changed him. He was in Hollywood, but not of it. The most rapid

[1] Kenneth Macgowan and William Melnitz, *The Living Stage: A History of the World Theatre* (New York, Prentice-Hall, 1955), 499–500.

and clear characterization of him came lately from Gilmor Brown, who wrote that "he belongs by himself as a creative writer and inspiration."

INDEX

Index

Index

Fogarty, Elsie: 177
Fordham University, N. Y.: 98
Fortunato: 156
Fountainhead, The: 97
France, American interest in her drama: 14
Frank, Bruno: 176
Freedoms Foundation, Valley Forge, Pa.: 170
French, Samuel: 229, 232n.
Freud, Ralph: 215
Fulbright scholars, dramatic training of: 90

Gale, Zona: 39
Galsworthy, John: 129, 176
Gard, Robert E.: 31–52; 1942 tour, 32; in Canada, 34–36; to the University of Wisconsin, 37–39; studies and work at Cornell University, 41–42; on folk drama, 44; on regional drama, 45–47; in England, 47; on road companies and current taste, 48–49; aims of the Wisconsin Idea Theatre, 51–52; biographical note, 273–74
Garfield, John: 257
Garland, Robert: 260
Gassner, John W.: 79, 84
Gate of Hell: 264
Gay, John: 191
Geddes, Norman Bel: 97, 167
Geraghty, Helen: 265
Germany, American drama in: 25–26
Gershwin, George: 14
Geyer, Emil: 146
Gielgud, John: 76, 80, 91
Glasgow, Mary: 17
Glasgow Citizens' Theatre: 91
Glaspell, Susan: 174
Glass Menagerie, The: 99, 116–17, 278
Gnesin, Maurice: 195, 220
Goethe, Johann W. von: 109, 234
Golden Boy: 76
Gold Rush, The: 230
Goodman, Randy: 68

Goodman Memorial Theatre, Chicago, lighting controls in: 220
Gorelik, Mordecai: 78, 79; quoted, 175–76
Granowsky, Alexis: 242–47, 253, 271
Grant, Lee: 67
Granville-Barker, Harley: 284
Grassroots Theater: 45, 273
Great Britain: recognition of drama in, 15; contrasts to the United States, 18ff.; drama since 1945 in, 90–92
Great Galeoto, The: 174
Greek Theatre, University of California at Berkeley: 127
Green Pastures, The: 246–47
Green, Paul: 6, 24, 148, 224–71; youth, 224; influence of Foerster on, 225; war and wartime reading, 226–27; undergraduate years, 228; graduate studies and teaching, 229; early successes, 229; Pulitzer Prize and first Broadway productions, 229; comments on Broadway, 231–32; on off-Broadway playing, 232–37; Guggenheim fellowship period in Germany, 239–47; visit with Shaw and return to Broadway, 248–57; symphonic dramas, 258–71; Far Eastern tour, 263–64; biographical note, 285–86
Greenlaw, Edwin: 228
Greenwich Village Theatre, New York City: 230
Gregory, Lady: 174
Gribble, Harry: 173
Gropius, Walter: 80
Group Theatre, New York City: 73, 76, 81–83, 108, 109, 257
Guggenheim fellowships: 239, 276
Guinness, Alec: 91
Gunther, John: 75
Guthrie, Tyrone: 91; quoted, 92

Haigh, A. G.: 236

291

Index

Index

Museum of Fine Arts, Richmond, Va.: 192; Artmobile, 193
Museum of Modern Art, New York City: 96, 98
Myers, Henry: 79
My Heart's in the Highlands: 96
Mysterious Universe, The: 74
Mystery of Hamlet, The: 163

Nathan, Vivian: 67
National Arts Council, Great Britain: 16–17, 91
National Recovery Administration: 72
National Theatre Conference: 55, 179; organized, 22–23; reorganized, 24; *Bulletin* of, 24; memberships, 24; war service, 150–53; releases of an Anderson play, 115; headquarters of, 134; founder, 134; influence, 135; aims of, 179
Native Son: 262
Neighborhood Playhouse, New York City: 82–83, 99
Nelson, Ruth: 257
Ness, Jens: 205
New Movement in the Theatre, The: 79
New Theatres for Old: 175
New York Herald Tribune: vii, 9n., 65
New York Times: vii, 236; quoted, 133, 137
Nicholson, James: 195
Nicoll, Allardyce: 16, 20n., 148
Night in the Old Marketplace, A: 242
No 'Count Boy, The: 229, 241
Noh drama: 264
Nolte, Charles: 67
North Carolina, University of, playmaking at: 21, 228–29, 248, 257–60, 270–71
Norvelle, Lee: 24, 152
Nutcracker, The: 70

O'Casey, Sean: 123, 129, 248
Odets, Clifford: 109

Oenslager, Donald: 195
Off-Broadway theatres: 94–95, 98–99, 108, 179, 232–36
Ojai Community Players: 113
Okhlopkov, N.: 175
Old Globe Theatre, Dallas, Texas: 117
Old Homestead, The: 141
Old Vic Theatre, Bristol, England: 91
Old Vic Theatre, London: 66, 80; school of, 90
Olivier, Laurence: 66, 91
O'Neill, Eugene: 108, 109, 143, 169, 176, 191, 230, 246
One-Third of a Nation: 191
On Whitman Avenue: 116, 278
On Your Toes: 76
Oracle Junction: 279
Oresteia: 236
Osborn, Frederick: 150
Othello: 86, 94, 136
Our Town: 26, 76
Ouspenskaya, Maria: 83

Pach, Walter: 138, 139n.
Pal Joey: 76
Panofsky, Edwin: 22; quoted, 23
Parke, James H.: 115, 153n.
Parker, John: 270
Pasadena Playhouse, Calif.: 6, 116; first structure, 165; benefactors of, 165–68; incorporated, 166; present structure, 168–69; the Play Box, 171–76; school of, 176–77; television training, 176–77
Pattee, Fred Lewis: 141–42
Pavlov, Ivan, quoted: 198
Payne, B. Iden: 126
Peer Gynt: 170
Peking Opera, The, in Paris: 95
Pelléas et Mélisande: 173
Pennsylvania State College, beginning of drama training at: 141
People Win Through, The: 178
Perdue, Judith: 196
Perigord, Paul: 168

295

Index

Ten Talents in the American Theatre

was set on the Linotype in W. A. Dwiggins' Electra, a type design which departs from traditional forms. One of its features is the use of square serifs instead of the bracketed serifs of old style or the hair-line serifs of the so-called "modern" faces. The general effect is sharp, swift-moving, appropriate to an age of speed and machinery. It combines best with contemporary style display alphabets, and is used on the title page with capitals of Alternate Gothic No. 1 from American Type Founders.